MEDIEVAL LATIN
AND THE
RISE OF EUROPEAN
LOVE-LYRIC

MEDIEVAL LATIN AND THE RISE OF EUROPEAN LOVE-LYRIC

BY

PETER DRONKE

*Lecturer in Medieval Latin in the
University of Cambridge*

VOLUME II

MEDIEVAL LATIN LOVE-POETRY

*Texts newly edited from
the manuscripts and for the most
part previously unpublished*

SECOND EDITION

OXFORD
AT THE CLARENDON PRESS
1968

Oxford University Press, Ely House, London W. 1

GLASGOW   NEW YORK   TORONTO   MELBOURNE   WELLINGTON
CAPE TOWN   SALISBURY   IBADAN   NAIROBI   LUSAKA   ADDIS ABABA
BOMBAY   CALCUTTA   MADRAS   KARACHI   LAHORE   DACCA
KUALA LUMPUR   HONG KONG   TOKYO

FIRST EDITION 1966
SECOND EDITION 1968

PN
688
D72
V. 2

PRINTED LITHOGRAPHICALLY IN GREAT BRITAIN

TO
URSULA

CONTENTS OF VOLUME II

(Where a number has an asterisk, the poem is one not recorded in Walther or Chevalier)

Contents of Volume II

Contents of Volume II

PRELIMINARY NOTE

In spelling I follow my manuscripts throughout (though I distinguish between u and v, and use capitals for proper names, for the sake of more immediate clarity). Contractions are expanded without comment; emendations are in italics. Supplementary words or letters obviously demanded by sense or by metre, as well as obliterated or uncertain manuscript readings, are in square brackets. The arrangement of lines and the punctuation, except when otherwise stated, are my own.

In each section the poems are printed as far as possible in the chronological order of the manuscripts. Further details about each manuscript can be found in the Bibliography. In manuscript references I follow Kristeller's convention of using each city's native name.

The texts include a certain number of poems previously printed, usually either because inaccuracies in the printed text prevent full understanding, or because the discovery of a new manuscript now makes a more complete understanding possible. In the notes to these poems I record readings of previous scholars, where they diverge from my own, with an initial (explained at the head of the notes), and emendations with the initial and square brackets. But I have not recorded minor misreadings or unusable conjectures, unless of some importance.

The great majority of the poems in this collection are not preserved in more than one manuscript. This means that textual problems are often insoluble, interpretations often uncertain. My translations are meant simply as aids to reading, as a tentative first attempt at making sense of the more difficult passages, and as a concise way of showing where the problems are, even when I cannot hope to have solved them.

TEXTS AND
COMMENTARY

Foebus abierat   subtractis cursibus;
  equitabat soror   effrenis curribus,
Radios inferens   silvanis fontibus,
  agitando feras   pro suis rictibus.
5 Mortales dederant   menbra soporibus.

Aprili tempore   quod nuper transiit
  fidelis imago   coram me adstitit,
Me vocans dulciter   pauxillum tetigit;
  oppressa lacrimis   vox eius deficit,
10 Suspirans etenim   loqui non valuit.

Illius a tactu   nimis intremui,
  velud exterrita   sursum insilui,
Extensis brachiis   corpus applicui,
  exsanguis penitus   tota derigui—
15 Evanuit enim!   nichil retinui!

Sopore libera   exclamo fortiter:
  'quo fugis, amabo?   cur tam celeriter?
Siste gradum, si vis   inibo pariter,
  nam tecum vivere   volo perhenniter!'
20 Mox me penitui[t]   dixisse taliter.

Roma, Vat. lat. 3251, fol. 178*⋆*   s. XII¹

. . . .

eq[uitaba]t soror   effr[eni]s curribus
radios inferens   silvanis frondibus

    . . . .

5 [mor]tales dederunt   mem[b]ra soporibus. O O

Veneris filius   sicut est solitus
. . . . . .   [vitula] . . .
. . . . . ra   ignotis ignibus—
ve mihi misere   que sum mortalibus
10 . . . . [O O]

. . . . [nu] per transiit
fidelis imago   coram me astitit
vocans . . . .
. . . . . .   [vox] eius defecit
15 [su]spirans etenim   loqui non valuit. O O

. . . .

velu[d exterr]ita   . . . [sur]rexi
extensis brachiis   corpus applicui

. . . .

20 [e]van[uit] . .   . . retinui. O O

Sopore liber[a]   exclamo . . .

. . . .

. . . . fortiter
nam tecum vivere   volo . . . .
25 . . . . [O O]

⋆The lines, which I read under ultraviolet lamp, are badly damaged and
almost illegible. Each dot denotes a missing syllable. A. Vattasso (*Studi med.*
1. 125) read some words, but could not judge the size of the illegible parts of
the poem.

Aperte fuerant   fenestre solii,
    fulgebant pulcriter   Diane radii—
    Heu me, heu miseram!   tam diu dolui,
        fluxerunt per genas   ploratus rivuli;
25   Donec in crastin*um*   nunquam abstinui.

14 MS. dirigui
14–15 MS. in reverse order
17 Cf. *CC* 48, l. 12
25 MS. crastino

Phoebus had fled, his voyage done. His sister was riding with unbridled span, shedding her beams in forest springs, stirring wild creatures to prey; men had laid their limbs to rest.

It was in the April which has just passed—the image of my true love stood before me. Softly calling me, he touched me gently. His voice failed, overcome by tears; he gave such sighs, he could not speak.

At his touch I trembled fearfully, I leapt up as if in fright, held out my arms and pressed my body to his. Utterly drained of blood I froze—for he had vanished! I was holding nothing!

Fully awake, I cried out loud: 'Where are you fleeing to, I beg you tell me, why so swiftly fleeing? Stay, or if you will, I too shall enter, for I want to live with you for ever!' Soon I rued that I had spoken in this way.

The terrace windows were open, Diana's beams shone in all their beauty, while I in my wretchedness grieved, ah so long. Streams of tears flowed over my cheeks—till the next day my weeping never ceased.

. . . . solii
fulg[ebant] . . . Diane radii
heu me miseram . . . . . .
. . . . . . [ploratus rivuli]
30 donec in crastinum   nunquam abstinui. O O

. . . .
. . . .
[.] prius fabulis   tempto describe[r]e
. . . .
35 . . quem diligo   curo transmittere. O O*

This is one of the most remarkable poems in Medieval Latin. In the swiftness and passionateness of its narration it achieves a kind of beauty which is rare in a 'learned' language, an atmosphere

> as holy and enchanted
> As e'er beneath a waning moon was haunted
> By woman wailing for her demon lover,

a mood evoked by some of the greatest ballads.†

The 'enchantment' of the story is at once apparent: the all-pervading moonlight, the lover's apparition at the window, the girl's giving herself, in terror and longing. There is great insight in the enigmatic line

> Mox me penitui[t]   dixisse taliter

* It is difficult to conjecture whether this MS. (V) contained the complete original song or is contaminated by additions. The refrain 'O! O!' may have been there from the start (for a general discussion of such refrains see Hans Spanke, 'Klangspielereien im mittelalterlichen Liede', *Ehrengabe für Karl Strecker*, 1931, pp. 171 ff.). It is arguable that in the earlier MS. (B) the transition between the first and second stanzas, as well as the end of the song, is abrupt. Too abrupt?—or is this precisely the kind of beauty of illogicality that one might expect?

In 3 I prefer B's reading, *fontibus*; in V 17 *surrexi* is clearly corrupt; in V 19–20 (B 14–15), V has probably preserved the right order of lines: the lover's vanishing is the fitting end and climax of the stanza; in V 30 (B 25), V has preserved the better reading, *crastinum*.

† See e.g. 'Fæstemanden i Graven' (S. Grundtvig, *Danmarks gamle Folkeviser*, No. 90) and analogues *ad loc*. But cf. also Laodamia's visions of Protesilaos (Ovid, *Her.* xiii, esp. 102–11).

While her sorrow at her lover's death★ is of tragic stature, is there not also a trace of chagrin, that she has broken the spell, and that her magnificent surrender is never to be known by him? ('Husband, I come!...') On being spoken to, the spirit vanishes. Nothing remains but the moonlit night and her tears.

In a sense 'holy' applies as well as 'enchanted'. There is more than ballad-matter here—the passionateness has something unearthly about it, but less in a faery sense than in another:

> Dilectus meus misit manum suam per foramen,
> et venter meus intremuit ad tactum eius.
> Surrexi ut aperirem dilecto meo . . .
> at ille declinaverat, atque transierat . . .
> Quaesivi, et non inveni illum;
> vocavi, et non respondit mihi. (*Cant.* v. 4–6)

In its language the poem has much in common with the dramatic 'Quis est hic qui pulsat ad ostium?' (*v. supra*, pp. 269 ff.), with which it is probably almost contemporary.

In its metre (rhythmic, as against quantitative, asclepiads)† and some of its expressions it can be related to the famous 'Manerius' poem in Vat. Reg. lat. 344 (*SLP* ii. 310), and to two poems in the Ripoll MS. (whose connexion with 'Manerius' has already been signalled by F. J. E. Raby): 'Quomodo primum amavit' and 'De somnio' (ibid. ii. 238, 242). These three poems are in two-, three-, and four-line stanzas respectively. The first of the Ripoll poems, like 'Manerius', opens with a young man hunting in the forest who loses his hounds, and at sunset searches for them. He does not find them, but is met instead by a vision: Manerius by the king's daughter, the other by the god of love. In its language, however, the Ripoll

---

★That he is dead rather than absent is, I think, entailed by both learned and popular conventions of the *revenant*. Here some motifs of 'ghost-lore' may be even more relevant than literary parallels such as Ceyx and Alcyone (*Metam.* XI. 650 ff.). The lover, like all *good* spirits, approaches sighing. Again, there are occasions when it is absolutely necessary to address a spirit—if he has made a promise (such as a lover's vow) which he was unable to fulfil because of sudden death, being spoken to may release him from his wanderings and give him rest. (*v.* H. Bächtold–Stäubli, *Handwörterbuch des deutschen Aberglaubens*, s.v. *Geister*.)

†Cf. D. Norberg, *Introduction à l'étude de la versification latine médiévale* (Stockholm, 1958), pp. 99 ff.

poem is closer to 'Foebus abierat' than to 'Manerius': not only does
it open with 'Aprilis tempore', but the lines

> Ad cuius monitus totus contremui,
> velut exterritus ad terram cecidi

seem a clear imitation of 11–12, and far closer to these than to the
comparable lines in 'Manerius'. Here it is worth noting that the Bodley MS. comes from the immediate ambience of Fleury, and very
probably from Fleury itself (as Mlle E. Pellegrin was kind enough to
confirm for me). There were strong links between Ripoll and Fleury
in the eleventh century. John of Fleury, a nobleman from Barcelona
who became a monk at Ripoll, went, after a time as abbot of Santa
Cecilia of Montserrat, to Fleury in 1013 accompanied by his brother
Bernard. He eventually became Abbot of Fleury, and all his life kept
up correspondence with Ripoll. (The letters are preserved in B.N.
lat. 2858, fols. 66^v–70^r, and are printed in part by R. Beer, *WSB*
clv (1907), 74 ff., and in *Recueil* x. 498.)

The other Ripoll poem, probably by the same poet as the first, is a
love-dream (once again 'Aprilis tempore'): 'Si vera somnia forent,
que somnio . . . .' As in 'Manerius' there is a king's daughter who
yields the young man her love. But the tone is quite different: this
is a humorous piece of wishful thinking. The princess is madly in
love with the young man, whom she finds the fairest on earth. She
woos him by offering him riches, echoing the words of Satan tempting Christ:

> plures tibi dabo, si gratus fueris,
> et ut te diligo sic me dilexeris.

Dr. Raby (*Speculum*, viii (1933), 204–8; x (1935), 68–71) illuminated 'Manerius' by analogues from the so-called *Dolopathos*, and
from *La naissance du Chevalier au Cygne (Elioxe)*. He concluded
from these that the Latin poet 'was well acquainted with the legend
of the "swan-children" and that, in an idle moment, he made its
opening scene the basis for his little poem' (x. 71).

There is one phrase in 'Manerius' which has never received attention: the king's daughter, falling in love at first sight,

> tota contremuit itura patria.

Where is she about to go? What is her *patria*? (Remember, they are
in the depths of the forest.) Surely, as in *Elioxe* (163–5), the answer
is: under the earth, in the caverns beneath—her *patria* is not of this

world. This king's daughter (like Elioxe herself, who, as H. A. Todd first pointed out,* is even once called 'la fée') is daughter of the King of Faery. 'Manerius' is a song about the union of a mortal huntsman with an other-world bride. Thus there are obvious correspondences with Breton lays, with their constantly recurring theme of the hero led by a deer he is hunting into the other world, to an enchanted queen or faery mistress (Pwyll in the *Mabinogion*, Guigemar, Tyolet, le Bel Inconnu, Floriant, Meliador, to name only a few). As in *Guigemar*, the huntsman's and the queen's way to love is thought of as a mutual 'counsel'—

> Bele dame, pur ce vus pri,
> Cunseillez mei, vostre merci . . .
> Cunseil vos dirai volentiers . . .
> Cunseillez me, ma duce amie
> Que ferai jeo de cest amur? . . .
> Cest cunseil sereit trop hastis.

However, while such parallels, and Dr. Raby's own, may illuminate one point or another in the Latin poem, they at the same time tend to obscure the essential difference: lays and fairy-tales are long and full of variety, the story is decked out with the trappings of romance and the trappings of magic, the episodic adventures and supernatural incidents are multiplied beyond number, everything is explained in detail. 'Manerius' and 'Foebus abierat' stand in complete contrast to this. They explain nothing, they add nothing, they tell only one happening with the greatest swiftness and intensity, an intensity which perhaps depends partly for its effectiveness on the audience's knowing (more or less) what will happen. 'Manerius' is, so to speak, *Guigemar* in its most concentrated form. Despite the extreme swiftness of narration there is great subtlety: the trembling girl, the young man who is suddenly aware that he is kissing her, the deliberations about love's fulfilment, taking place amid the kisses. 'Manerius' is not (as one might be led to think from Dr. Raby's analysis) the opening of a lengthy, complicated fairy-tale: it is a ballad, with its own appropriate unity and decorum.

'Manerius' owes much of its narrative art to 'Foebus abierat'. Even more strikingly, the newly found poem shows us an archaic ballad of the lover's ghost, as it was adapted by a brilliant eleventh-century poet for an audience of clercs. The two Ripoll poems are

* *La naissance du Chevalier au Cygne*, *PMLA.* iv (1889), vii.

literary exercises based on the two ballads. The first, 'Quomodo primum amavit', is comparatively slight; the other, 'De Somnio', has delightful elements of burlesque. But it is the earliest of the four poems which is a masterpiece.

Augsburg, Bischöfliches Ordinariat 5, fol. 1^r s. XII in.*

Ritimus

1a 'Parce continuis,
    deprecor, lamentis:
    nimium queraris
    legem Amoris—
5 neque vinculeris!'

1b 'Duris in cotibus
    [Ro]dope aut Ysmarus
    illum progenuit,
    neque nostri generis
10 puerum [aut] sanguinis.

2a 'Non reluctanti
    cedit, aut rebelli,
    sepe consilia
    [falli]t exquisita;
15 gaudet lamentis,
    gaudet querelis,
    ridet et ex[an]gues
    miseros amantes,
    ridet et precordia
20 trahere sus[p]iria.'

2b 'Cunctos evasit
    nexus infortuniis
    qui sola compede
    stringitur amantis:
25 placet honestas,
    urit utilitas,
    herent et verba
    nobis tantum unica,
    non tantum sermonibus—
30 solis loquar fidibus!

3   'Vivit aduc Piramus,
     Tispe dilectissimus,
     et amorum concia
     parietis rimula,
35 primum illis cognita,
     qua sibi colloquia
     dividebant intima;
     obtimus colloquiis
     sed infidus osculis,
40 disparabat corpora
     paries, spiritibus
     solis quidem pervius.

*v. p. 347 n.

4a 'Fo[r]ma, voce, lingua bona
gratus erat unic̣e
45 solus Tracas inter omnes
Orfeus Euridic̣e,
cuius capta federe
gestit omnes fugere;
dumque fugit procu*m*, illam
50 dente petit laetifer,
calce pressus coluber.
Orfeus illam modulis
urget insolabilis.

4b 'Quercus illam fatam sequi
55 su*b*igeba[n]t cytthare
dulces modi, quos vocali[s]
temperas, Calliop*e*—
sed non curas pecto[re]
efficax est demere.
60 Sola[m] vates non adesse

queritur [Eu]rid[ice]n,
ingemit Eu[ri]dicen,
atque solam fidicen
rettulit [Eu]ridicen.'

'Cease your endless laments, I beseech you! You may complain too much of Amor's law—may you not be bound by it.'

'He was brought forth on hard rocks by Rhodope or Ismarus. This boy is not of our race, does not have blood like ours.'

'He does not yield to any who resist or rebel, often he plays havoc with the best resolutions, he delights in laments, delights in plaints, and laughs at wasted, wretched lovers. He laughs at hearts that draw out sighs.'

'That man has avoided all ensnarement in misfortunes who is bound only by the lover's bond. Its honourableness pleases me, its value fires me, and words so unique abide in us (lovers)—not so much in discourses, I shall speak by song alone!

'Even now Pyramus lives, Thisbe's most beloved, and the little cleft in the wall lives, that they were the first to find, where they shared their inmost dialogues. The wall divided their bodies, wall best for love-talking, hopeless for kisses, penetrable indeed only by their souls.

'For his looks and voice and eloquence, Orpheus alone among all Thracian men was loved uniquely by Eurydice. Overcome by his love, she longs to flee from all others, and while she flees from her pursuer, the harbinger of death seeks her with his bite: the serpent, crushed by her heel. Orpheus, inconsolable, strains after her with his songs.

'The lute's sweet melodies, which you temper, tuneful Calliope, compelled the oaks to follow that fateful spirit—yet this does not succeed in removing the heart's sorrow. The poet laments, his one-and-only Eurydice is not there. He bewails Eurydice. And the lutanist brought back his one-and-only Eurydice.'

F: Firenze, Laurenziana Edil. 197, fol. 131ᵛ, written in France early s. XIII (*v. infra*, p. 553). Mr: Wilhelm Meyer, 'Zwei mittellateinische Lieder in Florenz', *Studi letterari e linguistici dedicati a Pio Rajna*, Milano 1911, pp. 149 ff. (prints 'Parce continuis' from F). V: Giuseppe Vecchi, *Pietro Abelardo, I 'Planctus'*, Modena 1951, pp. 72 ff. (derives from Mr, adding incomplete and inaccurate MS. readings from F).

3–5 F neque vincularis legem amoris nimium queraris [Mr nec qua]
6–10 Cf. Verg. *Ecl.* VIII. 43–45|
10 F sanguis [Mr sanguinis]
11–12 F non reluctanti stetit ut rebellis [Mr Non reluctantes cedit ut rebelles]
15–16 F gaudet querelis gaudet et lamentis
21–22 F contos, infortunii [Mr Cunctos evasi]
23–24 A F Tui sola compede stringor F adamante A et amantis Mr cui [qui] *Compede string*itur echoes *vinculeris* of the opening stanza. For the man who rails at it, love can be a danger; for the devotee it is a source of strength.
26 F urit urit utilitas [Mr unit utilitas]
28 F tandem
29 F non altis
30 F loquar? Mr loquor F 2 stanzas not in A
31 ff. Cf. *Metam.* IV. 55 ff.
32 A dilitissimus
39 *sic* AF [Mr invidus—from *Metam.* IV. 73]
42 F 1 stanza not in A
43 ff. The chief details (Eurydice fleeing from the suitor and treading on the serpent, Orpheus' repetition of her name) from *Georg.* IV. 453 ff.
43 F bonus
45 F trarchas—a scribal confusion with 'tetrarchas' in the song 'Dant ad veris honorem' later on the page (*v. infra*, p. 367)? MrV trarehas [Thracas]
46 A euridicen
47 F capto
49 A fugit procus F procos fugit illa
50 F letifer
51 F calle [Mr calce]
52 F illa [Mr illam]
54 F illum vatem
55 F subigebant A sugeba[n]t
56–57 A vocali temperas calliopes F vocalis temperat calliope Cf. Hugh Primas (Langosch 25, Meyer III): 'Orpheus Euridice sociatur, amicus amice, Matre canente dea. . . .'

58 F nec

60 A adessei (?)—as if the scribe had begun to write 'adesset' and had checked himself.

63 F semel fidicen   [Mr semper]

64 A: the last word is followed by the letters *li* and (after a space of three letters) *nq*. F continues with 4 stanzas and a coda not in A, beginning 'Liquid auras superiores'.

The remaining stanzas in F

After 2b:

> Quantos preterita
> genuere secula
> quos † . . . stabili
> nexu graciosa
> 5 vinxit amicicia:
> Nisum ut Eurialo,
> Pirothoum Theseo,
> Pollinicem Tideo.

> Quid David et Ionathe
> 10 fedus venerabile,
> quid amici memorem
> planctum lacrimabilem
> postquam Saül cecidit,
> Ionathas occubuit,
> 15 dum sederet Sichelec
> ceso victor Amalech?

After 3:

> Sevus Amor ultima
> urget in discrimina—
> non ignis incendia,
> 20 Bosfori non aspera
> perorrescit equora,
> quas dum sepe salebras
> iuvenis temeritas
> superasset, vincitur
> 25 tandem maris estibus:
> operitur Sestias.
> Sestias in speculis
> ponto perit iuvenis.

After 4b:

> Liquid auras superiores,
> 30 placet inanes visere sedes

> Tandem mitis carmine vatis
> superum terror, inferum
> rector

fidibus in querulis
incombendo modulis.
Manes sistit, penas fug*a*t,
Cerberi domantur ora,
35 Cerberi, Proserpine
dire manent lacrime,
prius incontigue.

40 'Tollat', inquid 'Orpheus
meritam melodibus,
lege certa: ne respect*et*.
Sola gaudeat dilecto
[ultra nostra limina]!'
45 Fallit Amor Orphea,
respicit ad premia.

Repetita lege
labitur Euridice;
rursus vates
50 parat ire Manes;
vector Stigio
prohibet ab alveo.
Luridus ab inferis
redditur auris
55 fata merens coniugis.

Vincit Amor omnia,
regit Amor omnia.
Fuga tantum
fallitur amantum.
60 Fraude subdol*os*
subnectendo modul*os*
manus, aures, oculi
strenua pati
vix negant cupidini.

65 Do quietem fidibus,
finem, queso, luctibus
tu, curas alentibus.

How many men have past ages brought forth whom gracious friendship bound by a† durable bond, as Nisus to Euryalus, Pirithous to Theseus, Polynices to Tydeus!

Why should I remind you of the admirable alliance of David and Jonathan, of David's tearful lament when Saul fell, when Jonathan lay dead, while the Amalekite sat victorious, with Ziklag destroyed.

Merciless Amor drives man into the extremes of peril. He does not shrink from conflagrations, or from the roughness of the Bosphorus. Young Leander's foolhardiness had often defeated those rough waves, yet in the end he himself is defeated by the sea's surges. The lady of Sestos waits. Before her very eyes, in the sea, Leander dies.

(Orpheus) left the upper air to visit the dwellings of the shades, devoting himself to melodies on his plaintive strings. He brings rest to the shades, drives their torments away. Cerberus' mouths are tamed. There remain the grievous tears of Cerberus and of Proserpina, who was never moved before.

At last the ruler of the underworld, terror of mortals, made gentle by the poet's song, said 'Let Orpheus take away her whom he has merited by his melodies. But with a certain proviso: let him not look back. Let this unique lady take joy in her beloved—[but not within our gates].' Amor deceives Orpheus. He looks back at his prize.

Summoned back by the law, Eurydice slips away. Again the poet prepares to visit the shades, but the ferryman debars him from the Stygian stream. Pale he returns from hell to the air, lamenting his wife's destiny.

Amor conquers all, Amor governs all. He is outwitted only in the lovers' flight (from love). Hands, ears, and eyes, deceitfully adding sly modulations, can scarcely say no to the longing to experience emotional stress.

Now my lute is still: I beg you, still the griefs that nurture cares.

3 MS. īs[ ]stabili MrV insolubili. The line remains problematic.

5 *sic* F   MrV iunxit

6 ff. Cf. *Anticlaudianus*, II. 181–96.

11 F quod

15–16 F sicheleo seso (em. Mr)

20 F borf[   ]ris (em. Mr)

33 FMr fugit   V Penas (sg. of *Penates*)

35–37 For *incontiguus TLL* gives only two instances, meaning 'qui non tangi potest'. Thus *incontigue* here goes not with *lacrime* but with *Proserpine*, and Mr was wrong to eliminate line 35 on grounds of verse-form. His emendation *manant* in 36 is plausible but not absolutely necessary (see my translation).

42–43 F respectat   [Mr ne respecta *sole* gaudeat dilect*a*] The retention of 35, and the assumption that a corresponding line has dropped out of this stanza, allow a simpler emendation of these difficult lines than Mr's, emending only one word instead of three. Mr's emendations *respecta*, *dilecta* are in themselves suspicious, in so far as the corresponding lines 33–34 do not rhyme with each other. 43 needs no improvement: *sola* is the poet's favourite word for Eurydice (cf. A 60–64).

60–61 F subdola, modula   I take it that *modula* (unrecorded elsewhere) is an error for *modulos*, and emend accordingly.

63–64 F sternuo paci vix negnant cupidini (em. Mr) Adopting Mr's emendation, the lines make even better sense if *cupido* is not construed as a name, as Mr would have it. (The god, it is worth noting, is called Amor throughout.)

Textual comparison

The relation between the Augsburg and the Florence versions of 'Parce continuis' presents difficult problems. The first is in two south German hands of the beginning of the twelfth century;* the second, in a French hand of the early thirteenth. Both Meyer and Spanke (*Speculum*, vii (1932), 371), knowing only this second version, were inclined to attribute the song to Abelard. This I have always found incomprehensible, not least if, like Meyer, one attributes to the man who saw his whole life as a 'Historia Calamitatum' the phrase 'Cunctos evasi / nexus infortunii'!† More important is that we have no evidence that Abelard ever wrote learned secular songs. We know he wrote love-songs for Héloïse, such 'ut etiam illitteratos melodiae dulcedo tui non sineret immemores esse' (*P.L.* 178, 185d). Whatever these were like, they cannot have been like 'Parce continuis'—cannot, that is, have been sequences full of classical learning, designed for solo performance to an intellectual clerical audience. The very thing that for Meyer spoke in favour of Abelard's authorship, the 'philosophisch-erörternde Ton des Gedichtes' (p. 157), should in fact have been seen as a strong point against it, if one remembers that Abelard himself wrote 'et si qua invenire liceret carmina, essent amatoria, non philosophiae secreta' (128c). At the same time, Meyer was puzzled by certain formal aspects of the song:

The nature of the rhymes is particularly striking. The poet certainly lived in the twelfth century, that is, at a time when two-syllabled rhyme was already very well known, and after 1150 was the rule. Nonetheless he is content with monosyllabic rhyme throughout, including even a certain amount of monosyllabic assonance.

The Augsburg MS. (the prototype of which can hardly have been written after 1100) now allows these considerations to appear in a different light. Not only is Abelard ruled out as a possible author, but the use of monosyllabic rhyme and assonance is precisely what we should expect in an eleventh-century sequence.

To compare the two MSS. in detail: in 1a. 3–5, F as it stands (*neque vincularis legem amoris nimium queraris*) makes no sense.

* B. Kraft, *Die Handschriften der Bischöfl. Ord. Bibl.* (Augsburg 1934), p. 18, described it as one eleventh-century hand; I am indebted for this correction to Professor Bernhard Bischoff (received after my chronological arrangement of MSS. in this section).

† A has, however, confirmed F's reading *evasit* (see below).

A seems to preserve the correct text, making Mr's emendation unnecessary. 1b. 10 A *sanguinis* confirms Mr's conjecture. The antinomy between this first pair of stanzas, in which the request 'Don't complain too much against Amor' (1a) is at once followed by a torrent of complaint (1b, 2a, answered in turn by 2b), indicates that there are two speakers, as in Vergil's Eighth Eclogue, on which stanza 1b is based.

2a. 11–12 A has the correct text, F (*non reluctanti stetit ut rebellis*) is garbled. A *cedit* confirms Mr's conjecture. 2a. 15–16 F may be slightly preferable, as syllabically closer to 2b. 25–26, but syllabic correspondence is often loose throughout.

2b. 21–24 The most difficult lines in the poem. Mr, knowing only the F text, emended:

> Cunctos evasi
> nexus infortunii,
> qui sola compede
> stringor adamante.

The two MSS., however, confirm each other in the crucial words *evasit* and *Tui* (though Mr read *cui* in F), as well as in *stringor*. In both A and F *Tui* clearly begins a new sentence. As this would give a peculiarly abrupt transition to the second person, Mr's emendation *qui* now seems to me almost unavoidable. This in turn implies that either *evasit* or *stringor* must be emended. As the song nowhere else gives a hint of autobiographical statement, to retain *evasit* and emend to *stringitur* seems preferable to Mr's solution. If this emendation is correct, the rhythm then demands a word close to A's *amantes* (*amantis*, or possibly *amante*) rather than F's *adamante*.

The two stanzas that follow in F cannot, as Meyer (op. cit., p. 153) and Raby (*SLP* ii. 315) have suggested, be intended to contrast the blessedness of friendship with the fatality of love. For each of the four friendships mentioned falls under the shadow of death. Even Theseus, who risks his life for his friend, is imprisoned in Hades, though in some versions of the episode ultimately restored. The examples of *amicitia* point, if anything, in the same direction as those of *amor*: no deep human attachment can remain permanently blessed on earth.

The pair of stanzas on friendship are, it seems to me, an addition to the original song. It is significant that the theme of *amicitia* is taken up nowhere else in the poem *in either text*. These stanzas have no intrinsic relation to those preceding or following. They are mere summaries of *exempla*, quite lacking the imaginative and evocative power of the stanzas on Pyramus and Thisbe, Hero and Leander, Orpheus and Eurydice. In each of these the poet subtly and swiftly evokes the feelings of the protagonists for each other through the events; the stanzas on friendship have nothing of this kind. The stanza on Hero and Leander, on the other hand, was presumably the counterpart of the Pyramus stanza in the original song (even though isolated stanzas were not unheard-of in eleventh-century sequences); it is similar to this stanza in its evocative technique and quality. It would perhaps be best interpreted as a rejoinder from the lover's friend, who can see a love-death only as showing Love's *saevitia*.

4a. 49 A *procus* and F *procos* both seem unsatisfactory. My correction *procum* is suggested by *Georg.* IV. 457: 'illa quidem, dum te [Aristaeum] fugeret . . . .' 4a. 50 A *laetifer*—is it possible to see a conscious irony in this spelling?

4b. 54 *illam fatam*—it is easy to see how the later MS., F, might have arrived at the obvious and conventional *illum vatem*; but how could a scribe seeing or hearing *illum vatem* have thought of changing it to the remarkable *illam fatam*? These words seem less strange if we remember two things. First the conclusion of the previous stanza:

> Orfeus illam modulis
> urget insolabilis.

Orpheus is straining after Eurydice; the trees are straining to follow Orpheus; so they too are in a sense following Eurydice.—Is not this poet capable of such an elliptical conceit? Second, it is significant that in the later medieval vernacular versions of the story, such as the English *Sir Orfeo* and the Danish *Harpens Kraft*, Eurydice explicitly becomes a *fata* (*fée*) after her death, and it is as *fata* that she is restored to Orpheus.

For the precise meaning of *fata* here, W. von Wartburg's note (*Franz. etym. Wörterbuch*, III. 433) is illuminating:

Fata is a rare feminine derivative form from *fatum*, 'fate'. Accordingly it signifies the Parcae. . . . The word [*fée*] always signifies an enchantress who influences human fate in a good or evil direction. Her origin in the myth of the ancient Parcae still shows itself clearly in the triads in which *fées* so often appear (cf., for instance, the *Jeu de la Feuillée*).

A's *illam fatam* seems to be the first instance of the transition from the stricter ancient sense (*fatales deae, v.* Forcellini, Lexicon and Onomasticon, s.v.) to the medieval (*v.* Du Cange, s.v. *fadus*). What is at stake is Orpheus' fate, embodied in the 'fateful spirit' of his beloved.

4b. 55–56 A's *calliopes* (like *euridicen* in 46) is clearly wrong. But the vocative (with *temperas*) in A seems poetically more subtle than F *temperat*. 4b. 63–64 A *solam* makes better sense than F *semel,* and makes Mr's emendation (*semper*) unnecessary.

In A the song finishes at this point, except that the second hand (which, as Professor Bischoff has kindly informed me, begins with *–icen* in 4b. 62) adds the four letters *linq.* As F continues 'Liquid auras superiores', these letters must be the beginning of F's stanza, here opening 'Linquit'. This stanza elaborates the beginning of Orpheus' attempt to win Eurydice back.

In an article 'The Return of Eurydice' (*CM* xxiii (1962), 198 ff.) I tried to interpret the Augsburg text by relating it to a literary context in which Orpheus succeeds in bringing Eurydice back from death. Both the Pyramus and the Orpheus stories, I argued, were intended in their different ways to show the triumphant, not the hopeless, nature of human love. It was a tentative and audacious argument, especially as there I only alluded to the question of the Augsburg text's conclusion (p. 210, n. 30), without discussing it in detail.—In F the stanza 'Liquid auras superiores' is followed by three further stanzas, which in fact tell of Orpheus' failure. Yet there is, I think, a noticeable difference in tone and quality from what has gone before. The stanza 'Liquid auras' still has something of the swift, allusive manner of the earlier narrative stanzas in A. The stanzas beginning 'Tandem mitis carmine vatis' have none of this conciseness. Pluto's speech is elaborated in a clumsy, non-lyrical way, and it is followed by *sententiae,* such as

> Fallit Amor Orphea,
> respicit ad premia.

—a brittle, cynical little couplet; the moralistic neatness is quite alien to anything in the A text.

Of the six stanzas and coda of which A knows nothing (5, 6, 8, 12–15 in Meyer's and Raby's text), only one (that on Hero and Leander) is allied in its specific techniques and qualities to the stanzas in the A text. The stanzas on friendship, and those from 'Tandem mitis' onwards, seem to me to belong to a different layer of writing. They are more 'moral', not at all 'romantic' like the rest. What prompted them? The friendship stanzas may have been added to give greater weight and respectability and, as I indicated above, to bring the stories of lovers into a graver, more pessimistic context. What prompted the stanzas on Orpheus' failure? Here I would conjecture—the notion of Orpheus' success. They were added to counter a notion which was morally unacceptable, and perhaps also unfamiliar, to the second writer. If 'rettulit Euridicen' in 4b. 64 meant 'he brought Eurydice back' (which the abrupt change from present tenses to a perfect makes *prima facie* more natural than 'he echoed her name'), then it is likely that the original not merely showed Orpheus' descent (in a stanza 'Linquit auras'), but in some way made clear in a concluding stanza that he really

> quite set free
> His half-regained Eurydice.

Can one go further and guess what such a conclusion might have said? It seems to me at least possible that the lines

> Vincit Amor omnia,
> regit Amor omnia

which (despite the Boethian Orpheus, *Cons.* III, m. 12) sound so unexpectedly in F, appeared in the original conclusion.

While the original 'happy ending' must remain a matter of con-jecture, and while I cannot hope to have finally solved the problems posed by these two MSS., the existence of a new layer of stanzas in F seems to me beyond reasonable doubt. It can be supported, more-over, not only by stylistic arguments but by a more 'objective' one, a consideration of F's coda, which, as Meyer saw, resembles that of Abelard's *Planctus David super Saul et Ionatha*:

Do quietem fidibus,	Do quietem fidibus,
finem, queso, luctibus	vellem ut et planctibus
tu, curas alentibus.	sic possem et fletibus.
	Lesis pulsu manibus,
	raucis planctu vocibus,
	deficit et spiritus.

Compare also F's lines on David's lament with some counterparts in Abelard's poem:

planctum lacrimabilem	Planctus, Syon filie,
postquam Saül cecidit,	super Saül sumite . . .
Ionathas occubuit,	victus rex occubuit . . .
dum sederet Sichele*c*	Amalech invaluit
*c*eso victor Amalech.	Israel dum corruit.

These parallels strongly suggest that whoever wrote the friend-ship stanzas and the coda in F was acquainted with Abelard's *planctus**—which the writer of A, and *a fortiori* the original poet, cannot, chronologically, have been.

*The alternative possibility, that Abelard should have been the borrower, seems barely conceivable. If we except the Old Testament sources themselves, I know of no point at which any of the six *planctus*—in form, matter, and language surely the most independent Latin poetry of their age—can be shown to be derivative.

Sankt Florian, XI. 58, fol. 83[v]   s. XI

Diplomatic text:

> Cantant o͞ms uolucers iā lucessit dies
> amica cara surge sine me p̱ por tans
> exire. Seten īarboribus dinumera
> cantibus ūte te tignibus eia &

A reconstruction:

> Cantant omnes volucres,
>   iam lucescit dies.
> Amica cara, surge sine me
>   per portas exire.
>
> [Volucres, quae omnibus]   5
> sedetis in arboribus
> innumeris cantibus,
> vertite virginibus, eia!
> et [servite amantibus, eia!]

All the birds are singing, already day is dawning. Rise, dear love, to go out through the doors without me.

[You birds who] sit on [every] tree, with your countless songs, ah turn to the young girls [in love! ah help them in their love!]

1 ff. These lines are written in a large, illiterate hand on the last page of an eleventh-century MS. of Boethius and Ambrose (bound into the present Sankt Florian MS.). The first stanza is the opening of a clerc's *alba*. In contrast to the famous, problematic 'Phebi claro nondum orto iubare' (Vat. Reg. lat. 1462, s. X ex., fol. 50ᵛ), which is about the dawn-watch of soldiers ('spiculator, [h]ostium insidie, preco'), this is the first extant medieval European *alba* of lovers (though dawn-songs of parting lovers probably existed long before this both in Latin and vernaculars; cf. Theodor Frings, *Minnesinger und Troubadours*, especially pp. 40 ff.).

This *alba* contrasts with the later medieval ones in that here it is the woman who has visited her lover; it is she, not he, who must leave at dawn without being seen. (It would also be grammatically possible, on the other hand, to read *sine* in line 3 as a verb: 'Rise, dear love, let me go out through the gates.' But this seems an unlikely situation: a lover who wants his mistress's permission to leave need not order her to rise.)

4 Compare the Middle English lyric 'Ne saltou neuer, leuedi' (*Leeds Studies in English*, iv. 44 ff.):

> Dore, go þou stille,
> Go þou stille, -e,
> Yat; hic abbe in þe boure
> Ydon al myn uylle, -e.

As in the παρακλαυσίθυρα of antiquity, there is a symbolic power about such doors: they evoke all that separates two lovers, and all that brings them together.

5 ff. The text of the second stanza is too corrupt to allow any certainty in interpretation. [tignibus—meaningless; on photograph I read *vignibus*, but the second, slanting stroke is only a blemish on the page.]

Cambridge, UL Gg. v. 35, fols. 438ᵛ–439ʳ   s. XI

Diplomatic text:

```
S . . . . . . . . . . nunn[a] . . . . fert
 . . . . . . . . . . . tempus adest
 . . . . . dum grōuonot gras in
 . rt . . .
Quid [uis ut faciā] s[a]go thu mir
 iu[n] . . . . . [turpis] hortaris unicā
 [rn] . . . . . . . . . [m]el . . . .
 . . . . . . . . . . . . . coro miner min
 n[e] . . . . . . . . [n]des [vir] . . . silve nu
 sing . . t . . . ela . . uualde
```

[I] am cant& philomela kristes
[u]uir . . . . cui me deuoui
. . . .
O [formosa] . . . . sagic thir
. . . . sede[ ] anīe.
. . . . [humele]
S[ed angilo] . . . . mia s . . . . [m]inne
. . . . u[o]k[ ]l[ ]s veradan.
C . . . . nunna choro miner
. . . . . . dabo tibi super hoc uuerelt
. . . . genuoc
H oc [euanescit] ome also uuolcan in
th . . . . umele solū xp̄ī regnū
th . . . . ineuum.
[Q uod ipse regnat cr]edo in humele
s[ ] scon[ ] . . . . . cus[ ]t dare
[ ]az [g]il . . . . uuare.
[ ] omin . . . . uuemir
. . . . [d]ere . . . . . m[ir]
. . ndi[s] . . . . . . inne.
[L aus] . . . . thaz her s[i]be
ker[e] . . . . [penetrabit] . . . . . also
s . . . . [e]ger . . . . . s[a]l

A reconstruction:

Suavissima nunna,   ach fertrue mir mit wunna!
Tempus adest floridum,   gruonot gras in erthun.

Quid vis ut faciam?   sago thu mir, iunger man.
Turpis, hortaris unicam   ferno themo humele dan!

5 Carissima mea,   coro miner minne!
Nunc frondes virent silve,   nu singent vogela in walde.

Iam cantet philomela!—   kristes wirt mine sela;
Cui me devovi,   themo bin ih gitriuwe.

O formosa domina,   sag ic thir mine triuwe—
10 Mee sedes anime,   thu engil in themo humele!

Sed angilorum premia   samt gotelicher minne
Te prement, animam   thines vogeles ver[r]adan.

Carissima nunna,   choro miner minna!
Dabo tibi super hoc   wereltero dan genuoc.

15 Hoc evanescit omne   also wolcan in themo humele:
Solum Christi regnum   thaz bilibit uns in ewun.

Quod ipse regnat credo   in humele so scono:
Non recusat dare—   thaz gileistit her ze ware!

Nomini amantis,   ther gitriuwe mir ist,
20 Tantum volo credere   thaz thu mir wundist mine sinne.

Laus sit Amori   thaz her si bekere,
Quam penetrabit ut sol,   also si minnen gerno nu sal.

He: [Sweetest] nun, [ah] trust [me joyfully]! [Blossom]-time has come, the grass is green on [the earth].

She: What do you want me to do, tell me, young [man]? You are wickedly urging your beloved [far away from heaven].

He: [My dearest one], put my love to test! [Now] the leaves in the wood [are] green, now [birds] sing in the wood.

She: Let the nightingale sing! [My soul] will be Christ's, to whom I vowed myself, [to whom I shall be true].

He: Oh lovely [lady], I am telling you [my trust], oh dwelling-place of [my] soul, [angel of the heavens]!

She: Yet the rewards of the angels, [together with] love [of God], [will force you] to betray [the soul of your] (little) bird.

He: [Dearest] nun, put my [love] to test! I shall give you, what is more, great [honour] in the world.

She: All such things pass like clouds in the sky: only Christ's kingdom [endures] for ever.

He: I too believe he reigns in heaven so beautifully: he does [not] refuse to give—that indeed [does he grant].

She: [I so want to trust] in the name [of my lover, who is true] to me, [that you are wounding my senses].

Praise [be to Love] that he is converting her, [her whom] he will penetrate [like the sun], as [now] she is eager [to love].

Palaeographical notes

The lines in the MS. have been twice mutilated, once by a medieval censor, and once in more modern times by a scholar who applied chemicals to the ink. I have studied the pages repeatedly under ultraviolet lamp, and have little hope myself of winning further readings. In my transcription each dot represents the approximate space of an illegible letter (or perhaps of an abbreviation, or of a space between words). But it must be stressed that in many lines it is impossible to tell where the first letter was written and where the last. Probable but uncertain readings are in square brackets.

I have been able to make considerable additions and corrections to the text of Strecker (*Carmina Cantabrigiensia*, *MGH* (Berlin, 1926), pp. 74 ff.), who worked only from Breul's facsimile edition (Cambridge, 1915) and from special photographs, not from the MS. In my reconstruction, my indebtedness to the brilliant suggestions made sixty-five years ago by R. Kögel (*Geschichte der deutschen Literatur*, 1. 2, 137–8) will be evident. In my translation, only the words that can neither be read nor accurately inferred from the MS. are in square brackets.

1 nunna—Strecker wrote (op. cit., p. 74) 'Sicher ist wohl nur, daß es nicht *nunna* lautete'; under ultraviolet lamp, however, *nunna* admits of little doubt; wunna—the principle of assonance between the Latin and German half-lines is established by 6 silve/walde, 14 hoc/genuoc, 15 omne/[h]umele, 16 regnum/euum, 18 dare/uuare.

2 gruonot—MS. grōuonot, ō possibly expunged.

4 ferno—highly conjectural (though there might easily have been another letter or two at the beginning of this line in the MS.).

7 wirt—MS. one minim, a space, three minims, r.

12 vogeles—MS. k beyond reasonable doubt, but I cannot suggest a palaeo-graphically more satisfactory word.

13 choro—h probably imported by the English scribe (*v. infra*, Bibliography, p. 552), by confusion with Lat. *choro*.

16 MS. in euum—Latinized (probably by the English scribe) from OHG *in ewun*.

17 Quod ipse regnat credo—legible in Breul's facsimile, but now obscured by mending of the page.

19 Nomini—MS. possibly *Homi*, but H and N are often alike in this hand.

18 I construe *thaz* as pronoun, and the German half-line as a separate clause in parataxis.

22 ut sol—too speculative? But *sal* (Kögel's suggestion) is almost certain, and requires an assonance in the Latin, and there is space for five letters after *penetrabit*. Subj. Amor?

Commentary: Ch. V, pp. 277 ff.

Plangit nonna, fletibus
inenarrabilibus
condolens gemitibus-
que consocialibus:
5   Heu misella!
nichil est deterius
tali vita!
Cum enim sim petulans
et lasciva,

10 Sono tintinnabulum,
repeto psalte[rium],
gratum linquo somnium
cum dormire cupere[m]
—heu misella!—
15 pernoctando vigilo
[cum] non velle[m];
iuvenem amplecterer
quam libenter!

Fibula n[on] perfruor,
20 flammeum non capio,
strophium [as]sumerem,
diadema cuperem,
heu misella!—
monile arriperem
25 si vale[r]em,
pelles et herm[inie]
libet ferre.

Ago trabe circulum,
pedes volvo per girum,
30 flecto capu[d] supplicum,
[non] ad auras tribuo,
heu misella!

Manus dans, [in] c[or]di[bu]s
rumpo pec[tus],
35 linguam [te]ro dentibus
verba promens.

Lectus est in pissinis,
filtris non tappetibus,
cervical durissi[mum],
40 subter filtrum palea—
heu misella!
[Vesc]or lance misera
et amara,
[e] succis farinule
45 et caseo.

Tunica tet[er]rima,
interula fetida
stamine conposit[a];
ceno[sis]† obicibus
50 —heu misella!—
[f]ex cupedes adolens
inter pilos,
atque lens per[fe]ritur,
scalpens carnes.

55 Iuvenis, ne moreris!
faciam quod precipis;
dormi mecum! s[i non v]is,
tedet plura dicere
—heu misella!—
60 atque magis facere,
perdens vita[m]—
cum possim e[r]u[e]r[e]
memetipsam.

A nun is lamenting with unutterable tears and moans, grieving deeply on behalf of her companions: Woe is me, nothing is more degrading than such a life! for, though I am made for love and play,

I have to ring the chapel-bell, to chant the psalter over and over, to leave my dear dreams when I long to sleep—woe is me—and stay awake all night against my will. How gladly I would fly into a lover's arms!

I have no brooch to enjoy, can wear no bridal-veil; how I'd long to put on a chaplet or tiara, woe is me—I'd get hold of a necklace if I could—and what joy to wear ermine furs!

I pace the floor, walking round and round, I bow my head submissively, not raising it heavenwards, woe is me; giving in, my heart bursts with grief, but as the words come out I bite my tongue.

My bed is in a pitchy place, with felt, not coverlets; the pillow very hard, under the bedding—straw, woe is me! I eat the wretched, bitter fare, tasting of a little flour and cheese.

The shift I wear is grim, the underwear unfresh, made of (coarse) thread; within these muddy walls—woe is me—there's a stench of filth in my delicate hair, and I put up with the lice that scratch my skin.

Young man, please don't delay! I'll do your bidding; sleep with me! If you don't want to, there's no more to say, woe is me, and no more to do, wasting my life—since I can still destroy myself.

V: M. Vattasso, *Studi med.* i (1904–5), 124.

While the text of this song is not as badly damaged as the fragment of 'Foebus abierat' in the opposite column (*v. supra*, p. 335), V's text had to remain incomplete. With the help of the ultraviolet lamp in the Vatican library and of an excellent photograph, I have been able to correct and add a number of readings and make a first attempt at a full text, though several passages remain problematic.

2–3 Cf. *Rom.* VIII. 26 ('sed ipse spiritus postulat pro nobis gemitibus inenarrabilibus').

4 MS. *que* seems fairly certain; V *dicens* (too long both palaeographically and metrically).

19 MS. (probably) n perfruor V ut perfruer

21 V sumerem

26 For the expression *pelles herminie*, cf. Du Cange s.v. *hermellina* V hermeu[m] (which I have not met).

27 *sic* MS. (beyond any doubt) V liberet

28 ff. A difficult stanza. In 28 *trabe* (perhaps *turbe*) is hard to translate, in 30 *supplicum* must be either for *supplex* or possibly for gen. pl. '[in the manner of] suppliants'. 31 *tribuo* seems to require some such obj. as *suspiria* rather than *caput*.

31 I cannot read anything after *supplicum*; V an . .

33 MS. perhaps more like *incendibus* (?)   V *iucundilis* (which I have not met)
37–38 Corr. in pessimis filtris, non t.   ?
38 MS. tāppetibus   V tam prepetibus. The *filtrum* is a rough piece of felt used instead of a mattress. In the *Vita S. Galterii* (s. XI ex.), 'Lectus eius filtrum erat, et vilis matta cilicio tecta' (Du Cange, s.v. *feltrum*).
44 farinule—cf. 3 *Reg.* XVII. 13.
47 Cf. *Ruodlieb*, X. 129 ('interulam male lotam'). The balance of lines 46–47 suggests that two garments are named rather than one—but cf. Apuleius, *Florida* 9 ('tunicam interulam tenuissimo textu'). *Tunica* may also mean 'dress' here (cf. *CB* 177. 2).
49 *ceno* is certain, *obicibus* probable. But between them are at least two letters at the end of one line and two at the beginning of the next: possibily *cenobali* (for some form of *coenobialis*?). Yet this is unlikely metrically. V ceno terre herbicibus (which I find unintelligible)
51 MS. [ ] ex cupides   V Lex
57 MS. dormi ue mecum s . . . . . is (*ue* may have a faint line through it) V dormi ut

The stanza-form, with its irregular half-rhymes and assonances, is a 'transitional' one; the song is pre-twelfth century, possibly contemporary with the (formally far more accomplished) song 'Foebus abierat' on the same page, and with 'Suavissima nunna' in the *CC*. While one can see this song against a background of eleventh-century vernacular *plaintes de jeune fille* (*v. supra*, pp. 27 ff., 274–7), it is even more important to see its individuality. The remarkable poetic use of sacred allusion at the opening, transforming the Pauline contrast between slavery on earth and the hope of heaven; the unflinching precision of descriptive detail throughout, best comparable to that in the *Ruodlieb* (cf. my discussion in *Germ. Life and Letters*, xvii (1963), 58 ff.); the careful progression from trivial complaints through physical revulsion to sheer despair—by such means the poet (or poetess) has created a lyric more complex and more serious than any of the later dance-songs (e.g. Bartsch, I. 33 and 34) on a comparable theme.*

*P. S. Allen, who discussed this song in his *Medieval Latin Lyrics* (Chicago, 1931, p. 75), saw nothing of this. To him it was 'scarce worthy of printing, but for one conspicuous fact . . . that it is imitated from the prototype' of a vernacular 'nun's complaint'. Did the eleventh-century vernaculars have complaints of nuns as well as of young girls and *mal mariées*? I cannot tell. But whether they did or not, the Latin poem can no more be reduced to an imitation of these than Yeats's *Crazy Jane* poems to an imitation of Irish folksongs.

München, Clm 14834, fol. 26ʳ s. XII

Iuvenilis lascivia
et amoris suspiria
tam sunt delectabilia
qu' En Rosseinos en cante.

5 Hec est amoris nuncia,
et hec inflammat basia
et accendit incendia
mei estus, que s'en vante.

· Audivi sepe merulam
10 dum movet ignis stipulam
et hec pungit puellulam
mil fiz desob quarante.

Que durior est marmure
et es habet in pectore
15 ut hanc audit sub arbore
tut est rendeu *ar*dante.

Hec est avis Cupidinis,
que post *i*ctum harundinis
movet estus libidinis
20 'oci! oci!' dum cante.

Youth's dalliance and sighs of love are such a source of joy that they are sung by Mistress Nightingale.

She is love's messenger, she makes kisses burn, she kindles the fires of my passion—so as to make boast of them.

Often I have heard the blackbird, stirring the little fiery blade that pricks a maid—who laments it a thousand times over.

Even she who is more unyielding than marble, whose breast is of bronze, hearing the nightingale from beneath a tree, is made utterly passionate.

Philomela is the bird of Cupid, she who, after the piercing of the arrow, inflames the senses with passion, singing 'oci! oci!'

M: R. A. Meyer, *ZfrP*, Beiheft 8, 108.

4 MS. quen, encantē   M que rosseinos   qu' En Rosseinos en cante—lit. that
Sir Nightingale (masc. form in the vernacular line, but fem.—philomela, avis—
in the Latin stanzas) sings of them.

8 MS. mei est usque

12 mil fiz desob quarante—lit. (she) complaining thereof a thousand times.
MS. (probably) desoh. M wrote '*mil fois de soi querant* dürfte kaum die richtige
Lösung sein. Gröber dachte an: *nuls . . . de so n(e)s guarante.*'

16 MS. (?) rēdezendante   M read 'rēdicendante' and emended at Gröber's
suggestion, to 'tout est rendu e' n chante'.

18 MS. dictum]M ictum] Another possibility is 'post dictum h*i*rundinis'
(i.e. 'after Procne's request' cf. *Metam.* VI. 424 ff., esp. 467–8; *Fasti*, II. 853–7).

20 MS. cantie

The form of this song (8aaa 7b) is virtually the '*zajal*-like' form (8aaa 8b)
of Guillaume's 'Pos de chantar m'es pres talentz' (xi).

fol. 26ᵛ

Virgo Flora,
tam decora,
tam venusta facie,
suo risu,
5   suo visu
me beavit hodie.

Visus eam
facit deam;
mens excedit hominem.
10   Frons est tota
sine nota,
sicut decet virginem.

Eius cultus,
eius vultus
15   recens est cottidie;
digna coli
cum nec soli
cedit in meridie.

Si sit cura
20   nostri, iura
per paludem Stygiam,
est firmandum

iusiurandum,
propter amiciciam.
25 Tantum gerit
quantum querit
species potentie;
letam labe,
plenam tabe
30 [reddunt excellentie].

The maiden Flora, so lovely, so fair of face, has blessed me today with her smile and with her presence.

Her aspect makes her a goddess, her mind is more than human; her forehead utterly unblemished, as becomes a maid.

Her attire and her features are fresh from day to day. Worship is due to her—she is not surpassed even by the sun at noon.

(You may) swear by the Stygian lake that she is all my care—an unalterable oath—so great is our affection.

She fulfils every potentiality towards which her being strives. [Her perfections make her] joyous even in adversity, full even in waning.

1 Flora—there are many 'Flora' poems in the twelfth and thirteenth centuries. On the one hand there are songs of love-worship, such as Arundel 3, 7, 8 (*CB* 83), 15, 16—in three others, 6, 9, 14 (*CB* 108) the girl is called Florula— or *CB* 106, 186, quite apart from the renowned *CB* 92, the *Altercatio Phyllidis et Florae*; on the other hand there are satirical pieces, such as Hugh Primas VI and VII (ed. Meyer; Langosch 19, 20). The Italian Flora, goddess of blossoms and spring, was known from the *Fasti* (IV. 945, V. 184 ff.). Pliny (*Nat. Hist.* XXXVI. 23) identified her with Korê, and her presence among the Charites (Martianus Capella, *De Nupt.* 888) made her akin to Venus *caelestis*. These are the connotations of Flora the beloved in medieval love-poetry, as in the present song. The satires and *meretrix* poems reflect the other half of the tradition. Flora was a common name among hetairai (cf. Juvenal I. 2, 49), and this was explained euhemeristically by Lactantius (*Inst.* I. 20) from the licentious aspects of Flora's feast, the Floralia.

10 MS. est est

19 ff. A difficult stanza. It may be interpreted as above, or else as addressed to a friend seen as a possible rival: 'Swear that she is mine (and won't ever be yours). You must swear this, for our friendship's sake.' In either case 'si' remains problematic.

28 Corr. ictam labe ?

30 The last line of this stanza, and possibly other stanzas also, are missing.

Commentary: Ch. V, pp. 287 ff.

Praha, UL Germ. XVI. G 23, fol. 46ᵛ   s. XII–XIII

> Quia sub umbraculum
> sedi, quem desidero
> amoris signaculo
> dilectissimus, quem video,
> 5   cor meum sic consignat
> ut generosa dignat.
>
> Surgat, ad me veniat,
> preelectus milium,
> amplexu me leniat,
> 10 pudoris sumens lylium
> quod illi soli servo,
> sub castitatis modo.

Because I sat beneath the shade, he whom I long for, my beloved whom I behold, seals my heart with the seal of love in such a way that it cherishes noble virtues.

May he rise and come to me, he who is unique in thousands, caressing me with his embrace, taking the lily of innocence which I save for him alone, incorruptible.

4 MS. dil'cis⁹ (corr. dilectus ?)
6, 9 MS. generosā (rightly ?), amplexū (impossible).

The poem's language is obviously coloured by that of the Song of Songs ('quem desidero; signaculo; Surgat . . . veniat, preelectus milium'), but there is no specific borrowing. The nearest phrases are 'Sub umbra illius quem desideraveram sedi. . . . Dilectus meus mihi, et ego illi, qui pascitur inter lilia' (*Cant.* II. 3, 16). In its simplicity this song seems to bridge the gulf between Solomon and the *winileodas*.

Roma, Vat. Reg. lat. 344, fol. 38ᵛ   s. XIII in.

> Nix transit et imber et frigus horidum,
> ver redit et estas et tempus floridum;
> iam gelu solvitur afflatu tepidum
> et mundus exuit quicquid est hispidum.

Iam arbor induit decorem frondium
et ortus floridus colorem varium;
in silvis resonat garritus avium,
spina rosas profert, odorem lilium.

Flos viole red[d]it campum purpureum
10 et aura temperat ignem ethereum—
qui modo non amat cor habet ferreum:
serenus est aer, tempus idoneum.

Cor habet ferreum si tempus transeat
ita ut amori curam non prebeat.
15 Amet, sed sic amet amor ut deceat—
indigno amori nemo subiaceat.

Formosam diligas, simplicem moribus,
et non meretricem instinctam fraudibus.
Ex corde diligas, non pro muneribus:
20 hoc est conveniens amoris legibus.

Snow and showers and harsh cold are passing, spring and summer and the time of flowers return. Now the frost, less cold, is
loosened by the breeze, and the world casts off whatever is rough.

Now the tree puts on its seemly dress of leaves, the garden in flower
takes on many colours, the warbling of birds resounds in the woods.
The thorn brings out roses, the lily its scent.

The violet's blossom purples the field, the breeze cools the
fieriness of the sun above.—Whoever does not love now has a heart
of iron: the air is serene, the time is made for love.

He has a heart of iron if the time goes by without his heeding love.
May he love, but love in all honour: let none be overcome by an unworthy love.

Love someone beautiful and unaffected, not a courtesan full of
deceit. Love wholeheartedly, not for the sake of gain—(only) this
is in accordance with love's laws.

11 ff. Cf. the refrain of 'Bruma, grando, glacies' (*MARS* iv (1958), 64):

> Serenus est aer, aura salubrior,
> marina resident, fit unda purior,
> qui modo non amat est ferro durior.

Firenze, Laurenziana Edil. 197, fol. 131ᵛ   s. XIII in.

[P]rimo quasdam eligo
et electas diligo
et dilectas subigo—
sum levis plus quam ventus;
5   nihil in me corrigo:
sic exigit iuventus!

In adolescencia
suadet nos lacivia
currere per omnia,
10 nihil iubet cavere;
nulla est infamia
hic legem non habere.

Senis obstinacio
est abhominacio:
15   iuvenis religio
fere nusquam laudatur—
viret in principio,
sed in fine siccatur.

Dum sum in hoc tempore,
20 dum fervesco pectore,
dum ignis in corpore
calet, semper amabo!
naturali frigore
congelatus, cessabo.

First I choose my girls, and those I choose I love, and those I love I
subjugate—I am lighter than the wind; I have no fault to find in me:
this is how youth should be!

When we are young a playful sense persuades us to experience
everything, not to be on our guard; it is no disrepute if there's no
measure here.

The inflexibility of the old is something horrible: youth's cult is
scarcely ever praised—youth, green at first, and dry at last.

As long as I am young and ardent in heart, as long as a fire burns

in me, I shall always be in love! When in the course of nature I grow
cold, I'll cease.

B: H. Brinkmann, *Gesch. d. lat. Liebesdichtung im Mittelalter* (Halle, 1925),
p. 33.
    1 B Prima
    2 MS. dirigo, corr. diligo
    4 B levi
    8 lacivia—i.e. lascivia (cf. lucinia, *infra* p. 392, l. 8, &c.)

fol. 131ᵛ

1a [D]ant ad veris honorem
        arida florem;
    flos in amorem
        spirat odorem.
5   En valor et calor
        est modo rebus,
    zodiaci petit
        ardua Phebus,
    omnia dant sua gaudia.

    . . . .

    . . . .

2a Tonat, prestat illi Parcas
    et decanas et tetrarchas,
    Musas ducit Stilbon Arcas,
        anxi[a]t Apollo.

3a Bello fera dat innumera
    Venus vulnera;
    tenet ethera,
    perimit Tartera.

4a Fles tu, o dia
    Filologia,
    flesque, Talia,

1b Color est Iri[di]
        ilaris serene,
    quia nunc †viri[di]
        [o]mne†madet pene;
5   saltant satiri
        voce Philomene,
    quos dire diu
        vinciunt habene.
    Nunc [cont]en[d]unt
        Venus et Minerva.
10 Pugnat Pallas egide
        proterva;
    clamat: Iovis me paterne
        serva!

2b Iuvant partes Citharee
    Ceres, Bachus, natus Ree,
    omnes simul fere dee
        adiuvant in bello.

3b Terga dat plane
    pompa Diane,
    capto Titane,
    teque, bifrons Iane.

4b casus Limitane.
    Catenato Pane
    rides, Volicane.

In spring's honour the barren places flower, the flower breathes its perfume into love. See the power of life, the warmth that is now in the world; Phoebus seeks out the high regions of the Zodiac, all things give forth their joys.

Serene Iris has a joyous colour, for now †on the green nearly every thing† is moist. Satyrs leap at the sound of Philomena, satyrs whom cords have long and grievously held bound. Now Venus and Minerva conflict. Pallas fights with her fearful Gorgon-shield. She cries out 'Aid me, Father Jupiter!'

He thunders, he offers her the Fates, and the decans and the tetrarchs; Arcadian Stilbôn leads forth the Muses, Apollo is ill at ease.

Ceres, Bacchus, and the son of Rhea (Attis?) help Cytherea's side; almost all the goddesses at once join in the battle.

Venus, fierce in war, inflicts countless wounds. She holds sway in heaven and ravages hell.

Diana's host turns tail entirely once the Titan is captured, and you, two-faced Janus.

You weep, Goddess Philology, and you, Thalia, weep at the calamities of Diana of the Crossways. And you laugh, Vulcan, because Pan is chained.

1a. 3 MS. 'odorem' deleted before 'amorem'. Cf. Baudri of Bourgueil, 237 (ed. Abrahams): 'Flos mittit florem, roseum rosa spirat odorem'; *CB* 163. 4: 'Flos in amore   spirat odore.' The strophic parallelism indicates that two lines are missing from this stanza.

5 ff. Cf. *Metamorphosis Goliae*, 65: 'Per hunc [Iovem] rebus insitus calor figuratur.'

1b. 1 MS. iri
3 MS. viri mne (5 minims and e)   The passage remains difficult, but a more radical emendation seemed inadvisable.

7 dire—possibly adj.
9 MS. minua
11 Iovis—a nominative used vocatively. Cf. 'Profuit ignaris' (*infra*, pp. 452 ff.) 40, 92, 160.

2a. 2 decanas—decanos? Cf. Martianus Capella, *De Nupt.* 200: '[Philologia] nunc tot diversitates cerneret formasque decanorum tunc octoginta quattuor liturgos caelo miraretur adstare.' Usually, however, there are 36 decans, one governing every ten degrees of the zodiac (*v.* W. Gundel, *Dekane und Dekansternbilder*, Glückstadt–Hamburg, 1936).

tetrarchas—Here, the powers that govern the four elements. Cf. Milton's 'Tetrarchs of fire, air, flood, and on the Earth' (*Paradise Regained*, iv. 201).

3 Stilbon Arcas—already in Aristotle Στίλβων was a name for the planet

Mercury. The names Stilbon and Arcas are synonymous in *De Nupt.* 24–25. Cf. also *CB* 70, st. 11b; Geoffrey of Monmouth, *Historia Regum Britanniae*, ch. 117 ('Stilbon Archadiae').

2b. 2 natus Ree—probably Attis. The identification of Rhea with Cybele was clear from *Fasti*, IV. 179 ff. (the festival of Magna Mater, and the story of Attis). Cf. Sir James Frazer's *Commentary*, III. 202. Rhea also occurs in *CB* 73, st. 2b, in Arundel 16, st. 2, and in 'Usus vite veteris' (*infra*, p. 370, and note).
   3 fere—possibly adj. *ferae*.

3a. 1 Possibly two lines, with a corresponding line missing in 3b.

4b. 1 Limitane—I take this to be genitive, 'of her of the boundaries' (*limitanus* = *limitaneus* in Priscian—*v*. Forcellini s.v.).
   3 Volicane—i.e. Vulcane.

Did the poem originally finish here?

The main theme of the poem (or of the fragment we have left) is the contest between Love and Reason (compare, three centuries later, Dunbar's *The Goldyn Targe*). On Minerva's side is every kind of law and order—Jove and the Fates, Apollo, the spirits of the zodiac (governing the laws of change in the universe), Mercury and Philology (the authority of Quadrivium and Trivium). Venus–Cytherea, aided by Bacchus and Attis and all the goddesses except Diana, holds sway over the upper regions (tenet ethera)—she is goddess of 'ethereal' love, *Venus caelestis*. Diana's train is put to flight, the sentry Janus (who according to Macrobius, *Sat.* I. 9, is 'quasi superum atque inferum janitorem') is captured. Yet Love's victory against Reason is not unconditional: Reason, by enlisting the cunning Vulcan's aid, has succeeded in chaining up Pan, who figures lust. The love that triumphs 'tenet ethera'—it is twice bless'd, born not only of Cytherea, but (st. 1a) of the barren earth and the spring.

Wien, CV 1565, fol. I^r 　　　　　　　　　　　　　　　　.s. XIII in.

      1a Usus vite veteris
         arma tulit Veneris,
            gravibus
             legibus
        subditus amoris;

1b Omni fruens Cipride,
   tryplici Caryptide
   florui,
   placui
   puellarum coris.

1c Nunc Bellone milito,
   Afros fluxus fugito,
   vinculo,
   cingulo
   abstraor et loris.

2a O Delio
   socio
   aliti et ereo,
   rex incinctus ense,

2b O studeo,
   hereo,
   obsequor Cillenio
   nupciali mense.

3a Mense Sol dat fercula,
   Bacus miscet pocula,
   Primus sedet Yparcon,
   Parce dicunt Togaton;

3b Sponsa sedet medio,
   una cum Mercurio,
   Noy Fyche proxime,
   dii, dee maxime.

4a Eoe
   Bache!
   Panes clamant Foloe,

4b Medii
   o y
   crepant saltus satiri,

4c Satrape
   pape
   risu linqunt a a e !

5a Corum ducit vox ninfarum,
   turmas trahens poetarum.
   Cum spondeo sonat iambus
   hinc resultat coliambus.

5b Metra sonant ydraulea,
   systra movet mater Rea,
   sonant tropi timpanorum,
   crepant bombi crotalorum.

6a Manticis prestigio
    Faunus caret pallio,
       Racio –o
    subridet Mercurio;

6b *Sileni* calvicia
    nudat Nigromancia.
       Talia –a
    dia ridet curia.

7a En ymenea
     corea
       sonat,

Fama velando,
    clamando
      tonat.

7b Ipse novene
     camene
      silent,

sistra canora,
    sonora
      vilent.

7c Livor ovantis
     clamantis
      vocet:

solus iniqua
    oblica
      docet.

8a Rex, Lex, Opifex
    archetiporum

8b Sternit livida,
    nudat invida.

I Et decreto nupciali L[ut]or pandit aditum.

9a Virtus ostia
    pandit regia,

9b Fama peribet,
    intrat quislibet.

II Meta placet,   Clio tacet,   lira vacet.

My old way of life bore Venus' arms, subjected to the burden-some laws of love. Enjoying every Cypris (that I met), I flourished in a thrice-perilous whirlpool, I gave delight to crowds of girls. Now I serve in Bellona's ranks, I shun the Syrtes (of love), I am drawn away from that chain, girdle, and scourge.

O royal (Mars), girt with sword, I now adhere and cling to Delius' companion, winged and air-borne: I follow Cyllenius at the wed-ding-feast.

Sol provides the table with food, Bacchus mixes goblets of wine. Yparcon is the first to sit, the Fates utter Togaton. The bride, (Philologia), sits in the middle, together with Mercury; Psyche next to Noys, the gods next to the great goddess.

Evoe Bacchus! shout the Pans on Pholoe. O! y! the satyrs in the middle make their leaps resound. The Pope's satraps die of laughing Ha! ha! he!

The song of the nymphs leads the dance, drawing forth the crowds of poets. Iamb sounds along with spondee, thence rings out the choliambic. The water-organ's measures sound, Rhea, Magna Mater, plays the sistra; modes of the tympani are heard, and castanets clapper.

By Manticê's illusion, Faunus (finds he) lacks his pallium. Ratio smiles at Mercury, while Nigromancia lays Silenus' baldness bare. The whole court of heaven laughs at such things.

But see, the wedding dance begins! By concealing and by proclaiming, Fama thunders abroad. The nine Muses themselves are silent, the sonorous singing sistra fade away. Let the envy of the uproarious shouter (Fama) sound forth—this alone insinuates wickedness.

The King, the Law, Fashioner of archetypes, overthrows malice, lays envy bare.

And he, the Purifier, lays open the way for the nuptial decree.

Virtus throws open the royal portals, Fama bears witness, whoever wishes enters.

The end is happy; Clio is silent; let my lute be silent too.

1a–2b. The train of thought seems to be: I was once a lover (1a–b), next a soldier, rejecting love (1c); then the soldier turns scholar (2a–b), handing his resignation to Mars, as it were, and becoming a follower of Mercury.

1b 1 Omni fruens Cipride—cf. 'nec Veneres nostras hoc fallit' (Lucretius, IV. 1185), or 'Venerum feritas saepe fit aura levis' (*A.L.* 2292)—though I have not found a parallel use of *Cypris.*

2 tryplici Caryptide—cf. Isidore. *Etym.* XIII. 18, 5:

Charybdis dicta quod gurgitibus occultis naves obsorbeat; est enim mare verticosum, et inde ibi laniata naufragia profundo emergent. Ter autem in die erigit fluctus, et ter obsorbet; nam accipit aquas ut vomat, vomit ut rursus accipiat.

In Martianus Capella, *De Nupt.* 512, Charybdis is shown to be synonymous with 'luxuria'.

3–4 MS. placui florui—I have reversed the order as it yields a much clearer sense.

1c. 2 Afros fluxus—the Syrtes (cf. Pliny, *Nat. Hist.* IX. 149, and *De Nupt.* 671-4, though not *ipsis verbis*). Less probably, an adj. formed from ἀφρός: 'the foamy (Aphrodític) waves' (cf. *Etym.* VII. 11, 76–77, and Macrobius, *Sat.* I. 8, 6).

2a. 1 Apollo's socius is Mercury (Cyllenius). *V. De Nupt.* 210.

3 ereo—i.e. aërio.

2b. 3 obsequor Cillenio—i.e. I am now a devotee not of Venus but of Philologia.

3a. 3 Yparcon—originally Ὁ Ὑπάρχων, in the pseudo-Dionysius, *De Divinis Nominibus*, v. 4.

4 Togaton—τὸ ἀγαθόν, the Platonic Idea of the Good. The 'suprema divinitas' in Bernardus Silvestris, *De Universitate Mundi*, II. 5, 24. Here, the Fates reveal this transcendent 'Fatum' which, *qua* transcendent, is inexpressible.

3b. 3 Noys (the neoplatonic Νοῦς)—following Bernardus Silvestris, the goddess who is 'bonum bonitatis divinae, plenitudo scientiae ... Dei intellectus' (I. 2, 152). I construe *Noy* as dative.

Fyche—MS. Fychem   Psyche is frequently written 'Fyche' in mythographic MSS., but I cannot understand the (? acc.) -em in this line. Psyche is found in a similar assembly in Bernardus Silvestris, II. 5.

4 Dea maxima—Noys. The 'dii' are probably the Olympians, rather than Yparcon and Togaton.

The link between the figurae of Chartrain philosophy and Martianus Capella's nuptials may be illuminated by the declaration of Thierry, the master of the Chartres school, at the opening of his *Heptateuchon*: 'We have married Trivium to Quadrivium, so as to increase the noble race of philosophers.' In the Platonism of Chartres, in other words, the arts of Philology were to be wedded to those of Mercury.

4a. 3 Panes—the plural form is found in *De Nupt.* 167 (Panes, Fauni, Fones, Satyri) and again in Bernardus Silvestris (Silvani, Panes et Nerei).

Foloe—i.e. Pholoe, actually a haunt of centaurs (*v.* Bernardus Silvestris, I. 3, 194–5).

4c. 1 Satrape—here 'cardinals'. *V.* Du Cange, s.v., and the Feast of Fools song 'Gregis pastor Titirus' (for the twelfth-century version from Saint-Martial, *v.* *MÆ* xxviii (1959), 192):

> Ad [h]onorem Titiri
> festa colunt baculi
> satrape et satiri.

In our poem too I think the incongruity is deliberate: the solemn wedding ceremony is preceded by wild Bacchic noises and music, and a grotesque dumbshow in which anything can happen. Though there is no external evidence, it is possible that this poem also has a direct connexion with the Feast of Fools. *Pape*—could also be the interjection *papae!*

5a. 1 MS. ducat
4 MS. resultet coriambus

5b. 1 The *hydraula* is twice mentioned among a series of instruments by Martianus Capella, but the adj. form *hydrauleus* does not seem to be recorded.

2 systra movet mater Rea—the sistrum was an instrument invented, as Isidore (*Etym.* III. 22, 12), quoting Juvenal, XIII. 93, states, by Isis. Rhea is here seen as equivalent to Isis (cf. Hippolytus of Rome, *Elenchos*, v. 9, 8).

3 tropi timpanorum—cf. *De Nupt.* 133:

. . . hymeneia dedere tripudia, sed ecce magno tympani crepitu crotalorumque tinnitu universa dissultant eo usque, ut Musarum cantus aliquanto bombis tympani obtusior redderetur, et cum sonitu introfertur lectica interstincta sideribus, cui ritu mystico crepitus praecinebant, qua mos fuerat nubentes deas in caelestis thalami pervenire consortia.

Hence the buffoonery preceding the actual *ymenea corea* in this poem (6a–b). But it may also have a more serious aspect: the lustful Faunus and Silenus are exposed and put to ridicule by two of Philologia's attendants.

4 MS. crotanorum

6a. 1 Manticê—i.e. Divination. In *De Nupt.* 6, a prospective bride of Mercury.

6b. 1 MS. Cilleni—but Silenus (*De Nupt.* 809) would fit far better.

2 Nigromancia does not occur in Martianus Capella. She is Manticê's darker counterpart. The distinction between them may well have been suggested by a passage in Isidore, where he says in connexion with Necromancia 'Duo sunt autem genera divinationis: ars et furor' (*Etym.* VIII. 9, 11–14).

3–4 There are two other possible ways of construing: 'Dia (the mother of Mercury—*v.* Cicero, *De Natura Deorum*, III. 22) laughs at such things in the curia', or again 'Talia (Thalia) laughs in the divine curia'. The second is quite attractive if we compare 'Dant ad veris honorem' 4a (*supra*, p. 367).

7a–c. There is a ritual permission for Fama and slander to have their last fling at the beginning of the marriage ceremony, a kind of 'clearing of the banns'. Compare the fescennine episode in Catullus' epithalamium *In Nuptias Iuliae et Manlii*.

I. Lutor—the reading is uncertain, owing to a smudge in the MS. The word might also be 'livor'—'and spite (itself) opens the way'.

II. The three-line coda in which the singer refers to his lute's return to silence is found also in the later version of 'Parce continuis' (*supra*, p. 345), and in a double form in Abelard's *Planctus David super Saul et Ionatha*. It may well have been Abelard's invention.

Oxford, Bodley Add. A. 44, fol. 70ᵛ   s. XIII in.

Ver prope florigerum, flava Licori,
iam rosam aspicis,   egressam tunicis,
credere celo tepidiori
tenera germina floris odori.

5 Iam iuxta garrulos   lascivit rivulos
flos dive Veneri gratus Adonis,
herba recentibus apta coronis.

Si declines   iuxta fines
fontis   euntis
10   vallibus   declivibus,

reddetur herba gracior,
    fons purior,
    mens lecior.

O si tamen   supra gramen
15   gressus repressus
      morulam ad parvulam,
inpresso celer basio
    Venereo,
     rem finio!

20 Cum flavi capitis develas verticem
comamque colligis in nodum simplicem,
ploratam Orpheo reddis Euridicem.

Sed digitis evagatis
circa locum voluptatis
25   discursu libero,
    sub crure manum
      tenero dum perfero,
Medis et Persis impero!

Cum motu lateris sentitur Veneris
30 illud et ultimum dulcescit operis,
amice mediis relabor brachiis—
dum respiraverim rebus Venereis.

Te quando vultu video
sidereo, depereo;
35   *sed* quando rides
      lecior, illicior
et levi causa capior
illecebris amoris.

Sed que placebas displices
40 si iuvenem non abdices
    ad quem transfertur
      oculus tam sedulus,
et nostri ridet emulus
suspiria doloris.

45   Si lascivo   more vivo,
     fame nitorem detero;
     sed misero sic vivitur
     cum debellatus animus
     ire sub hastam cogitur.

50   Vale dicturus paginis,
     vale dicturus artibus,
     tibi, Licori, milito—
     tuis concedo partibus.

When spring is almost in flower, golden Lycoris, you watch the rose, arising from its dress, trusting the tender buds of its fragrant flower to a warmer sky.

Now Adonis' flower, the joy of goddess Venus, luxuriates by babbling streams, now fresh garlands can be plucked from the grass.

If you recline at the brink of a fountain that passes down curving valleys, the grass will be made lovelier, the fountain purer, the mind more full of joy.

But oh if only on that grass, staying my steps for a brief little delay, imprinting a passionate kiss, I could swiftly reach love's goal!

When you unveil your golden hair and bind it into a simple knot, you are giving back to Orpheus his lamented Eurydice.

But when my straying hand roves freely in the domain of bliss, brought between your tender thighs, the world—Persians and Medes—is mine.

When the body's movement feels the transport of love, and the act grows serene at last, I fall back into my beloved's arms—till I revive in love.

When I see you with your starry face, I am undone; when you laugh so joyfully, I am beguiled, and easily caught in love's allurements!

But you who pleased me well will please me ill, unless you give up that young man to whom your ardent gaze now turns, while he, my rival, laughs at my sighs of grief.

If I live wantonly, I dim my reputation's brightness—yet that is how a wretch must live when the defeated spirit is forced to pass beneath the spear.

I'll say farewell to my studies, I'll say farewell to the arts; it is you I serve, Lycoris—I've come over to your side.

A: Auxerre 243, fol. 18ʳ (1358). V: A. Vernet, *Mélanges Félix Grat*, ii. 260 ff. (ed. from A). W: A. Wilmart, *MARS* iv (1958), 60 ff. (ed. from O).

1 A liquori   For the name 'Lycoris', cf. (outside the Roman poets) *CB* 63 and Arundel 2, and *infra*, p. 465.

2 Cf. Alanus, *Anticlaudianus*, IX. 405: 'E tunicis egressa suis rosa purpurat ortos.'

4 *sic* OA   [W et tenera—unnecessary, and syntactically and rhythmically awkward]

5 A iusta

6 *sic* OA   [W Veneris]   Cf. Servius *in Ecl.* X. 18.

7 A recemptibus

8 A iusta fontis fines

9 A euntes

18 A venerio

20 A vertice   V verticem

21 A nundum

22 i.e. 'you bring about an inconceivable, miraculous joy'. A reddes erudicem   O euridicen

27 A tenere   V tenero

28 Cf. Horace, *Carm.* III. 9, 4; Walter of Châtillon, Saint-Omer, XXXI, st. 3, 7–8.

29 A sentitu   V senatu

30 A ad, dulcessit   V dulcescit

35 O si quando

37 A a levi

39 A Sed quia

44 A suspirio   V suspiria

45 A Sed

47 *sic* OA   [W misere]

48 *sic* OA   [W altero]

50 *sic* OA   [W parcito: paginis *absurde* O]

52 Cf. Horace, *Carm.* III. 26: 'Vixi puellis nuper idoneus / Et militavi non sine gloria.' Also Apuleius, *Metam.* IX. 9: 'Veneri militabant nudi milites'; Marbod, *R. Archidiacono*, 8 ff. (*P.L.* 171, 1659); Peter of Blois, 'Olim militaveram / pompis huius seculi'; Walter of Châtillon, 'Hactenus immerito / militavi creature . . . Creatori milito'; Saint-Omer, XXIII, st. 6–7 (playing on Ovid, *Am.* I. 9), XXV. 4 (*militantium* of those who serve); *Causa Acis et Polyphemi*, 9 (Walther, *Streitgedicht*, p. 234).

53 A tuus concedo devotus partibus

45–53 The situation here is not merely that of choosing to be a lover rather than a scholar (as in Arundel 14, 'Vacillantis trutine'). The lover, broken and humiliated, feels that for him, as for his faithless Lycoris, only 'La Ronde' is left. The last two lines suggest not 'I've been won over to love, like you' (this had happened long before), but, more bitterly, 'I enlist in your (faithless) kind of love, as you have convinced me I must'.

Form: a *descort*. It may be helpful to distinguish four basic types of (accentual)

line: a dactylic tetrameter, with slight variations (*a*); a trochaic or iambic dimeter (*b*); an adonic (*c*); and an 'echo' of four syllables, heavily stressed on the second, preceded by a dactyl (*d*) or alone (*d'*). The rhythmic structure can then be clarified as follows:

aaaa [or aacca] aaa bcdbd'd' bcdbd'd' aaa bbccdb aaaa bbcdbb bbcdbb bbbbb bbbb

As no melody survives to provide further evidence of the metrical scheme, I have adopted this as the arrangement of the lines.

Paris, B.N. lat. 3719, fol. 23ʳ   Before 1210

1a Ex ungue primo teneram
        nutrieram
      ut te, Lice,
      prima vice
5 aetatem circa puberem
        exigerem
      et caperem
    primitias pudoris!

1b Fovisti viros gremio
        propicio,
      iam iam vivis
      cum lascivis—
    septennis adhuc fueras
        —te reseras—
        admiseras
    illecebras amoris.

2a   Me meo memini
      scripsisse legem inguini—
        pro foribus astaret,
        nec molestum virgini
        profundius intraret!

2b   Audax virguncula
    maiora multo iacula
        suscipere decrevit—
        votum, licet parvula,
        femineum explevit.

3a   Pubertatem
        per etatem
        dum stultior
        operior,
5   Lice! Lice!
    Lice, sexu ducta femineo,

    virgo virum nosti, et doleo,

    doleo! doleo! doleo!

3b   [Te futuram
        iam maturam
        dum studeo,
        custodio,
        Lice! Lice!
    corpus adhuc impube,
                tenerum,
    furtim vendis, migrans,
                adulterum—
    doleo! *doleo! doleo!*]

I'd looked after you in tenderness from your earliest youth, Lycê, that as soon as you reached womanhood I might demand you and take your maidenhead.

You've welcomed men to your accommodating lap, now you live with lights-of-love—you were only seven then, but, laying yourself open, you'd already been allured by love.

I remember ordering my weapon to stay outside, not to hurt a little girl by going in too far—

But that impudent little creature thought she'd like far bigger spear-thrusts—though so small, she got all that a woman desires.

While I, like a fool, wait for your nubile years, you, oh Lycê! Lycê! under the spell of sex, know a man while still a maid, and I am sad—sad, sad, sad!

While I was diligently taking care of you till you grew up, oh Lycê! Lycê! secretly you sell that still so tender little, flighty and lascivious little body of yours—I am sad, sad, sad!

P2: B.N. lat. 3719, fols. 37v–38v (a later gathering). A: Auxerre 243, fol. 18r. S: H. Spanke, *Speculum*, v (1930), 431 ff. (ed. from P2). V: A. Vernet, *Mélanges Félix Grat*, ii. 262 ff. (ed. from A).

1a. 1 A ab ungue teneram—supply *te* from 3.
4 A [lice] vicem etatem
6 P1A exigerem P2 (possibly) erigerem

1b. 2 *sic* P2 P1 pro precio A propreio V precio
3 *sic* P1P2 A Iam vivis
7 *sic* P1 (one word) P2A word-division doubtful SV ad miseras

2a. 2 P2 virgini
3 A astare
4 P2A ne P1 virginis
5 A intrare

2b. 2 A multa V multo
4 A nomen lice—an 'improvement' (λύκη = lupa)?

3a. 4–6 A operior lice sexui duta (*sic*) V sexu ducta
7 P2 virum viro
8 *sic* P1 P2 adds *doleo* twice more, A omits this refrain-line.

3b 1 ff. only in A
4 AV custodio corpus I supply the refrain here and in l. 8.
6 A tenero V tenerum
7 V ad alterum On microfilm I read 'adulterum', but cannot decide if there has been a correction.
8 A et doleo

This sequence has been twice printed, but never yet from its earliest and best text, in the older gathering (P1) of the Saint-Martial songbook B.N. lat. 3719. Both the slightly later version in this MS. (which was completed in 1210) and the much later one in Auxerre 243 (1358) are textually independent of P1 and of each other. They can be used to correct and complete, but only P1 can serve as the basis of a critical text.

While the lover's grief at the girl's hardness, and the name Lycê itself, bring to mind the associations of Horace's ode III. 10, the παρακλαυσίθυρον, the song in fact takes its departure from III. 6:

> Motus doceri gaudet Ionicos
> Matura virgo et fingitur artibus
> Iam nunc et incestos amores
> De tenero meditatur ungui . . .

'Ex ungue primo teneram' may be regarded as a witty variation on Horace's theme. With 'septennis adhuc fueras' the poet calls to mind the episode in *Satyricon*, 25, the deflowering of Pannychis ('quae non plus quam septem annos habere videbatur') and the delighted recollections of Quartilla ('minor est ista, quam ego fui, cum primum virum passa sum? . . .' Compare also 'maiora multo iacula' with Quartilla's 'maioribus me pueris applicui').

The song is remarkable not only for its frivolous, *risqué* qualities (which set it apart from the other profane songs in the Saint-Martial repertoire), but for an intellectual sophistication, a *facetia* which could have been enjoyed only by an élite. One imagines it meant for private performance among a small group of worldly and widely read young clercs. A similar theme is treated, though more delicately, in *CB* 88, st. 6 ff.

fol. 40ʳ⁻ᵛ

> Ecce letantur omnia!
> queque dant sua gaudia,
> excepto me, qui gracia
> amice mee careo—
> 5 quod corumdam invidia
> evenit, unde doleo.
>
> Amor amoris lancea
> me vulneravit aurea—
> mallem ego quod plumbea!

10 nam sic in illam ardeo,
non est catena ferrea
que me teneret laqueo.

Est equidem res anxia
amor, plenus miseria:
15 nam tunc dat mihi gaudia
cum velle mentis abeo,
item preb*et* suspiria
cum cupitam non teneo.

Amore nichil gravius,
20 nichil amore levius,
nichil eo felicius;
gravat corde lapideo,
mutatur ex lascivia—
en felix cum possideo!

25 Quod sunt arene littore,
quod folia in arbore,
quod rami sunt in nemore,
tot dolores sustineo:
ob oc infirmus corpore,
30 quod anc tenere nequeo.

Rursus, quot sunt in etere
astra, vel quod sub aere
omines credo vivere,
tot vicibus congaudeo
35 cum possum man*u* tangere
quam semper mente video.

Nulli fit ammirabile
quod facit amor femine
me non carere crimine—
40 nam sub trono etereo
non est que pulcritudine
anc vincat, cui me debeo!

E

See how all things are full of joy, all send their joy abroad, except for me who lack the grace of my beloved, which was lost through the envy of certain men, so that I grieve.

Love has wounded me with the golden lance of love—I wish it were a leaden one! I am so much afire for her, no iron chain could hold me in its snare.

Love indeed is an anxious thing, full of wretchedness: it gives me joy when I possess my mind's desire, then, when I lack the desired one, offers sighs.

Nothing is heavier than love, nothing is lighter, nothing happier; it engraves even on a stony heart, it is transformed out of sensuality— ah I am happy when I possess love!

As many sands as are on a shore, leaves on a tree, boughs in a wood, so many griefs do I endure, faint in body because I cannot hold her.

Yet again, as many stars as are in heaven, as many men as I think live beneath the sky, so many times I rejoice, when my hand can touch her whom I see for ever in my mind.

It is no wonder that a woman's love can cause me to be slandered, for beneath heaven's throne is none who can surpass her in beauty, her to whom I owe myself.

D: E. Du Méril, *Poésies populaires latines du moyen âge* (Paris, 1847), p. 234.

17 MS. prebent
18 D cupita   MS. stroke over *a* uncertain.
19 ff. *v. supra*, p. 293.
24 MS. ē   D est
35 MS. mane
37 D sit
41 D qui

Commentary: Ch. V, pp. 293 ff.

fol. 41^r

Nisi fallor, nil re*cep*tum —o—
est in terris, et adeptum.
  O fila, sui mi lo d*u*n io!

Unam novi sine fraude —o—
claram fama, dignam laude:
  f[ila, sui mi lo d*u*n io!]

Quod in parte sui tota —o—
quod sunt sui bona †iura.†
  O f[ila, sui mi lo dun io!]

10 Amor, ergo, hoc adeptus —o—
iam non queror ut deceptus
  'f[ila, sui mi lo dun io!']

Iusta ista que videntur —o—
iam non visa comprobentur!
15   O f[ila, sui mi lo dun io!]

Fronsque, labra, pectus, venter —o—
sunt formata tam decenter
  —o f[ila, sui mi lo dun io!—]

Ut nil visum emendandum —o—
20 sed sit omne collaudandum!
  O f[ila, sui mi lo dun io!]

If I'm not wrong, nothing, o nothing on earth is both promised and won. (O my fair one, while the game lasts, follow me!)

I've come to know one girl without deceit—o she is bright in name, deserving praise: (my fair one, while the game lasts, follow me!)

What she is in every part she is entire—o hers are the powers of goodness! (O my fair one, while the game lasts, follow me!)

So now, Amor, now that I've won her, o I don't lament like a disappointed lover, 'My fair one, while the game lasts, follow me!'

If those parts that are seen are fair, o how much should the unseen be praised! (O my fair one, while the game lasts, follow me!)

Forehead, lips, breast, loins—o they are formed so perfectly (o my fair one, while the game lasts, follow me!)

that nothing we can see should be improved—o no, let every part be praised! (O my fair one, while the game lasts, follow me!)

S: H. Spanke, *Beziehungen*, p. 17.

1 MS. repertum [S perfectum]

As this is a *carole*, rhythm is all-important, and syntax is often loose or over-concise. But there is no need to suppose (like S) that a stanza is missing.

2 S adeptum, o. But in the MS. o belongs to the refrain.

3 MS. dan Lit.? 'O ma fille, suis-moi là (au cours) d'un jeu.' Spanke suggests the improbable 'Mädchen, folge Milo von Anjou'.

5 MS. laude. F. (in the second and fourth stanzas the refrain is indicated by 'F', in the rest by 'o. F'). S laude, o. (et sic in 8, 11, 14, 17, 20)

7 *sic* MS.   S Est in parte

8 *sic* MS.   S bona nota (possibly acceptable as an emendation). This couplet is awkward and elliptical. The meaning seems to be a *courtois* compliment like Florizel's to Perdita:

> Each your doing,
> (So singular, in each particular)
> Crownes what you are doing, in the present deeds,
> That all your Actes, are Queenes.

13 *sic* MS. (for *Iuxta*)   S Iuxta illa

16 S notes the parallel with *Laudes alterius amice* in Ripoll 74 (*SLP* ii. 245):

> nasus, dentes, labra, venter
> sunt formata tam decenter . . .

Cf. also *CB* 117, st. 8–9:

> humeri, pectus et venter
> sunt formata tam decenter;
>
> Frons et gula, labra, mentum
> dant amoris alimentum . . .

The rhyme is an obvious one, and the similarities may well be pure coincidence.

18 *sic* MS. Omission of initial *o* might be expected here.

fols. 87ᵛ, 91ʳ

> Plures vidi margaritas,
> preciosas, exquisitas,
>   et diversi generis;
> Marg[arita] tamen una
> 5 quantum stellis preest luna
>   tantum preest ceteris:
> Preciosa M[argarita]
> per se valet, non polita
>   manibus artificis.

10 Nam qui tangit eam calet,
et, ut dicunt, multum valet
[propter] pudiciciam.
Noster presul eam servet,
quia, quando sanguis fervet,
15 tunc affert remedium.
Non est sumpta de tesauro,
nec inclusit eam auro
aurif*ex* Lemovicis.
M[argarita] non est lapis,
20 immo res est animalis,
et est subicibilis;
Non est lapis M[argarita]
quia lapis caret vita
et est interibilis.
25 Nata diae Citheree,
vultum habet Galatee
et cultum Tindarid[is].
Felix fatum, felix omen!
M[argarita] preter nomen
30 nichil habet lapidis.
De colore si requiris,
coloratur modis miris
velut arcus Iridis;
Si requiris de colore,
35 talis color est in ore
qualis erat Naidis.
Probo formam et etatem;
preter bonam voluntatem
nichil habet Thaidis.
40 Ut in loco sit securo
custodita, clauso muro
consul*to* pontifici*s*.

I have seen many pearls, precious, exquisite, and of diverse kinds;
but there is one Pearl who excels the rest as the moon outshines the

stars: this precious Pearl has value of herself, not polished by a craftsman's hand. Whoever touches her glows with love, and, as men say, she has great worth because of her virtue. May our bishop protect her—for she can assuage the fever in men's blood. She is not taken from a treasure-hoard, nor has the goldsmith of Limoges set her in gold. This Pearl is no stone, but a living creature, and conquerable—she is no stone, for a stone is devoid of life and corruptible. A daughter of divine Cytherea, she has Galatea's face and the splendour of the Tyndarean. Oh happy omen, happy destiny, that Pearl has nothing stonelike but her name! If you would know her colouring—it is miraculous as Iris' bow; if you would know the colour of her lips—a Naiad had such lips as these. I salute her beauty and her youth; she is in no way like a wanton, except in being kind. May she be protected in a safe place, in a cloister, according to the bishop's plan.

18 MS. auri fax.

25 diae—*sic* MS. This is the last word on fol. 87ᵛ; fol. 91ʳ continues 'Citheree'.

42 MS. consulo pontifici (but I think the poem must have closed, like the previous stanzas, on an -*is* rhyme). Spanke (*Marcabrustudien*, p. 69) printed twenty-seven lines from various parts of this song, with numerous errors and omissions.

The concluding verses, and phrases such as 'Noster presul eam servet' and the Limoges allusion, tempt one to try to identify Margarita. Geoffrey de Vigeois (*Recueil*, XII. 426) mentions three women of that name, two of whom come into the right span of time for the MS.: (1) the daughter of Raimond I of Turenne, whose first husband was Adémar IV, Viscount of Limoges from 1139 to 1148; (2) the daughter of Adémar V (1148–99). It seems to me far likelier, however, that the Margarita of this poem is of less distinguished birth, that she was an orphan and the ward of the Bishop of Limoges. Thus it would be that, whatever her beauty and perfections, she would not have the dowry for an appropriate marriage, and the poem suggests, if she is to remain incorruptible and not to satisfy the desire of a clerc, she must enter a convent. (As in the case of Héloïse, herself an orphan and niece of a canon of Notre Dame, virtually no other life would have been open to her.) Yet I think the suggestion of the final verses is made humorously—she must be put firmly out of sight or her beauty will drive the clercs of Limoges to distraction!

Stuttgart, HB Asc. I. 95, fols. 22ʳ-23ʳ　　　　s. XIII

1a　O quam formosa,　　　　1b　Metro nec prosa
　　quam decens quam diligo!　　　parem se non ambigo,
　　　rubet ut rosa　　　　　　　textu *nec* glosa,
　in qua visum figo.　　　　laus cui cor ligo!

2a　Candet plus quam lilium,　2b　O status amantium
　　formas vincit omnium,　　　vota consequentium—
　　in qua meum gaudium,　　　o me*a* Clicerium,
　　　pro qua genas rigo.　　　　pro te me affligo.

3a　Mea pro te macra faties,　3b　In me thelum iaties,
　　turpem facit maties;　　　mortis et spem vite
　　　　　　　　　　　　　　　　　　　　quaties,
　　immo velle meum faties!　　hiemps non, nix neque
　　　　　　　　　　　　　　　　　　　　glacies
　　　spe longa cor aret.　　　me infrigidaret.

4a　Figo in te oculorum acies,　4b　Intuitum oculorum
　　　　　　　　　　　　　　　　　　　　saties—
　　te diligo: foris paret!　　　cor deficit cum te
　　　　　　　　　　　　　　　　　　　caret.

5a　　　O deus, quid agam?　5b　　Rursus porta serta,
　　　　iam plagam　　　　　　deserta
　　amoris,　iam foris　　　　obscurant,
　　　　　　　　　　　　　　　　　　　obturant
　　monstro, tolero intus;　　edera, therebintus;
　5　fero mentem vagam,　　　sensus inexperta,
　　　presagam　　　　　　incerta
　　　maioris　doloris.　　　qu*i* curant,　cor
　　　　　　　　　　　　　　　　　　urant
　　O qualis laborintus!　　quatuor atque quintus.

6a　Tam est forme grate　　6b　Talem nec a vate
　　fameque late,　　　　　spectam putate;
　　　nil delirum　　　　　　et qu*o*d mirum

est hinc—hanc amate,   (si in veritate
5   o regum nate   hac vehar rate)—
   omnes per girum!   non novit virum.

7a Hec est sole pulchrior   7b Credite, non mentior,
   et celo perfectior,   res est dicto verior,
   ista nusquam melior   solus hac prestantior
   nec tam bona scitur.   deus invenitur.

Oh how beautiful, how comely is she I love—she is like a red rose, on whom I fix my gaze!

In verse, in prose, in text, in gloss I hold she is unparalleled. Praise be to her to whom I bind my heart!

More radiant than a lily, she excels all women's beauty, she in whom I find my joy, she for whom I weep.

Oh happy state of lovers who obtain their prayers—o my Glycerium, I am afflicted for your sake.

For your sake my cheek is lean, making me pitiful to see. If only you will do my will—my heart is dry with hoping long.

You will pierce me with a dart, make tremble my hope of life and death. No winter, snow or ice would cool me (then).

I direct all the strength of my gaze on you, I love you—as can well be seen.

May you utterly fill my field of vision: when you are not in it my heart fails.

O God, what shall I do? That wound of love—I show it without, endure it within. My mind is distraught, foreboding greater grief. Oh what a labyrinth!—

With the door closed again, ivy and terebinth darken, shut in the wasted space; the four senses, and at last the fifth, all bent on what is untried, uncertain, cause the heart to burn.

She is of such perfect beauty and such wide renown, there is no folly here. Love her, all you daughters of kings throughout the world!

Do not think such as she was ever seen by poet; and, what is wondrous—as my sail's mark is truth—she is still a maid.

She is lovelier than the sun, more perfect than heaven, nowhere can men know a better lady, or one as good.

Believe me, I do not lie, the reality is truer than the words: if any can be found more perfect than she, it is God alone.

D: G. M. Dreves, *A.H.* xx. 158.

1b. 1 The contrast could be between metrical and rhythmic verse, but I think this less likely.

3 MS. ut glosa

2b. 3 MS. meum

Clicerium—i.e. Glycerium, Terence's Lady of Andros. Walter of Châtillon gives the name to the girl in his love-lyric 'Declinante frigore' (Saint-Omer, XVII). But compare also Hermann of Reichenau, *Opusculum* (*ZfdA* xiii. 385), 32 ff. (Musa ad Sorores):

> vobis gliceriis suis
> selectisque sororculis
> quaedam carmina pangere . . .

Thus G. need not be a proper name, and the phrase could simply mean 'o my sweetheart'.

3a. 1 D marcida

3b. 1 D transposes this line with 2, presumably for closer metrical equivalence. But this makes less good sense, and in any case the neums show that the musical structure of 3a and 3b is AAAB AAAB.

5a. 5 D mente

5b. 4–5 D (without break) terebinthus sensus—which I find unintelligible.
7 MS. que curant

6b. 1 *sic* MS.   D anate [annatae]
3 MS. quid

7b. 4 MS. continues:

O nobilis,	amabilis,	Placabilis,	affabilis,
in te sensus mei.		esto memor mei.	

Da facilis	me agilis	Prestabilis,	laudabilis
a spe ad rem vehi;		esto, mater dei.	

> O Maria,   plena gratia
> celi via,   da celestia
> a-m-e-n.

These pious jingles have no intrinsic connexion with the love-lyric that precedes them, which is the first of the four remarkable love-songs in the MS., followed later, fol. 73^r, by 'Cogito plus solito' (*SLP* ii. 320), fol. 73^{r-v} 'Vale tellus, valete socii' (*CB* 119), and fols. 77^v–78^r 'Rumor letalis' (*CB* 120). The question remains, are the lines 'O nobilis, amabilis' a hymn not separated clearly enough from 'O quam formosa' in the MS. by a larger capital? or were they deliberately tacked on to the love-lyric, as though to provide it an edifying conclusion? (Compare the 'transformation' of 'Instar solis

ave', *infra*, p. 518. Here on the other hand it is hard to see how the
plaints of a hopeless, consuming passion for the Virgin Mary, and
such lines as 'velle meum faties' and the *double-entendres* 'foris paret',
'plagam amoris iam foris monstro' could fail to sound sacrilegious).
As the MS. contains many very short hymns and tropes in which
the words are there for the music's sake and have no poetic merit, I
am inclined to think that the apparent continuity between the two
pieces is a scribal accident. D, printing 'O nobilis, amabilis' without
comment as a part of 'O quam formosa', seems to have been
oblivious of any transition.

München, Clm 4603, fol. 135ᵛ   s. XIII

> Propter frigus hiemale
>   cantu non deficia*m*:
> mittam carmen speciale
>   Rose cui serviam.
> 5   Rosas minus querito—
>   pro hac Rosa
>   dulcorosa
>   corde sto sollicito.

I'll not abandon song because of winter's cold—I'll send a special
song to the Rose whom I shall serve. For (other) roses I search less—
it is for this Rose, this sweet-scented one, that I am troubled in heart.

2 MS. deficiar

Fragmentary lines, the prelude to a love-lyric. This 'Farai un vers'
type of opening is rare among Latin lyrics.

Firenze, Laurenziana Plut. XXIX. 1, fol. 228ʳ⁻ᵛ   s. XIII ex.

> Flos in monte cernitur,
>   gaudet cor amantis.
> Circa florem, nemora:
>   nulla vox clamantis,
> 5 locus est ydoneus
>   placito mandantis—
> fiat amor aureus
>   gratia donantis!

Odor florum iuvenem
10   renovans amore,
multa secum cogitans,
florem tangit ore;
flexo genu gratulans
floris in honore,
15 florem carpit manibus—
non [est] tempus more!

The flower is seen on the mountain-side, the lover's heart grows glad. Around the flower there are groves: there is no sound of human voice, the spot would suit a seducer's will—may love grow golden by the giver's grace!

Renewed in love by the scent of the flowers, deep in his thoughts, the lover touches the flower with his lips. Giving thanks on bended knee in honour of the flower, he plucks the flower with his hands—now is not time for delay.

D: G. M. Dreves, *ZfdA* xxxvii (1895), 365.

3 MS. ? Cura—for sg. verb with neut. pl., cf. A. Blaise, *Manuel du lat. chrét.*, p. 124.

6 mandantis—lit. of one who commands.

7–8 gratia donantis—i.e. if the Flower gives her love graciously, then it is no longer merely a man's imperious will (6), but becomes 'amor aureus'.

9 ff. Compare the great narrative counterparts to these lines in *CB* 77 'Si linguis angelicis' (see above, Chap. V, pp. 318 ff.) and (slightly later) in Guillaume de Lorris's part of the *Roman de la Rose* (especially 1649 ff., 3476 ff.).

13 Flexo genu—cf. *CB* 77, st. 7:

surgensque velociter   ad hanc properavi
hisque retro poplite   flexo salutavi.

15–16 Are the last lines an ironic deflation of the reverence shown in 13–14? I think not. They simply say 'Carpe diem'—so that if 13 is interpreted as the lover's thanksgiving for the Flower's assent to love, there is no change of tone. The song is probably complete as it stands, yet the extreme lyrical conciseness leaves it in some measure enigmatic. This makes it (dare I say it?) poetically more subtle than its renowned modern counterpart, Goethe's 'Heidenröslein', though there are remarkable affinities between the two, and for a moment, at the opening

Sah ein Knab ein Röslein stehn,
Röslein auf der Heiden,

one has the uncanny illusion of a contrafactum.

fols. 228ᵛ–229ʳ

Veris ad imperia   eya!
renascuntur omnia; eya!
amoris proemia   eya!
corda premunt sautia—
5 querula melodia,
gratia previa—corda marcentia.
Media vita, vernat flos intra nos!

Suspirat lucinia—   eya!
nostra sibi conscia [eya!]
10 impetrent suspiria, eya!
quod sequatur venia.
Dirige vite via,
gratia previa, vie dispendia
gravia vite—verna, flos, intra nos!

At the commands of Spring, eya! all things are born again, eya!
The first stirrings of love, eya! weigh upon wounded hearts,
languishing hearts, with plaintive melody, with guiding grace. In
the midst of life—the flower blossoms in us!

The nightingale sighs—eya! Would that our sighs, eya! of which
she knows, eya! brought mercy to be shown. On life's way, with
guiding grace, control the harsh expense of spirit of life's way—oh
flower, blossom in us!

D: G. M. Dreves, *A.H.* xxi. 36.

1 ff. The form and melody are identical with those of the Provençal 'A
l'entrade del tens clar, eya' (B.N. fr. 20050, s. xiii, fol. 82ᵛ—facs. ed. Meyer-
Raynaud, *Le chansonnier français de Saint-Germain-des-Prés* (Paris, 1892);
transcr. Gennrich, *Formenlehre*, pp. 85 ff.).

1–3 D omits *eya* in each line, and again in 8 and 10.

5–6 querula melodía—musically and metrically the stress is on the penulti-
mate (cf. 12 'Dirige vite via', and the fifth line in the Provençal stanzas, as
'kele est si amoróuse'). querula melodia, gratia previa—a subtle contrast in
which love's *dulce et amarum* are, as always, inseparable. D Corda marcentia /
Media./ (I find this unintelligible.)

7 vita—*sic* MS. D Vitae vernat flos   The line, however, is a deliberate antithesis to 'Media vita / in morte sumus' (Mone, i. 397).

9–10 MS. conscia impetrent

14 verna—*sic* MS.   D Vitae vernat

fol. 352ᵛ (first stanza only); Oxford, Rawlinson C 510,
fol. 10ʳ⁻ᵛ (complete) s. XIII²

Veneris
prosperis
usa successibus,
turba, nascentibus
5   floribus teneris,
ex[s]equaris
priscum morem,
ad amorem
accingaris,
10   sceleris
pretermissis ceteris!

Solitum
debitum
reddite Veneri,
15 iuvenes teneri!
Laudes et meritum
is enervat
iuventutis
qui virtutis
20   formam servat.
Libitum
pueris est licitum!

Iupiter,
arbiter
25 rerum, instituit
nichil dum libuit
fieri turpiter.
Sic edixit,
sicque, votis
30 usus totis,
suo vixit
iugiter
edicto conformiter.

Vivere
35   tenere
satagam igitur—
qui Iovem sequitur
non degit temere:
fixo telo
40   voluntatis
voluptatis
utar velo,
sidere
navigans sub Venere.

All you who are devoted to Venus' happy coming when the
tender flowers are born—follow love's ancient rule, be girt for love,
casting all that is base aside.

You youngest lovers, pay Venus her established debt. Whoever
keeps up an appearance of virtue diminishes youth's merit and its
praise. For the young, joy is the law of life!

Jupiter, judge of all things, arranged that nothing should be wicked
when it pleased him—that's what he decreed and so, fulfilling all his
wishes, he always lived in keeping with his law.

I therefore am determined to live a lover's life—to follow Jupiter
is not to live unguided: I'll use the sail Delight, fixed to the mast of
Will, navigating under Venus, my star!

D: G. M. Dreves, *A.H.* xxi. 158.

23–27 cf. Ovid, *Her.* iv. 133.

35 O temere

38 *sic* O   D agit

39 ff. O fixus telo voluptatis utar vero voluptatis   The virtuoso stanza-
form helps to indicate the corrections. Alternatively, 'fixus telo voluptatis,
voluntatis utar velo' [R.M.] 'pierced by the arrow of delight, I'll sail at will'.
D voluptatis utar natis voluptatis

fols. 429ᵛ–430ʳ

Vitam duxi iocundam sub amore,
plus libitum   quam licitum
attendens,

sed a vita resipisco priore,
5   plus studiis   quam *neniis*
    contendens.
Ut que causa? Compellor unica:
ne me Fama suo privet favore
    dum sub vita vivo filargica.

10 Impendisse libet tempus amori,
    ne nesciam   cum cupiam
      fugisse:
malis namque medela certiori
    occurreris   cum poteris
15   novisse.
Ergo, sciens quid sit illicitum,
redeunti non concedam furori,
    sed vitabo malum precognitum.

Potest namque, ne dampnemus amorem,
20   vel veniam   vel gratiam
      mereri:
reddit enim amantem minorem
    affabilem   et d[o]cilem,
      vereri
25   quicquid turpe putat—et amplius,
non nihil est: ne forte preter morem
    dum carpitur fructus Venereus.

I have led a joyous life of love, caring more for pleasure than for measure. But now I am recovering from that life, struggling more with studies than with ditties. Why is this?—only one reason moves me: that Fame should not deprive me of her favour, while I live a life of ease.

I am glad I have devoted time to love, lest I should not have known it when I want to shun it—you can surely face ills with a better remedy if you can recognize them. So now, knowing what is forbidden, I'll not yield to the madness when it returns, but shun the evil by anticipation.

Yet love (let us not condemn it) can indeed deserve indulgence or grace: for it makes an imperfect lover courteous and gentle, it makes him fear whatever he thinks base—and what is more, for an important reason: lest perchance he overstep gracious behaviour in plucking the fruit of love.

D: G. M. Dreves, *A.H.* xxi. 156.

5 MS. seriis (emend. B. Bischoff).—The sense requires an antithesis to *studiis*; *sericis* [R.M.] would be closer to the MS., but lacks double rhyme.
13 MS. naque
22 MS. minorem amantem
24 *sic* MS.   D Veri
26 ne forte preter morem—*sit* understood.

Commentary: Ch. V, p. 294.

fol. 469[r]

Iam ver aperit   terre gremium,
Flos letitie   dat incendium,
Ergo resonet   vox letantium:
'Hyemps exulat
5   in ortu Floris,
Renovatio
         verni temporis
pellit tedium
         pigri frigoris.'

10 Corda refovet   Flos amantium,
Flos [letitie   dat incendium],
nova revehit   estas gaudium!
Hiemps [exulat
         in ortu Floris,
15 Renovatio
         verni temporis
pellit tedium
         pigri frigoris].

Benedicite   patris filium
20 —Flos letitie   dat incendium —
qui dedit Floris   benefitium.
Hyemps ex[ulat]
          in or[tu] Flo[ris],
Re[novatio]
25   v[erni] t[emporis]
pellit tedium
          pigri frigoris].

Now spring opens the lap of the earth, the Flower of joy makes
passion flare; may the voice of those in joy ring out: Winter is put
to flight in the Flower's birth, spring's renewal drives out the
weariness of the dull cold.

The Flower of lovers kindles hearts again, the Flower of joy
makes passion flare, a new summer brings back joy. Winter is
put to flight. . . .

Bless the Son of the Father—the Flower of joy makes passion
flare—who has given the Flower's grace. Winter is put to flight. . . .

D: G. M. Dreves, *A.H.* xx. 94.

1 The opening image is a sexual one. But this song does more than meta-
phorically to unify the ardour of nature in spring and the *incendium* of human
love. It shows the human 'Flos amantium, / Flos letitie' as God-given—as if
there were one single Flower (simultaneously divine, human, and natural)
whose resurrection banishes 'wintriness' in every sense of the word. The thought
has its origins in Boethius, *Cons.* II, m. 8:

> O felix hominum genus,
> Si vestros animos amor
> Quo caelum regitur regat.

and in Paulinus of Nola (*Epist.* XXXI. 49 in Peiper's ed. of Ausonius), where
Christ is 'Sol aequitatis, fons bonorum, flos dei'. (See further my excursus *Flos
florum, supra*, pp. 181 ff.)

5 ff. MS. Floris (similarly in 14, 21, 23)   D floris (thoughout)
10 *sic* MS.   D flos
12 *sic* MS.   D aetas
21 MS. benefititium   D beneficium

München, Clm 18628, fol. 12ᵛ   s. XIII–XIV

1a Fatorum prodigia,
   que tanta est licencia
   ut superum ignavia
contulerit tantam vim
      alme Veneri?

1b Hec dea virtutibus
   ius confert animantibus,
   pulcris et deformibus
mortalium †mulcet†, legere
      quoque sinceri.

2a Hic me victum sencio
   Dyonis inperio
     cum puellula,
     cum iuvencula
5 precandidula,
felix quia cum illa
     pusilla
   morari mora liceat.

2b Hec tota laudabilis
   et nimis amabilis,
     generositas,
     speciositas,
5 morum probitas
tanta datur sibi,
     describi
quod perfecte non valeat.

3 Hanc ut novi vario
decorum beneficio
ornatam, colloquio
†cui sedulo
5 sibi placito
omnimodo iungere.†

4a Nam si nocte dormiam
   vel servem vigiliam
   te desidero,
   semper recolo:
5   numquam potero
   [de] memoria digna,
     benigna
quavis hora negligere.

4b Tu vite subsidium
   mortisque suplicium
   esse poteris:
   tu me deseris,
5   mori pateris;
   dulcis et amena,
     serena,
tu me noli despicere.

5a   Scis quod amo,
     quod inclamo te.
   Scis quod volo,
     quia colo te.

5b   Scis quod nosco,
     quia posco te.
   Scis quod spero,
     quia quero te.

6a	Brevis tua sit responsio,	6b	Cum mea longa sit peticio.
7a	Cur moraris annuere	7b	Quod conaris perficere?
8a	Hec me videns et subridens obmutuit,	8b	Quod speravi, quod rogavi iam voluit.
9a	Ad amplexus mille nexus mihi contulit	9b	Et post ludum †manens dudum esse poterit.†

Oh monstrous fates, what licence is so great as this, that the gods' cowardice has conferred such power on bountiful Venus? This goddess with her powers imposes her law on all living beings; among men she †caresses† both the beautiful and the ugly—even those untouched know this from books.

I feel myself vanquished under Dione's sway, by a slip of a girl, young, surpassing white, happy if I may linger with my little one for a while. She is entirely praiseworthy and utterly lovable, she has so much nobility, beauty, and honour that it cannot be fully told.

As I knew her graced with manifold charms, her for whose sake †I strive in every way to converse as pleases her† . . .

For whether I sleep at night or wake, I long for you, I always return in my thoughts: I shall never at any time be able to disregard this high and gracious memory. You can be my source of life or death; if you abandon me, you let me die. You who are sweet and lovely and serene, do not disdain me.

You know I love you and invoke you, you know my wish, because I worship you; you know my mind, because I ask for you; you know my hope, because I seek for you.

May your answer be short, though my plea is long.

Why do you delay in promising what you yourself are longing to fulfil?

She, seeing me and smiling, was silent—what I hoped, what I pleaded for, she granted then.

She entwined me a thousand times in our embraces, and †after this sport perhaps she will stay a while.†

1a. 4 The scansion here and in 1b. 4 remains problematic; the deletion of *mulcet* (unexpected with the datives) would give syllabic equivalence.

1b. 5 MS. q̄q̄ɜ (queque?)

2a. 5 Precandidula—cf. Maecenas, in Isidore *Etym.* xx. 32, 6: 'nec precandida (*al.* percandida) margarita quaero'.

2b. 1 MS. laudibilis

3–4a. The break in sequence-form makes it probable that a stanza parallel to 3 is missing. 3 as it stands lacks a principal clause; 'sedulo' is perhaps best construed as implying a verb, but the lines remain obscure.

4a. 2 MS. servam   4a. 4–5 MS. numquam potero semper recolo

9b The text is corrupt, but I do not know how to improve it. A later hand (s. xv) has bracketed the poem, with the words *falsum totum*!

Cambridge, Caius 418, fol. 94^r s. XIII–XIV

In vere virencia   loca iuvant vere,
In estu calencia   iuvatque cavere
Et umbris frigencia   dilectat habere;
Bruma cum celia   iuxta prunasque sedere.

5 Requiem laboribus   decet concinnare
Et plausum, meroribus   planctuque cessare,
Quibusdam temporibus   ac ludis vacare,
Dando corporibus   solamen particulare.

Nulla quidem corpora   quibunt convalere
10 Per prolixa tempora   vel sana manere,
Si cogantur onera   semper sustinere—
Si fuerint pecora   que sunt fortissima vere—

Pusilli precipue   nequeunt studere
Semper et continue   scolisque merere,
15 Quin requirant mutue   quieti favere,
Nam vivit fatue   qui vult sine fine dolere.

Studiorum pulvere   quapropter studentes
Finem nunc accedere   termini scientes,
Incoant applaudere,   mutuo dicentes
20 'Surgamus propere!   non hic ultra remanentes.

'Nostra vero capita satis doluerunt,
Gaudia sunt reddita que diu fuerunt;
A nobis abscondita diu latuerunt.
Nobis per merita sanctorum iam patuerunt.

25 'Clamemus nunc igitur: totum est de festo!
Terminus consumitur— vie sumus presto.
De magistro dicitur nichil. Sed adesto,
Consors qui fruitur consortis amore modesto.

Ex hoc nunc proponimus nunquam verberari,
30 In agris appetimus lepore[m] venari,
Omnia qui agimus, omnes aucupari
Et statim volimus ubicumque placet spatiari.'

In spring the green places are a true delight, there is delight in avoiding scorching places and in having coolness in the shade—or again in winter, sitting with a tankard by the fire.

Now we must prepare our rest from labours, and now applaud, making an end of grieving and complaining, at certain times have time to play, giving our bodies the comfort they must have.

For no bodies are able to grow strong, or to stay healthy any length of time, if they are compelled to bear a constant load (indeed as if they were the strongest beasts of burden)—

Thus specially the very young must not study all the time, and be continually depressed in school—rather they'll try to enjoy a spell of rest—it is a senseless life to be always miserable.

So the students, amid the dust of studies, knowing that the end of term is coming now, begin to applaud, saying to each other 'Up and away! Let's not stay here!

'Our heads have ached quite long enough, the joys which existed long ago are restored; they have long lain hidden from us. Now they lie before us, through the merits of the saints.

'So let us shout, all is in holiday. The term is dwindling away! We are ready to be off. Not a word about teachers! But be ready, lover, to delight in the delicate love of your lass.

'From now on we're determined not to be beaten again, we long to hunt the hare in the fields, all of us who pursue all things, we want to go fowling and from this moment walk wherever we please.'

1 ff. A student's celebration of the beginning of holidays, comparable in theme (though not in quality) to the famous 'Omittamus studia' (*CB* 75). It is worth noting that among the many Latin spring songs the 'end-of-studies' topos occurs only rarely, and is not, as has often been thought, the most typical *Vagantendichtung*. On the other hand, the form of this poem is one of the commonest variants of the 'Goliardic measure' (*Vagantenstrophe*), in which, instead of the usual four rhythmic lines, the last is replaced by a (not always successfully classical) hexameter, at times a quoted (or misquoted) one, at times, as here, improvised. The rhyme-scheme remains aaaa. This hexameter close was possibly an innovation of Walter of Châtillon's. A frequent additional complication is the caesura-rhyme, here extended even to the hexameter (for other instances of this, *v.* Walther, *Initia* 8167 [from this MS.], 19031).

4, 15, 19 minim errors: MS. Bruna, mitue, mituo
4 celia—probably the noun rather than the proper name.
9 MS. Ni illa
15 requirant—MS. doubtful.

Ll. 25, 26, 30 are echoed in another poem in this MS. (fol. 87ʳ), 'Ferule frangantur', ed. S. Gaselee, *The Oxford Book of Medieval Latin Verse,* no. 86.

London, B.M. Arundel 102, fol. 1ʳ s. XIV

Me cogit amore quedam speciosa
cuius gene niten*t* velut rubens rosa;
super omnes feminas est multum formosa,
vite delectabilis est, et virtuosa.

5 Gemo ut opinor (pote*s* et cogitare)
quam dul*ce* et quam suave est illam amare!
Quem vult potest ledere et potest sanare;
eius me servici*o* volo subiugare.

Heu dolor[e] conteror, nequeam sperare,
10 nam stilum cum stimulo non vult ex[c]itare.
Sed tu, flos Vacessie, ge[mm]a, dedignare
sicienti gratie potum propinare.

A certain lovely lady compels me to love. Her cheeks are radiant as the blushing rose, she is exceedingly beautiful, beyond all other women, her life is a delight, and full of excellence.

I sigh as I think (you too can imagine it) how blissful and how sweet it is to love her. She can harm or heal whomsoever she will; I willingly submit myself to serving her.

Alas, I am worn away with grief, I cannot hope, for she will not

take out the shaft with its goad. Yet deign, you flower of (?) Va-
cessia, you jewel, to give a draught of your grace to one who thirsts.

1 MS. amare?
2 MS. nitens
5 MS. genio?, potest
6 MS. dulcis
8 MS. servicium
11 *sic* MS. Corr. Vacerie (i.e. Vachères)? vaccinii ?   dedignare—for *dignare*?

Auxerre 243, fol. 18ʳ   1358

  Predantur oculos, captivant animum
    vocalis Orphei
     siderei
vultus et simplices risus E[u]ridices.

5   Qui solis animos luneque menstruos
        rimari solitus
         circuitus,
       celo fugam siderum
        per numerum
10   notatam,

     Iam nunc ad alteram traductus operam,
       mutato studio,
        de basio,
      de amplexu loquitur
15   et sequitur
           amatam.

   In flammam abiit totus philosophus,
     amantis spiritum
      solicitum
20 tacente cithara stupebant Ismara.

     Non vult E[u]ridice
      de suplice;
    preces perdat vacuas—
      sed ianuas
25   pudoris

> et gremium
> dat pervium
> discursibus
> et lusibus
> 30   amoris.
>
> Su[m]pto libamine
>   de virgine,
> suam tandem fidicen
>   Eur*i*dicen
> 35   cognovit,
>   et lirico
>   sub cantico
>   iam spiritum
>   sollicitum
> 40   removit.

Eurydice's starry looks and innocent laughter ravish the eyes of singing Orpheus, captivate his mind.

Orpheus, whose habit was to research into the spirits of the sun, the monthly orbit of the moon, the numerically established courses of the stars in heaven,

now led to a pursuit of another kind, his studies modified, speaks of kissing, of embracing, and follows his beloved.

The philosopher has quite gone up in flames—Ismarus stood amazed at his love-lorn spirit, while his lute lay still.

Eurydice will have none of her suppliant—he would waste his prayers in vain, but then she opens the gates of her womanliness, and devotes her body to the sallies and sports of love.

Taking the first fruits of her maidenhead, at last the lutanist possesses his Eurydice, and now, playing a melody, he dispels all his cares.

V: A. Vernet, *Mélanges Félix Grat*, ii. 261–2.

1 *sic* MS. [V animos (to rhyme with 'oculos')—incorrectly, because the corresponding line (17) in the antistrophe has no internal rhyme.]

2–3 possibly 'of star-gazing Orpheus the singer' (cf. *Ex Ponto*, iv. 16, 6).

4 vultus—MS. v, 3 minims, t⁹ V vin[c]tus (which makes the stanza unintelligible).

MS. erudices But the rhyme, fidicen / Euridicen (guaranteed by that of the antistrophe, vacuas / ianuas) shows the form the poet must have used.

5 ff. For Orpheus as cosmologist, *v.* Lactantius, *Inst.* I *passim*, Augustine, *De Civ. Dei*, XVIII. 14, 37; these 'testimonies' recur even in Aquinas's commentaries on Aristotle (*in Metaph.* I, lect. iv; XII, lect. vi; *in De Anima*, I, lect. xii). solis animos—cf. Cicero, *Somnium Scipionis* (*De Re Publica*, VI. 15): 'hisque [hominibus] animus datus est ex illis sempiternis ignibus'; Macrobius, *in Somnium*, I. 21.

11 ff. For this theme, cf. Henri d'Andeli's *Le lai d'Aristote.*

13 MS. de de basio

16 MS. amotam

20 MS. continues: nam misero sic vivitur Cum debellatus animus ire sub hastam cogitur (ll. 47–49 of 'Ver prope florigerum', interpolated from the second to fourth lines of this column, fol. 18ʳᵇ).

21 MS. erudice [V Erudices, which spoils both sense and rhyme. V wants to rhyme with *preces*—but the metrically equivalent *suam* (33) in the antistrophe has no rhyme.]

23 ff. The meaning seems to be, Eurydice refuses to be conventionally courted, but gives herself spontaneously.

34 MS. eurudicē V Eurudicem (again spoiling rhyme)

36–37 *sic* MS. V Et luito subcavato The correct reading was suggested to me by Professor Bischoff before I had seen the MS.

38–39 spiritum sollicitum—probably refers to Orpheus rather than to Eurydice (cf. 18–19).

Is there any link between this song and 'Ver prope florigerum' (*supra*, p. 374), which immediately precedes it in this MS.? There are certain analogies of rhythm: particularly frequent in both songs is the short four-syllabled 'echo' that rhymes with the preceding word ('Orphei / siderei, solitus / circuitus; vallibus / declivibus, morulam / ad parvulam'). And in both songs Orpheus and Eurydice are brought into a context of happy, sensual love. Again, 33–34 might suggest a link with 'Parce continuis' (*supra*, p. 342) in the splendid rhyme 'fidicen / Euridicen'—but given the subject of Orpheus and Eurydice the rhyme must have come almost inevitably to a clever lyrical poet, and the affinity between these songs lies rather in their allusive (perhaps bewildering) narrative concision in lyrical form.

What is truly remarkable about this song is the poet's free play with his mythological characters, completely disregarding the famous story and treating them wittily, affectionately, as if they were a pair of lovers in his circle of friends. This goes beyond the play with mythological *names* in the Arundel lyrics; the form, too, (which was seriously distorted in V's text) is more sophisticated than any in the Arundel collection. Thus it is difficult to assign a date or provenance. The datable lyrics in the Auxerre MS. are twelfth-century ones, two (*Licê* and 'Quam velim virginum', which recurs in Arundel) are from Saint-Martial (B.N. lat. 3719). So there is every chance that 'Predantur oculos' likewise belongs to the great flowering of the secular sequence and conductus at Saint-Martial.

(i) *Bruxelles, Archives générales du Royaume, Fonds de S. Gudule MS. Arab. Ka. 758 (fly-leaf)*   s. XIV²

> Vos, quid admiramini,
> virgines, si virgini
> pre ceteris eligende
> dignati fuerimus
> 5   nubere? dum nupsimus
> tamquam valde diligende:
>
> Ista pulcra spetie,
> humilis manerie
> ac op[er]e virtuosa;
> 10   turpis vestrum altera,
> ausu nimis aspera,
> necnon virtutes exosa.
>
> Ista lux, vos nubila;
> ista velox aquila,
> 15 vos, colubres gradientes!
> Ista super ethera,
> regnat, vos in misera
> valle languetis egentes.
>
> Ista virgo regia
> 20   dulcis est amasia,
> mea sponsaque pia;
> rex ego sum, hec regina!
> Quid tanta referimus?—
> nos qui cuncta novimus
> 25   dignam preelegimus
> et ut rosam hanc pre spina.

      Surgite vos igitur
      (quia tempus labitur
      et mors nos prosequitur)—
30 huic servite, hanc vocate!
      quod si neglexeritis,
      illam non videbitis
      gloriam quam cupitis—
      vos, e y a, properate!

(ii) *Ivrea, Bibl. Cap. 115, fols 8ᵛ–9ʳ*   s. XIV²

      'Gratissima
            virginis species,
      quam decorat
            carnis mundicies,
5 usque centrum
            placasti intima
      mei cordis
            plaga dulcissima.'

      'Intra stillans
10   amoris spiritum
      nescientem
            pectoris exitum,
      gratissime,
            simili vulnere
15 peperisti
            mundum me ledere.'

      'O regina,
            tuum amplectere
      astringendo
20   pectus cum ubere
       . . . .'

      'O rex regum,
            occulum occulo
      et os ori
            iunge pro osculo,

25 ac inspira
            verbum in labia
        quo recepto
            fiat caro dia.'

(i) You girls, why do you wonder that I have thought it fitting to wed a girl who is peerless beyond the rest?—since I have married one as lovable as can be.

She is beautiful in looks, gracious in manner, and excellent in deed. Any other girl among you is worthless, far too rude in forwardness, contemptuous of excellence.

She is light, you are clouds, she a swift eagle, you, creeping serpents. She reigns beyond the skies while you languish, deprived, in a wretched valley.

This royal maiden is a sweet mistress, and my devoted bride. I am a king—she is my queen! Why do I tell all this? I who know everything have chosen a lady of worth, one who is as a rose surpassing thorns.

Arise, then, all of you (as time slips past and death pursues us)— serve this lady, call upon her! If you neglect this, you will never see the glory for which you long—ah, come quickly now!

(ii) [He:] Most beloved beauty of a girl, graced by the radiance of your body, you have made the depths of my heart serene to their very centre, with the sweetest wound.

[She:] Raining down the spirit of love, spirit that knows no way out of my breast, you, most beloved, have made an implement to strike me with a wound like your own.

[He:] O queen, to be entwined in your embrace, your breast . . .

[She:] O king of kings, let my eyes meet yours, let our lips meet in a kiss, and breathe into my mouth the word through which my body may become godlike.

C: Cambrai, Bibliothèque Municipale 1328, s. xiv², fol. 11ʳ (often illegible). D: Durham Cathedral Library C. I. 20, s. xiv², fol. 337ʳ.

Note—The music of these two lyrics, which were set as a motet by Philippe de Vitry (c. 1291–1361), has twice been edited, first by H. Besseler, *AfMW* viii (1926), 250–3, and recently by L. Schrade, *Polyphonic Music of the Fourteenth Century*, i (Monaco 1956), 76–81, *Commentary* (1956), 104–6, from I and

C, though without textual consideration of C. Neither musicologist, however, attempted to make sense of the difficult poetic texts. The most accurate text of 'Vos, quid admiramini' is in B, which Besseler and Schrade did not know.* Despite one slip, I gives the best text of 'Gratissima' (which breaks off in B at l. 5). The readings from D and, wherever legible, C, exclude purely orthographical variants.

(i) 1 *sic* BD, I qui *Virgines* is better read as voc. than as obj. of *admiramini* (cf. 10 *vestrum altera*), and thus prompts the decision in favour of *quid*.

3 *sic* BD, I pro
5 *sic* BD, I nuptuis
8 For the meaning of *humilis*, cf. the discussion *supra*, I 158 ff.
13 DI vox nubila
15 D vox
18 *sic* BD (B possibly deleted length-mark), I languentis
21 *sic* BCI, D meaque sponsa
23 *sic* BCI, D quis
24 *sic* BDI, C tanta
26 *sic* BD, I rosa, C ut spina
27 *sic* BD, I urgite, C surgite vos leg[itur?]
29 D vos, DI persequitur
30 CDI servire
30-34 Cf. the conclusion of 'Deus amet puellam' (*supra*, I 265 ff.).
33 I om. quam

These lines contain several phrases of a type found in hymns to the Virgin Mary—'virgo regia', 'rosam hanc pre spina', 'huic servite, hanc vocate'. Most strikingly, 'in misera valle languetis egentes' could well be an echo of 'gementes et flentes in hac lacrimarum valle' in the famous *Salve, regina*. Despite this, it seems to me highly unlikely that the Virgin could be the 'bride' and beloved whom the other girls are here asked to venerate: there is a certain flippancy in the tone, and in particular such phrases as 'Rex ego sum' and 'nos qui cuncta (corr. *cunctas*?) novimus' seem to belong to the exuberant lover's *gab* (cf. *CB* 83, st. 4; Arundel 3, st. 3). The song belongs, I think, essentially to this genre, despite the adaptation of sacred phrases.

(ii) 6 CD plagasti I's *placasti* may not be merely a variant spelling but a deliberate subtlety, for as love is 'compounded of opposites', its wound and its peace may be seen as inseparable.

9 Intra—possibly imperative and not adverb? stillans—*sic* D; I stiulans (*stimulans* would be hypermetric); C, uncertain, but not *stillans*.
13 gratissime—possibly adverb and not vocative?
15 *sic* CI, D pepercisti
20 I vebere The stanza, which is incomplete, was presumably cut by Philippe de Vitry in order to achieve musical symmetry.

* I am most grateful to Dr. F. L. Harrison for telling me of the MSS. B and D, and for lending me photographs of the relevant pages.

21–28 The last eight lines are spoken by the beloved. It seems likeliest that she is addressing her lover, calling him 'rex regum' in answer to his 'regina': if in their embrace he breathes words of love for her, her body will pass into a 'divine', ecstatic state. Another possibility, however, is that in the last stanza she is praying to God ('oh let my eyes meet his . . .'), asking that she may be able to express physically for her lover the divine power of love she feels shut within her incommunicably ('nescientem pectoris exitum').

27 CD quod receptum

München, Clm 17289, fol. 144ʳ   s. XIV²

   A. dulcis roris unda,
   n. stella cordis munda,
   n. fer solamen moris,
   a. dulce verbum oris,
5 profer ut quadruplo rore
   sit vox una sic in ore
   ut ita 'a. n.' bina
   pars mea sit de mina.

A, sweet shower of dew, N, pure star of my heart, N, give me the solace of your gentleness, A, sweet word upon my lips, come forth that in the fourfold dew it may be still one name, spoken in such a way that, coining my double 'Ann', I come upon my golden 'mine'.

2 MS. doubtful: may read *stilla*.

3 *sic* MS. To correct to amoris' would spoil the syllabic equivalence of the first four lines.

5 MS. .4. Cf. *Genesis*, II. 10. The conceit seems to be that as the paradisal river that sheds dew on the earth is fourfold and yet one at its source, so her name, the sound of which refreshes the lover, is four letters and one name.

7–8 There is a word-play on the coin *mina* (the 'pound' of *Luc.* XIX. 13) and, presumably, MHG *mîn*—that Anna may be my share of what is 'mine'. (Compare Shakespeare's 'Either was the other's mine' [i.e. 'source of wealth' and 'own'], as well as the 'angel' puns in Elizabethan love-lyrics.) In addition the letters 'a' and 'n' which make up Anna's name are 'pars' (i.e. half) of the word 'mina'. The lines are virtually untranslatable. I include this as a rare instance in medieval Latin of love-verses used for an almost wholly private *jeu d'esprit*. It is this quality which makes interpretation specially difficult, and I cannot vouch for the correctness of my attempt at solving the riddles.

Praha, UB germ. XI. C. 9 (2033), fols. 130ʳ–131ᵛ　　s. XV

Iam entrena　　plena	Man sihet lawber　　tawber
stet, et metu,　　fletu	vor dem walde　　palde
gemens,　　tremens	reysen,　　greysen
tellus erbida,	syt man perg unde tal;
qua　　gramina　5	val　　uber al
Aperilis virens dans eduxit.	ist nu perg unde anger awe
	leider.
Animalem　　talem	Vogelein singen,　　clingen
per livorem,　　morem	ist vorstoret—　　horet
cedit,　　redit	wynde　　swynde
ros odibilis,　　10	wehen durch den walt;
vis　　iam nivis	kalt,　　ungestalt
orida brumalis hinc eluxit.	ist nu mancher hande sumer
	cleider.
Prochdolor!　　omne cor	Winter lank,　　dein
	getwanck
iam algor　　pruine mor-	machet crank　　sundir wank
biferum turbavit;　　15	sumerliche schone,
medianis　　ramis	daz ir varbe　　garbe
iam rosarum　　parum	mus vorbleichen,　　weychen,
spirat,　　girat,	rosen　　lozen
omne dum lugens	musen iarlank me;
ens　　condolens 20	we,　　kalder sne,
pia feris pruina nunc fugavit.	du pist ane mase in awen hone!
Sic in duris　　curis	An dir, swere,　　were
irretitur,　　scitur,	iarlank weibes　　leibes
avis　　suavis—	dicke　　blicke
omnis conticet,　　25	wol eyn meyendach—
et　　sublatet	ach,　　wer gesach
tectulis algore sauciata.	besser frewde den bey schonen
	weyben?

Sed quid miri,   viri
mens turbatur?   datur
verum   merum   30
medicabile
     de   femin*e*
vultu, quia [est] predulco-
          rata.

Eius vox   non atrox   34
clangens, mox   longa nox
iocis breviatur,
per amplexum,   nexum,
femininum   vinum,
bonum   donum,
tactus virium,   40
     dum   mi*l*ium
avium garritus recitatur.

Eius visus   risus
ex amenis   genis
morum   florum   45
dat flagranciam,
     tam   fulgidam,
prenitentem luce febiali.

Ornamentis   centis
in festitu,   ritu   50
daris,   gnaris
†pratis omnibus,
     plus   omne r*us*†
excellens decore feminali.

Os rubrans   sic ovans,   55
annum stans   inovans
aureis coronis—

Wy doch eyne   reyne
frawe twynget,   bringet
herzen   smerzen
mir vil senden man,
     kan   und mich lan
ane trost und mus [auch] alzo
          bleiben.

Roter munt,   thu mir kunt,
frewden funt   zu aller stunt,
hab mich dir vor eigen;
la nicht von weiden scheiden,
mich bedenk[e],   wenke
suze   gruse,
liplich zu mir sprich—
     sich,   do von ich
herz und munt dir ganz zu
          dinst wyl neigen.

Schult ich tummer   kummer
durch dich leiden   meyden
sere,   were
mir den senden mut!—
     thut   frawen gut—
daz vorkere mir zu libem
          heile.

Thu mich swere   lere,
frawe, mache   swache
meine   pein[e],
freye mir den leip,
     bleip,   selig weip,
fast an mir mit ganzir
          mynneteile.

Fuge mir,   frawe schir,
sulche gir   zo daz wir
liplich uns gezweien;

eius nempe   Tempe
generosa   rosa
dignum   signum—   60
carmen hoc tibi
      qui   sum tui:
sic contenteris [in] istis donis.

pei dir sunne,   wunne,
frawe schone!   lone,
hewer,   stewer
mich aus sorgen var,
      zwar   wo ich var
dir zo sing ich, frawe, dysen
      reien.

Now let the grassy earth be full of tears, moaning, trembling, in fear, in weeping, earth from which verdant April, the giver, made the grass to rise. Out of living spite, hateful wetness works its will, returns—the fearful wintry power of snow has become apparent here. Alas, the cold of hoar-frost has troubled every ailing heart, now too few roses blow, circle in the midst of boughs, since the dutiful frost has put every mourning, sorrowing creature of the wilds to flight.

So the sweet birds are ensnared in their harsh cares, we know: every bird is still, and, hurt by cold, hides in the eaves. What wonder if a man's mind is troubled then? (Yet) there's a true, reviving wine in a woman's lips, in one surpassing sweet. Her voice has no harsh sound— soon the long night's made short, in sport, in entwining, winding embrace, that wine a

Soon one sees lifeless foliage drift before the woods, sees hill and dale grow grey; everywhere, alas, hills and grassy banks are pale. The singing, sounding of birds is done away with—hear the swift winds blowing through the woods. Many a one's summer clothes are now cold, ill shapen. Your tyranny, long winter, constantly drains the strength of summer's beauty, so that her colour must grow utterly pale, dim, roses must fall, perpetually more—woe to you, cold snow, you are arrogant beyond measure on the green shores.

A woman's frequent gaze would always be a May-day in your midst, you (time of) heaviness—ah who ever saw greater joy than among lovely women? Yet one glorious lady rules me, brings me heartache in my great love-longing, and can leave me comfortless, and so I must remain. Let me know you, you red lips, source of joy at every moment—take me as your woman's gift of grace, two straining together, while the chatter of a thousand birds is remembered.

The looks, the laughter in her lovely face shed a fragrance such as flowers have, so radiant, shining with Phoebus' light. In your dress adorned a hundred-fold you are presented in the rite, in †our familiar meadows, surpassing every region† in womanly beauty. Red lips rejoicing, renewing the lingering year with golden garlands—indeed the noble rose of Tempe is their fitting symbol—I (give) you this song, I who am yours. May you be content with these your gifts.

own! do not cut me off from joy, think of me, send me sweet salutations, be near me, speak to me, then see how I'll devote my heart and lips wholly to serving you.

If I in my inexperience am to avoid grievous suffering for your sake, grant me the spirit of desire, as is good for women to do, and turn it for me into love's remedy. Let me be void of heaviness, lady, make my griefs less, make my life free, blessed lady, cling to me with all the love you possess. Grant me such longing, bright lady, that we may unite in body. With you, beautiful lady, is sun, is joy— give reward, make serene, guide me out of the danger of my cares, and wherever I go, lady, I'll sing this song to you.

V: Vipiteno (Bolzano), Archivio Comunale, cod. s.c., s. xiv ex., fols. 35ᵛ–36ʳ. This MS., lost in the Second World War, was described by I. V. Zingerle, *WSB* liv (1866), 293 ff., who printed the German stanzas of this song from it (and the incipits only of the Latin ones). The readings from V given below are based on Zingerle. It is likely that the V text was as poor in the Latin stanzas as in the German. I exclude purely orthographical variants.

1 entrena—from the rare Gk. adj. ἔνθρηνος? (*v.* Liddell–Scott, s.v. ἐνθρηνέω). Du Cange records *trenus* (=lamentabilis), as well as *threnosus* and *threnare*.
6 MS. apealis, das
16 MS. mediamnis ramnis
18 MS. girrat
21 MS. piam, pruinam
*1 V tŏwer
*6 (*12 in V) V sten nw   *12 (*6 in V) stet noch maniger
*13 V Ach winter
*15–16 V sumerlicher schone das ir gelwe varbe   MS. zo daz
*18 V losen rosen
23 MS. irritetur   V irretitur citur
32 MS. feminee

38 Cf. Baudelaire, 'Franciscae meae laudes': 'divinum vinum, Francisca'.
40 lit. the touching of strengths.
41 MS. mirium
*22 V Vor die were swere
*25 V ist wol
*27 MS. y besser   V zarten frawen
*29 V brenget tzwenget
*33 *sic* V   MS. mus alzo
*36 MS. und hab
*37–38 V gar vor laide schaide mir nicht wencke dencke
*42 V leib und hertze das dint dir gantz vor aigen
48 febiali (i.e. Phoebiali)—a hapax legomenon?
50 ritu—probably a May-feast ceremony (*v.* 56, and Commentary).
52 This line and the next are corrupt, but the rhyme-scheme makes further emendation hazardous.
53 MS. ros
60 MS. digna signa
*44–46 V meiden leiden meren seren mir den sweren
*49–52 V lere swere frawe mache swache lache und erfrewe
*55 V fuge an mir
*58–59 V so die sunne wunne varbe. lone schone
*61 V war
*63 V dir sing ich liep in gantzen frewden

The Latin stanzas form a song complete in itself. Syntax and meaning link the opening of the second Latin stanza to the close of the first; the opening of the third, 'Eius visus', continues the description of the lady's effect on her lover, beginning 'Eius vox' (34), broken by the German stanza, which is a plea for love. And the three last lines of the Latin are clearly an *envoi*.

While the first German stanza repeats the thoughts of the Latin, the second and third contradict it. Where the Latin is about fulfilled love, whose joy could defy the cold, about a beloved for whose bounty there was no winter, the German becomes a plea to a (still unyielding) lady to show pity. Unlike the Latin stanzas, the three German ones cannot stand on their own—the first German lines can hardly have opened a song.

Thus there is no doubt not only of the independence of the Latin stanzas, but also of their priority (one of the very rare instances where this can be determined from internal evidence alone). The German stanzas were added, made to be sung to the same melody as the Latin, for the greater enjoyment of an audience not confined to clercs (see my discussion of this in *PBB* lxxxiv [1962], especially pp. 182–3).

The Latin canzone emerges from its winter setting into a new year of life—its last stanza evokes 'le sacre du printemps', and the beloved becomes the queen of the rites, *inovans annum*. This recalls the radiant song to the May-bride, 'Annualis mea' (*CB* 168), as the description 'prenitentem luce febiali' recalls the lines in *CB* 169 (discussed above, pp. 315 ff.):

> In Amoris hec chorea
>   cunctis prenitet,
> cuius nomen a Phebea
>   luce renitet

—a song which Schumann (*CB* i. 2, 256) suggested was by the same author as *CB* 168. Did the writer of 'Iam entrena plena' know either of these songs, or both? It is hard to conjecture. What is certain is that the Latin stanzas are earlier than their German contrafacta, and that even these (as their garbled condition in V, which according to Zingerle was late fourteenth-century, indicates) are considerably earlier than the two MSS. themselves. So the Latin stanzas may well go back to the world of the Carmina Burana, or near it. Their virtuoso form can scarcely be paralleled anywhere in Medieval Latin. In the vernacular, Heinrich Frauenlob's *aubade*, 'Durch dinster vinster, nebel dicken blicken' (ed. Ettmüller, pp. 260 ff.), offers an analogy.

Wien, CV 5371, fol. 216ʳ   s. XV

1a Iam vernalis amenitas
    et temporum serenitas
    aureque flatus lenitas
      se mundo presentavit.

1b Nunc avium garrulitas
    et nemorum viriditas,
    nunc terrarum fecunditas
      tristiciam fugavit.

2a Florum nu[m]erositas
    ac odorum suavitas
    torpentes sensus excitat
    quos ad amorem incitat.

2b Quis enim tam ferreum
    cor habens vel lapideum
    quin flectatur tam variis
    donorum beneficiis?

3a Hec temporum mutacio
    rerumque delectatio
      iam cuncta renovavit,

3b Hinc Veneris imperium
    ge[n]us omne viventium
      iam sibi subiugavit;

4a Ac iugo quoque virginis   4b unius iam pre ceteris
     subdi confiteor   amore torqueor;

5a Que nunquam a memoria 5b sed intra cordis saucia
     mei languentis labitur   tanquam presens resolvitur.

6a Cuius generositas   6b Nam suis virtutibus
     et probitas   et dotibus
   et forme speciositas   cunctis quidem virginibus
    meretur commendari,   non potest coequari.

7a Huius amor me cruciat   7b sed nisi me reficiat
     intolerabilis,   non sum curabilis.

8a Cor meum miserabile   8b et non erit sanabile
    pre cunctis hanc desiderat hec ni solamen conferat.

9a Eius ridentes oculi   9b Frons libera extenditur,
   scintillant ut carbunculi   candore gena pingitur
   cuius ic*tibus* iaculi   cui rubor interseritur,
    cor meum sauciatur.   eius coma crispatur.

10a   Ora serena,   10b   Vultu benigna,
     nectare plena,   laudeque digna,
   melle magis dulcia,   abilis per omnia.

11a   O decora,   11b   Salvus ero,
     sine mora   nec despero
   medela mihi sis!   si me sanare vis.

12a   Dulce solamen,   12b   Sis relevamen
    Anthea, spei   vulneris mei;
   mihi faveas,   semper valeas!

13a Propter te doloris finem 13b Tu dolori miserere
   quero, quia crucior—   quèm pro te suffero;
 nisi *venias, reclinem*   ne permittas me languere—
 morte infelicior.   iug*um* non desidero.

Now the loveliness of spring, the time's serenity, and the gentleness of the breeze are manifest in the world. Now the chattering of birds, the verdant groves and earth's fertility have put melancholy to flight.

The countless flowers with their sweet perfumes rouse the dull senses and incite them to love. Has anyone a heart so iron-hard or stony that he does not yield with so many blessings given?

The change of seasons, the delight of creatures has renewed all that is—thus Venus' rule has made every race of living things submit.

I too confess I am yoked under a girl's will, tormented by the love of one girl beyond the rest.

She never, as I languish, eludes my memory, but freely enters my heart's wounds, as if present there.

Her nobility, her honour, the beauty of her shape deserve all praise: in her perfections, her endowments, she cannot be compared with any other girl.

An unbearable love for her tortures me, I am incurable unless she revives me.

My piteous heart longs for her surpassingly, and will never be healed if she does not give solace.

Her laughing eyes sparkle like carbuncle-stones, my heart is wounded by the piercings of their dart. Her brow set wide, her cheek blended of radiant white and red, her hair in waves;

Her lips serene, full of nectar, sweeter than honey; merciful in her looks, worthy of praise, accomplished in every way.

O glorious one, be my cure without delay—I shall be well, I'll not despair if you are willing to heal me.

Grace me with the sweet solace of hope, Anthea, be the lightening of my wound. May you flower always.

Because of you I seek the end of sorrow, afflicted as I am—if you do not come, let me, too unhappy, rest in death. Have pity on my sorrow, which I suffer for you; do not let me languish—it is not I who wish this yoke.

8a. 1 MS. m'isabile

9a. 3 MS. ictu seu

13a. 3-4 MS. quem nisi facto (?) vinculis tero (faulty in sense, rhythm, and rhyme)

13b. 4 MS. iugis

London, B.M. Add. 12195, fol. 64ᵛ s. XV²

My sol my sol my fa re my fa sol

Erat quedam domina
Valde dives et clara,   my sol

Et dilexit puerum,
Iuvenum pulcherimum,   my sol

5 Et intravit cameram
Osculando dominam—   my sol

'Scis tu, scis tu, clerice,
Quid tu debes facere?   my sol

Debes me supponere
10 Velud vis ter opere.'   my sol

Quando *fact*um *f*uerat
Clericus ploraverat.   my sol

'Tace, tace, clerice,
Volo tibi solvere;   my sol

15 Dabo tibi tunicas,
Tractas et camisias.'   my sol

Clericus tunc tacuit,
Quia sibi placuit.   my sol

Once there was a lady, very rich and famous, and she loved a lad,
a very handsome lad. And he went into the chamber, kissing his
lady-love. 'Scholar, scholar, do you know—what you must do now?
You've got to take me now three times, in any way you like!' When

he had done his mistress' will, the clerc began to weep. 'Quiet, quiet now, my clerc—I want to pay you now. I'll give you lots of daytime clothes, some woollies and some shirts.' The scholar became quiet then, because he liked this well.

1 ff. A clerical ballad, probably sung with a *Klangspielerei* as refrain between each couplet. A different version, 'Fuit una domina', was printed by J. Feifalik from Wittingau Archiv A. 7 (*v.* Bibliography ad loc.).
6 MS. Et osculando
7 MS. Sis tu sis tu
11 MS. st͞m sn ˆ erat [R. M.]
16 tractas—*v.* Du Cange, s.v. *tractae.*
18 Followed (in the same hand) by the words 'Nunc finem feci da michi quod merui quod Leke'.

München, Clm 24539, fol. 69ʳ s. XV²

    Brumalis temeritas
    et nivis asperitas
      prata violentat,
    que venti severitas
5   et eius celeritas
      graviter eventat.
    Hec est rei veritas:
    tota se prosperitas
    veris sic absentat.

10 Si pratorum spacia
    desunt, tunc solacia
      requiras in stupis,
    ubi mentem sacia
    puellarum gracia
15   quas habere cupis!
    et sua fallacia
    fallatur audacia
      ut morbus syrupis.

    Nunc in habitaculis
20 stupe ferit iaculis
      Amor cor internum,

sed in tabernaculis
Bachi carens maculis
   bibitur phalernum.
25 Istis sub umbraculis
obstetur obstaculis
   nivis in eternum!

Cunctis in temporibus
sub virtutum moribus
30   Mariam honora—
estu vel algoribus,
nive vel in floribus,
   virginem implora;
veris in dulcoribus,
35 pruina vel roribus,
   semper hanc adora!

Winter's temerity and the snow's asperity ravage the fields, which
the wind's severity and celerity fans with vehemence. This is the
matter's verity: all spring's prosperity has gone its way.

If you cannot walk in the fields, then look for comfort in the warm
baths—there sate your mind with the loveliness of all the girls you
long to possess. May their elusiveness be eluded through your own
bold confidence, as sickness is through cordials.

Now in the buildings of the baths Amor strikes the inmost heart
with darts—but in the taverns men drink Bacchus' irreproachable
Falernian. In these refuges may snowdrifts be kept out for ever!

At every season, honour the Virgin Mary by virtuous behaviour.
Whether there's heat or cold, snow or flowers, pray to the Virgin;
in spring's sweet graces, in hoar-frost or in dew, adore her always!

1 ff. The gallimaufry of themes—nature, voluptuousness, wine, religion—
the parade of jingling rhyme, and the delightfully inconsequential trains of
thought, go to make this a neat burlesque of the secular Latin lyric. It is done
almost straight-faced, with a deftness that a literal translation cannot convey.

6 eventat—*TLL* gives *evento* only as a technical medical term (chiefly in the
Latin transl. of Oribasius); Baxter–Johnson gloss it for the twelfth century as
'to fan'. Compare OFr *esventer, esventeler*, meaning 'rafraîchir par un souffle'
(Godefroy), 'anblasen, lüften' (Tobler–Lommatzsch).

12 stupis—*v. stuba* (Du Cange): vaporarium, hypocaustum,
22 tabernaculis—*v.* Du Cange, s.v. 1. *tabernaculum*, pro *taberna*.

THE LOVE-VERSES FROM
REGENSBURG

München, Clm 17142, fol. 92ʳ   s. XII in.

1   Contempnens uvas   huius regionis acerbas,
    Vulpes ad campos   ibat saturanda Falernos.
    Ut venit, placidum   dederat iam vinea mustum,
    Ut rediit, nostras   calcator presserat uvas;
5   Tandem perdoluit,   quia sors utrobique fefellit.
    Sic ego, dum raras   capio male sanus amicas—
    His etiam carui   poteram quibus aptius uti!

Looking down on the sour grapes of this region, the gourmand
fox went to Falernian vineyards. When he came there, the vines had
already yielded their soft must, when he returned, the treaders had
already pressed our grapes. Then the fox grieved, for in both places
fate had tricked him. So too do I grieve, when rashly I try to win
choice girls—I have lost even those whom I could so well have
enjoyed!

fol. 93ᵛ

II Advolat et stillat,   pugnat Vulturnus et undat.
    Qui procul est oculis   procul est a lumine cordis.
    Odero si potero,   si non, invitus amabo,
    Nec recolens fusum,   nec anus—iam pergito lusum!
5   Commoda qui sacrat   stolida sibi dona rependat!

The Volturno flies on, trickles, fights its way and winds. He who is
far from my eyes is far from the light of my heart. I shall hate him if
I can, if not, against my will I shall love him. I am not toilbound or

old—let love's play go on! May whoever condemns delights find reward in his own brutishness.

fol. 94ᵛ |

 III Quicquid flos flori,   rutilans sub tempore verni,
  Hoc demandat ei,   pariter ludos ymenei
  Qui te pre cunctis   amat: excole nomen amantis.
  Nunc effrenatis   venis redit ardor amoris.
 5 Proh dolor, ahc quid agunt?   Me dulcia somnia ludunt.
  O dum dormito   tua se presentat imago,
  Oscula defigit,   complectens ipsa recedit.
  Tu mihi, tu cura,   timuique fugatior aura,
  Instabilis stabiles   nimium deludis amores.
 10 Sed cur fervet amor,   ferus, intolerabilis ardor?
  Fervor—ahc restringuam?—   stimulat summam
                 medicinam.
  Quid medicina valet?   quid nobis herbida confert?
  Nil confert nobis: non est medicabilis herbis.
  Sed quam formosa,   tu salubris medicina!
 15 Tecum dulcis amor—   amor est dulcissimus ardor,
  Sed lactas steriles,   perdulce tempus, amores.
  Si mihi plus cedis,   vel ad oscula danda patebis. . . .

As flower asks flower, radiant in the spring, so he who loves you beyond all asks you for the sports of wedded love: cherish the name of lover! Now love's ardour returns to my impetuous veins. Alas, what tumult is in them? Sweet dreams tantalize me. While I sleep your image reveals itself, presses kisses on me, and even in embracing vanishes. You who are mine, my care, more fleeting, I fear, than air, utterly inconstant, you make sport of constant love. But why does love, that fierce, insupportable ardour, continue to burn? This fervour—ah shall I restrain it?—challenges the greatest medicine. What use is medicine? What can herbals give us? Nothing to us— herbs cannot heal it. But how beautiful you are, you health-giving medicine! and with you is sweet love. Love is the sweetest pain, but you, season of delight, are giving suck to barren loves. If you yield more, or will allow kisses. . . .

IV Simia dicaris,   vel spinx, quibus assimularis
     Vultu deformi,   nullo moderamine comi!

You should be called monkey, or sphinx—you are like them in
your ill-shaped face and unkempt hair!   *fol. 95ʳ*

V Mittit vestalis   chorus ad vos xenia pacis,
    Concedens vestre   dominandi iura caterve,
    Sic tamen, ut precium   Virtus sibi reddat honestum.

The band of maidens sends you a peaceful welcome, granting
your company rights of dominion, but in such a way that Virtù
gives us an honourable esteem.

VI Corrige versiculos tibi quos presento, magister,
     Nam tua verba mihi reputo pro lumine Verbi.
     Sed nimium doleo, quia preponas mihi Bertham.

Correct the brief verses I am sending you, master, for to me your
words are like the light of the Word. But I am very sad, because you
prefer Bertha to me.

VII Gaude quod primam   te sors mihi fecit amicam.
      Me turbat graviter   qui crebro defluit Ymber,
      Nam vereor nostris   hanc vindictam dare culpis.

Be glad that destiny made you my first love. I am sorely troubled
by 'Rain' who drops down so often—I fear she will take revenge for
our faults.
[Ymber, D. Schaller suggests, may hide a German name (of the
abbess or prioress) beginning Regen-/Rein- ('rain' by popular etym.).]

VIII Mens mea letatur,   corpusque dolore levatur,
       Idcirco quia me,   doctor, dignaris amare.

My mind is full of joy, my body is raised up from grief, because
you, my master, honour me with your love.

IX Quas docuit Virtus   ad honestum vergere pignus
    His mittunt vere   mei cordis et oris amice . . .

The true friends of my heart and lips, girls whom Virtù has taught to look to an honourable vow, send you with these [verses] . . .

X Te [ ] cunctis   que plus amplector amicis
   Sollicitat rerum   graviter me causa tuarum.

Your situation gives me grievous anxiety, who embrace you [. . .] more than all women who are loved.

XI Salva sis, inmensa   pro scriptis laude repensa.
   Quamvis, amor care,   scriptum velut innuit a te.
   Non tamen, oro, meis   de rebus solliciteris:
   Sat quia cautus ego   de re per cuncta cavebo.

May you prosper, showered with immense praise for what you have written. Although just a letter, dear love, it was like a trace of you. But I beg you not to be anxious about my situation—enough that, being wary, I shall take care in every way.

XII Optet ut ista tibi,   tua sic mihi litera scribi.
    Eice, Christe, tua   tenebras de corde lucerna,
    His qui sancta tui   querunt vestigia verbi.

May your letter wish to be written to me, even as mine to you. Christ, with your lamp cast out the darkness from the heart of those who seek the holy traces of your word.

XIII Es dilecta mihi   quia munera cara dedisti:
    Vas bene tornatum   nitidumque, bibentibus aptum,
    Allia preterea,   mea que poscit medicina.
    Si tamen addideris   plus, grates semper habebis.

You are dear to me because you have given me dear gifts: a well-turned, sparkling bowl, ideal for drinking, and garlic too, which my medicine requires. But if you add more, I am bound to you for ever.

XIV En ego quem nosti,   sed amantem prodere noli!
Deprecor ad vetulam   te mane venire capellam.
Pulsato leviter,   quoniam manet inde minister.
Quod celat pectus   modo, tunc retegit tibi lectus.

It is your lover who writes—do not betray him! I implore you to
come to the old chapel at dawn. Knock softly on the door, for the
sacristan lives there. Then the bed will reveal to you all that my
heart now keeps hidden.

XV Prepositus vetule   mandat tibi fausta capelle,
H, quam primam   sibi sors bona fecit amicam.
Prima tamen non es,   quia duxerat antea bis tres:
Septima venisti,   supremaque vix placuisti.

The provost of the old chapel wishes you joy, H, you whom a
happy chance has made his leading lady. Yet you are not the first—
he had previously known six others! You have come seventh—and
hardly pleased him best.

fol. 96ʳ

XVI Sicut christallo   iacinctus fulget in albo
Fulges mente mea,   mihi tempore quoque serena.

As a jacinth sheds radiance in bright crystal, you irradiate my mind,
you who are serene to me at every moment.

fol. 96ᵛ

XVII Hunc mihi Mercurius   florem dedit ingeniosus
Quo possim viciis   precibusque resistere fedis—
Ius igitur nullus   retinet de me quoque stultus,
Qui nostris longe   sociis discordat ab ore.
5 Quos incesta iuvant,   consortia nostra relinquant—
In quorum numero   si converseris, abesto!
Vix admittuntur   qui rebus mille probantur,
Sed tamen hos modice   complectitur atque
                                        modeste[. . .]
Denique quîs Virtus   nostrum vult credere pignus,

10 Illos extrema   curat bene fingere luna,
   Ut sermone bono   clam crescant atque perito,
   Moribus egregiis   sint undique rite politis.
   Ergo quam venias   prius ad nos, instrue pennas,
   (Si quas imposuit   Ratio tibi, quando creavit),
15 Ne qua parte dolo   sis oblitus inveterato.
   Quem similis morum   sibi iunxit fama bonorum,
   Illi vestalis   chorus obtat dona salutis.

The shrewd god Mercury gave me this flower that I might resist unworthy frailties and entreaties. So no one who is foolish has any power over me; such a man strikes a jarring note in our set. Let those whom lewdness delights be banished from our company—if you are one of that sort, stay away! Even those who are proven in a thousand ways are only just admitted, but [our circle] welcomes them to some extent, and discreetly. As for those to whom Virtù wishes us to commit our pledge, she takes care to mould them well, when the moon is at its end, that secretly they grow in excellence and courtesy of speech, that they are duly refined in every way with manners of distinction. Therefore, before you come to us, preen your feathers (if Reason gave you any when she created you), lest you are fouled in any part with ingrained falsehood. For the man who has acquired a reputation for courtesy like ours, our maidenly company desires the grace of joy.

fol. 97ʳ

XVIII Explorare mei   te credo munia voti
      Quod perpendiculum   rogitas a me tabularum.
      Prospice re parva   mea sit devotio quanta,
      Que non tarda tuis   favet oficiosa petitis.
    5 Ergo tuo lateri   dum iungas quod tibi feci,
      Interiore nota   cordis me sedulo porta.

I think you are putting the obligations of my vow to the test by asking me for a holder for your tablets. In this small request you may see how great is my devotion, instantly ready and eager to do what you ask. So when you place what I have made for you at your side, keep me with all care at the centremark of your heart.

XIX Sum merito tutus,   perfectos quosque secutus,
     Et sic semper ero,   quia fit mihi litera medo.
     Cur paterer tali   quod lederer a moniali?
     Immo viros pellam—   multo mage vinco puellam!

I am not in danger, and this is only right, for I have followed
perfect masters. I shall always remain so, with literature as my mead.
Why should I allow myself to be hurt by such a nun? Surely if I am
to control men, how much easier to cope with a girl!

XX   Anulus in donis   missus fit pignus amoris,
     Ergo de more   fedus studeamus inire.
                              ★
     Fedus quod narras   nutrix mea nescit Honestas,
     Nec prorsus talem   voluit me discere morem.

He: The ring I sent among my gifts is a token of love, so let us in
all courtesy strive to submit to love's law.

She: My nurse Reputation does not know the law you mention,
and indeed does not wish me to learn such courtesy.

XXI Non valeo crebrum   de te sufferre regressum:
     Ad te cum nostre   concurrant queque puelle.

I cannot bear to leave you so often, when all our girls are flocking
to you.

fol. 102ʳ

XXII Quos docuit Virtus   ad honestum tendere fedus,
     Hos non amoveam,   sed dignis digna rependam.
     Non autem didici   privato federe iungi [. . .]

Those whom Virtù has taught to strive towards a worthy vow of
love I shall not dismiss, but shall return honour for honour. I have
not, however, been brought up to enter a secret attachment [. . .].

fol. 103ʳ

XXIII Est amor electus   sub amico pectore tectus.
      Qui tacite currit   amor omnia federa vincit.

A wondrous love lies hidden in my lover's heart. Love that runs
silently overcomes all laws.

fol. 103ᵛ

XXIV Cetera si possem   laudare, beatior essem—
       Permanet in voto   mens mea firma suo.

If I could commend other things, I might have greater joy, but my mind remains unshaken in its vow.

fol. 104ᵛ

XXV Reddo vicem digne,   pensans tua scripta benigne.
       Pectore devotam   te scripsisti mihi totam:
       Sic ego devotus,   quamvis sim carne remotus.
       Spiritus ipse quidem   tecum sit semper et idem!—
  5 Spiritus est unus,   fidei servans sibi munus.
       Si mea mens talis   frustretur vota sodalis,
       Hanc renitam nequam!   Quis nequam dixerit
                                     equam?
       Hoc fidei pignus   semper servabo benignus,
       †Ne qua succedat   sic, *ut* omnis forma recedat.†
 10 Dicimus ante vale   quam desint carminis ale.

I give you answer in all worthiness, musing with delight over what you wrote. You wrote that in your heart you were utterly devoted to me—so too am I, though far away in body. May that spirit also be with you for ever unchanged. There is (in us) one spirit, keeping for itself the gift of constancy. If my thought ever deceive the vows of such a beloved, I shall resist that base thought! Who could call such iniquity right? I shall freely hold this pledge of constancy for ever, †that it should never come to pass that all beauty fails.† We say farewell before the wings of poetry fail.

XXVI †. . . senta† iam dicam   blande moniturus amicam.
       His versus isti   respondent †*quos* potuisti†:
       Verba quidem saltum   demonstrant pectoris altum.
       Cum descendisti—   sed dic, ubi me posuisti?—
  5 Totus eram tecum,   sperabam te quoque mecum.
       Iste sed accessus   me commovet atque recessus.

Descendens ad me,   quo nescio cesseris a me.
'Sto, stas': sic stamus!   mutuo sic nos adamamus
Unum si velle   sit nobis, sit quoque nolle!

I shall now say . . . sweetly to admonish my beloved. These verses
are an answer to those you were able (to write), and indeed words
can show the heart's high leap. When you came down to me—but
tell me, where did you place me then? I was utterly with you, I
hoped that you also were with me, but this approaching and with-
drawing troubles me. As you come down to me, I do not know why
you are taken from me. 'I stand, you stand': thus do we stand, thus
love each other, if all we will and unwill is the same.

fol. 105ʳ

XXVII . . . .

  1★ †Munere donatis   Cesar vixisse tabellis.†
      Credimus esse parum   nisi demus nos quoque
                                     donum
      Temporibus festis   et moribus utile nostris.
      Immo tibi, frater,   dat amor tibi munera noster
      [H]aut de materie   producta sed ex ratione,
  5 Iusta relativis   que dictant munia flammis,
      Ut videas inopes   non prorsus egere sorores.
      Mercurii nate   sunt tres et Philologie,
      Quas pater ingenii   iussit nobis famulari,
      Ne titube*t* studium   sub inepta negotia flexum.
  10 E*u*propho*r*en docti   primam dixere Palesgi,
      Commo*te*[nque] bonos   blande receptat amicos,
      †Engialen† aliam,   susceptis officiosam,
      Virtutum robur,   comes his Basi*l*ea locatur,
      Ex habitu casto   quod agit decorans et honesto.
  15 Has tibi contiguum,   si vis, prestamus in usum,
      Condicione tamen   facias vit*am* specialem,
      Distans hospitibus   quibus est vaga mens uti corpus.
      Te decet ut placide   fidas venereris ubique.
      Unda calens patrie   movet ut sis fervidus igne,
  20 Igne salutari   quo virtus debet am*a*ri.

[. . .] We think at the very least we too should give a present at festive times, as befits our way of life. Or rather, dear brother, it is our love offers you these gifts, made not of matter but of reason, according to what obligation allied with ardour dictates, so that you may see the sisters have not been wholly helpless. Three daughters were born of Mercury and Philology, whom the father of talents asked to serve us, lest our studies falter, bent under foolish tasks. The wise Pelasgians called the first Euprophorê (ease of speech), the next, Commôtê (the embellisher), receives good friends with sweetness; the third, Engyalê (? the giver of gifts), obliging to her pupils and firm in all virtues, accompanies the other two as queen, adorning all she does in her chaste and honourable way. We shall give you these ladies, if you will, for intimate use, but with the proviso that you lead a special way of life, remaining far from those guests whose roving minds are like their bodies. It behoves you serenely to venerate those true mistresses everywhere. The warm waters of your birthplace make you glow with that wholesome fire by which virtue should be loved.

XXVIII Carmine dives eram   cum paucis rebus egebam,
    Carmina posthabui   postquam ditescere cepi;
    Iam non est tutum   contendere carmine tecum!
    Prolem Mercurii   tibi testaris famulari—
  5 Illa mihi sobolis   sunt munia Mercurialis;
    Quin ipsam doctam   scio te docuisse Minervam,
    Que dedit ignitum   vultum tibi, corque peritum,
    Teque saginavit   vel *se* cognoscere iussit
    Ne late[at] quantas   gestent tua pectora flammas—
  10 Flammas et turpes,   quibus et me, torrida, torres!
    Longe precellis,   longe me carmine vincis.
    Victum me fateor   tandemque manus dare cogor.

I was rich in song when I was poor in certain things; I have neglected my songs since I began to be enriched (by you): it is no longer safe to vie with you in song! You show that Mercury's daughter waits upon you: such gifts, it seems to me, are the gifts of Mercury's daughter. Indeed I know that learned Minerva herself has taught you, she who gave you glowing features and a sensitive heart, who nurtured you, and what is more, bade you acknowledge her, lest your heart hide the fires it contains, as well as those poor fires by which you in your blaze kindle me. You surpass me by far, your poems far surpass mine, I confess myself vanquished, and at last am compelled to surrender.

xxix Treicius vates   iustas reperit sibi clades,
  Presumens vestrum   scribendo lacessere sexum;
  Risit ventosas   Tritone Marsia buccas,
  Hinc cute detracta   defluxit ut amnis in arva—
 5 Femineisque mares   cesserunt litibus omnes!
  Sic satis exemplis   me commonitum memoratis
  Hanc ut devitem   (quia non sum par tibi) litem.

Orpheus wins the disastrous death he deserves, daring to provoke your sex in his poetry. Marsyas laughed at Minerva's puffing cheeks, and so, flayed, he was washed away, like the stream (Marsyas) through the fields—men have always been vanquished in their struggles with women! Thus you remind me, who am more than warned by such exempla, that I should avoid this contest, because I am not equal to you.

fol. 105^{r–v}

xxx Quod me collaudas   —tanquam Tritonia Pallas
  Fecerat ignitam   metrique sub arte peritam
  Me—non ingratum   mihi, quamvis gratia verbum
  Hoc tua prestiterit   potius quam res solidar*it*.
 5 *Sed* laus quam *fatur*   dilectio non reprobatur.
  Sed dare velle manus   *te* miror, cum neque vinctus
  A me dicaris   neque penam promerearis.
  Treicius vates   et Marsia, quod vehementes
  Extiterant animo,   diras meruere profecto.
 10 Nos nihil astute,   nihil illicitum meditate,
  Ne sine muneribus   discedere te sineremus,
  Unanimes sobolem   dedimus tibi Mercurialem—
  Quam si fastidis,   melioraque dona requiris,
  Iunonis comitem   dabimus, quacunque placentem.

15 Attamen est forma   pulcherrima Deiopeia—
    Hanc cape promissam   tibi, princeps Eole,
                                 quondam:
    Spernimus antiquas   non *propter nomina* nimphas.
    Nunc ne plura tibi   scribam commo*tio* regni
    Famaque terribilis   prohibet tristissima nobis,
20 Virgis mobilibus   avium vice qu*e* residemus.
    Es*to* memor nostri,   vivas ubicunque morari
    Te iubeat dominus—   nos denique corde videmus.
    Iam valeas animo,   valeas quoque corpore tuto,
    Sic ut *neve minus*   deposcat sors tua nec plus.

You praise me as if Tritonian Pallas had kindled my fires and made me skilled in the art of verse, and I am grateful, though it is your courtesy rather than my accomplishment that has prompted what you say. And yet the praises uttered by love cannot be rejected. But I am amazed that you want to surrender, when I have never called you captive, and when you deserve no punishment. Certainly Orpheus and Marsyas, with their unbridled spirits, deserved their misfortunes. But we who have thought no guile, no impropriety, must not let you leave without farewell gifts. All together we give you a scion of Mercury—if you disdain that, and look for better gifts, we shall give you a companion of Juno who is delightful in every way. Deiopea indeed is fairest of shape—take her, Prince Aeolus, she was promised to you long ago: we do not despise the nymphs of old because of their names. Now the turmoil in the land and the fearful, tragic news prevent us from writing more —who are perched like birds on shaken branches. Remember us, live wherever the Lord bids you; we, let me conclude, shall see (you) in our hearts. May you be safe and well in body and in mind, in such a way that your lot may leave nothing to be desired, more nor less.

XXXI . . . .   cum matre Cupido
    Qui tibi spe vacua   promisit federa nostra,
    Ut scribas penna   te decipiens fugitiva—
    Sed tamen ille puer   tibi dictat inepta, magister!
  5 Quomodo nos primas   tibi demonstravit amicas?
    Erras nimirum,   nec habet te Legia natum,

Si nos mol[l]itis   pariles vis esse puellis.
Illos diligimus   quos sculpsit provida Virtus,
Quosque Modestia se   monuit spectare modeste.
10 Ergo correcti   cape sanus munia voti,
Et vome pestiferam   Veneris puerique cicutam
Ridentis flentes   mutilatum fedus amantes!
Denique si tibi se   fautorem Iupiter ipse
Adderet, et cithara   peteret nos Phebus acuta,
15 Omnibus adiunctis   in vota nefaria divis,
Spes tua concideret   et leto fine careret!
Te non castorum   decepit miles Amorum
Ovidius, qui te   [per]suasit car*men* amare
Quo subvertuntur   miseri, non erudiuntur.
20 Si condonamus   tibi culpas, diiudicamus
Anti*do*to sane   rationis te valuisse;
Posce tamen puerum   mordax sedare flagellum—
An te castigat   quem spes mendosa fatigat?
Gratia domnarum   quicquid prestabit honestum;
25 Hoc illi reddit   qu*i* cuncta modesta requirit.

. . . .

Cupid and his mother, who promised you my love, was feeding
you on vain hopes, tricking you on the wing, that you would write.
Come, sir! what foolishness the blind boy dictates! How did he prove
to you that I was your most beloved? You are quite wrong, you are
no true son of Liège, if you think we are like girls who yield at once.
We love only those whom prudent Virtù has moulded, whom
Gentleness has trained to look on her with deference. So be sensible,
restore your devotion to its true standard, disgorge the poisonous
hemlock of Venus, and of her son who laughs at lovers weeping over
broken vows. Even if Jupiter came to aid you besides, if Apollo
visited me with his keen lyre, if all the gods helped you to an unworthy love, your hopes would be dashed and you would fail.
Ovid, that knight of the unchaste 'Amours', has deceived you, per-
suading you to love the poem by which unhappy men are seduced
and not made finer. If we forgive your faults, it is because we per-
ceive you have come to yourself again, through the antidote of
right reason. But tell that boy Cupid to lay down his biting whip—

or does he chastise you for the false hopes that vex you? A lady's grace will grant whatever is honourable—this she will give to one who always asks with due deference. . . .

fol. 106ʳ

XXXII 'Salve' mitto tibi   quod non queat adtenuari
     Tempore vel spacio   terrarum centuplicato.
     Dextra dei cunctos   spectans virtute probatos
     Assit ubique frequens   tibimet felicia mittens.

I send you a greeting which cannot be diminished by time, or space of lands a hundredfold. May the right hand of God, who looks upon all who are tried in excellence, be with you everywhere abundantly, sending you happiness.

fol. 106ᵛ

XXXIII Quid tibi precipue   scribam nequeo reputare,
     Qui laudes multas   esse mihi memoras.
     Num tamen ista ioco   dicas an corde sereno
     Me latet, et dubius   pendet adhuc animus—
5 Nam pretermissis   que sunt insignia cunctis
     Laudasti formam,   sit quasi digna, meam.
     Si quid laudis habet   res quam febris horrida sorbet

   . . . .

I cannot think out just what I should write to you, you who say so much in my praise. Whether you say these things in jest or out of a serene heart, I cannot tell—my judgement is still in the balance. For, leaving out all that is truly worthy of note, you praised my beauty—as if that deserved it. If a creature consumed by a ghastly fever deserves any praise . . . .

XXXIV Si puer est talis,   quo iungi me tibi gestis,
     Ut quocunque ferat   solidum voto sibi cernat
     Et maneat constans,   idem fervens nova captans—
     Sit procul a nobis.   Nam siquis perstat ineptis,

  5 Luctus adest grandis   dum vult persistere ceptis,
       Nec quandoque viam   percurrere consulo ceptam.
       Hec tibi ne nimias   reddant, peto, scripta querelas,
       Nam mihi res suadet   quicquid mea litera pro*d*et;
       Sed nec honor medio   quemquam desistere cepto,
10 Esset et aucta magis   contractio suspicionis.
       †N*e* quid ames nimium,   incaut*e*, sit† utile
                                           [pri]mum.

       Sic placet et nostrum   'differri tempore ceptum
       Tutius ut nostris   vincamus noxia culpis'.
       Est tibi vana fides,   non est dilectio perpes!
15 Qui 'Fortis' nomen   tibi iunxit perdidit omen.
       Quid prodest nomen   si non retinebis honorem?
       Nomine fulgebunt   tali qui fortia querunt.
       '*Ignavus*' potius   sis amodo iure vocatus.
       Nunc breviter dicam   cur hec enigmata solvam:
20 Istud nempe tue   vicium successio culpe.
       Cum tibi versiculos   misi ratione politos
       Non mihi responsum   curasti reddere dignum
       Sed mihi rescrips*t*i,   vetuit turbatio regni.
       Tu solus pesti   potuisses huic medicari …
25 Nec lorica tuum   pectus protexit ineptum,
       Ensis namque tuus,   multa ferrugine tectus,
       Etsi percussit   hostem, sine vulnere mansit.
       At miror clipeum   tua qu*e* ferret manus aptum?—
       Dextra reor: timido   nam convenit hoc bene
                                             sclavo.

30 Sed forsan dicis   'deerat mihi nuntius omnis'.
       Que tibi porrexit   mea scripta, mihi tua ferret,
       Mittere si velles,   vel si componere scires.

If the boy (Love), by whom you desire me to be bound to you, is
such that he would hold soundly under any condition, and remain
constant while at the same time aspiring to new heights— I'll yet
have none of him! For if anyone is stuck in foolishness, great grief
comes of it if he wants to persist as he began. Sometimes I think a
course begun should not be pursued to the end. Don't be too sad

at what I am writing—for I am sure it is all exactly as I say. It would not be honourable for a man to break off in the middle of what he began, and people's suspicion would be increased. †Lest you should love anything too much, incautious one, let expediency be your first concern.† So it is right for our relationship to be 'postponed', that we may the more securely avoid all harm for our faults'!— Yours is an empty faith, no everlasting love! Whoever gave you the name 'Brave' failed in his augury. What use is such a name if you cannot maintain its honour? Only those who aspire to courage are adorned by such a name. Henceforth you should more fittingly be called 'Coward'.

Now in short I shall tell you why I would dismiss these quandaries. Everything was spoilt through your own fault. When I sent you verses, the best I could, you did not bother to reply properly, but wrote only that the civil commotions prevented you from writing. Only you could have provided a remedy for this sickness (of mine)…. But you had not even armour on your foolish breast, and indeed your rusty sword, even if it struck an enemy, could not have inflicted a wound. I wonder which of your hands held a shield, for effective protection?—your right hand, I imagine, for this is what a timid slave would do. But perhaps you will say: I had no messenger. She who brought you my letter would have brought me yours too, if you wanted to send one, or knew how to write one.

fols. 106ᵛ–107ʳ

xxxv Nolo meis culpis   assignes quod cita scriptis
    Non responsa dabam,   que dare debueram.
    Non servo nonum,   quod amicis scribo, per

                           annum;
    Peniteatque 'sclavi'   consimilesque tui,
5 Huius desidie,   nosti, quia causa fuere:
    Illorum subitus   me latuit reditus.

I wish you would not blame me for not replying to your verses quickly, as I should have done. I do not keep what I write to friends till the ninth year. (You) and your companions should feel sorry for the 'slave', because, you know, they were the cause of this dilatoriness. I did not know they would return so suddenly.

XXXVI . . . .
> Sed quia certa meis   non das responsa lituris,
>   Quid scribam dubius   non mihi fert animus.
> Id tantum doleo   quod iactas ore protervo
>   Ex nobis multa   noscere te stolida.
> 5 Non cure nobis   est si quid inutile garris—
>   Si laudas etiam,   spernimus ut nebulam.
> Ergo virgineis   fugiat procul ille choreis
>   Agnis infestus   qui solet esse lupus!

But because you give no definite answers to my blotted lines, my mind wavers, and offers me nothing I can write. I can only grieve that shamelessly you go about saying you have learnt many things which are not nice from us. We do not care if you chatter disparagingly—even if you praise, we despise it as vapid talk. So let the wolf who harasses lambs stay well away from the parties of girls!

XXXVII Ut valeas animo   quamvis irata rogabo.
> Ipsa re didici   mihi divos insidiari—
> Nam sub amicicia   tu me deludis inepta,
> Me verbis, alias   opera complexus amicas.
> 5 Quid queror? adversis   mihi fiat quod precor illis:
> Fert quoscumque coma   serpentes dira Medusa
> Nimphis insiliant   que nunc tua federa temptant!

Though I am angry with you, I shall wish you joy. I have learnt from experience that the gods are out to ensnare me—for under a vain cloak of friendship you deceive me, embracing me in words, other women in deed. Why should I complain? May my wish come true upon my rivals: may every snake in grim Medusa's hair leap upon the nymphs who tempt your constancy now!

XXXVIII Me quia fecisti   letari sede decenti
> Invidie iaculo   de multis ledor amaro.
> Sed ne me noceant   et ad imum vulnera condant
> Iam tua prevideat   pietas illasque repellat.

Because you gave me joy and enthroned me with great honour, I am hurt by many women's grievous darts of envy. Lest they should harm me and wound me to the quick, I hope your devotion will anticipate them and ward them off.

fol. 107ᵛ

XXXIX Vos proficiscentes   prohibetis nos fore tristes,
  Presertim verni   qu*ia* temporis huc redituri.
  Crederet hoc durum   pia mens—si non daret unum
  Solamen nobis   domni comitatus Hugonis.
 5 Hic o! o! quantos   secum deduxit amicos,
  Vestibus insignes,   et verbis se reputantes
  Omnes victuros   quos Norica nutrit ephebos!—
  (Non nobis horum   placet experientia morum).
  Si steterint clari,   vos flebitis inde reiecti;
 10 Si fuerint victi,   cantabitis inde recepti.

On the point of departure you forbid us to be sad, especially as you are coming back in spring. A devoted mind would find this (separation) hard—if Sir Hugh's entourage did not give us a certain consolation. But, my goodness gracious, how many friends he brought with him here!—so elegant, and all thinking they could out-talk the young men of Bavaria! (We are not impressed by such elaborate manners.) If their courtesy remains untarnished, you'll be cast off, and weep; if it is flawed, you'll be welcomed back, and sing.

XL Nobis Pierides   ferrent si vota fideles,
  Optarent tibi que   vellet Apollo bene—
  Sic vite laute   sonus oblectaret ubique
  Et nil quod cantet   Iupiter esse putet!
 5 *N*os tamen has hilares,   quamquam dis inferiores,
  Odas exprimimus   quas notat alta Salus.
  Ergo tibi festum   sit salve centuplicatum:
  'Expectatus ades,   gaudia certa fer*es*.'
  Denique non stolide   *tibi* dicimus, hinc abeunde,
 10 Quod pax atque salus   sit tibi iam reditus.
  Nunc igitur nobis,   quia gaudes, flos probitatis ...

If the loyal Muses answered our prayers, for you they would choose what Apollo well might wish—then the sound of a fine life would give delight everywhere, and then let Jupiter consider its song naught! But we, though lower than the gods, give expression to those joyful songs which Salus dictates on high. So we give you a hundredfold festive greeting: 'Long-awaited, you are here, you will bring us true delights.' Indeed with all courtesy we tell you, you who must leave, that your return will be peace and bliss. Then, flower of courtesy, as you are in joy, (tell) us now. . . .

fol. 109ʳ

  XLI Nos quibus ornatum dominus dedit et dabit aptum
     Laudis yperbolice non oblectamur honore;
     Nec tamen indignor quia pulchra venustaque
                   dicor,
     Si modo simpliciter venit hec laus, non
                   petulanter.
    5 Sic detestor eum qui cor gerit insidiosum
     Quasque iac*it* madide nigro sunt felle sagitte.

We, whom God has given some fairness, and will give as much as is right, are not amused by exaggerated tributes of praise. It is not that I am angry because I am called beautiful or attractive, provided such praise is unaffected and not forward. Thus I detest a man who wears a deceitful heart, and lets fly arrows dripping with dark poison.

fol. 110ʳ

  XLII Que mihi prima novum dederat bene prodiga
                   nummum
     Semper amanda mee statuetur filia dextre.

The first girl who so generously gave me a new coin—let her be set as a daughter at my right hand, I shall love her always.

  XLIII *Se* tibi dantis amor quasi dulcis ros fluat in cor,
     Cingarisque nova per centum gaudia zona!
     Gaudeo me *numeris* sambuca nitescere comptis

Docta peritorum   posuit quos dextra virorum.
5 Si mihi Pierides   hoc plus tribuere sorores:
Quod recinit laute   Limnat*idi* turba Diane [. . .]

May the love of one who offers herself to you flow into your
heart like a sweet dew, and may you wear your new cincture in joy
a hundredfold! I am glad that, playing the zither, I shine in the
elegant rhythms that the accomplished hands of wise men have
taught me. If the Pierian sisters gave me this also: that of which
people sing to glorious Diana Limnatis [. . .].

fol. 111 ᵛ

XLIV Pulverulenta no*v*is   bene verritur area scopis!
      Mercurii famule,   scribendo loquendo perite,
      St*a* mecum, ne quid   presumptio garrula possit.
      P*a*rvulus ergo cave   tibi, ne gravius cruciere
    5 Quam c*o*rvus niveam   cum dempsit lingua figuram.

Dusty ground is well swept by a new broom! You, Mercury's
disciple, eloquent in writing and in speech, stay with me, lest
jangling presumption cause me harm. Then beware, little fellow, or
you'll be made to suffer worse than the crow when a jangling tongue
deprived him of his snow-white form.

XLV Sum tibi cara gene   pro sede ruboris amene;
      Turturis in morem   mihi serva fide pudorem,
      Sponsi post obitum   iam non habitura maritum.

You love me for the seemly blush upon my cheek: then help me
loyally to keep that modesty, and, like the turtle-dove, not take
another husband after the first has died.

XLVI Hesperidum ramis   hec mala recepta superbis
      Doxa puellarum   dat regi Palladiarum.
      Hercule nobilior,   quia non tulit omnia victor.

These apples, taken from the resplendent boughs of the Hes-
perides, the 'glory of girls' gives to the king of Pallas' maidens. He
is nobler than Hercules, because, though winner, he did not take all.

fol. 112^r

XLVII Hoccine pro scriptis   precium mihi, perfida, reddis:
       Ut fugias a me   nec, inepta, velis meminisse
       Quot vel quanta pii   dederim tibi munia voti?
       Si tibi plana fides   esset, secreta venires—
    5 Ac mihi deferres   secreti quicquid haberes!

Faithless one, is this the reward you give me for my verses—that
you flee from me, and discourteously refuse to remember how many
and how great were the vows of holy love I gave you? If your faith
were perfect you would come to me in secret and you would bring
to me whatever secrets are yours!

XLVIII Nunc autem non re   sed in astu vis agitare
        Ut tibi me dedam,   licet agnoscas alienam.
        Denique lauta bone   non aufers signa puelle.
        Ut tibi plus scribam   vetat indignatio, que iam
     5 Me monet ut queram   meliores, teque relinquam.

Now you are trying not truthfully but by trickery to move me to
give myself to you, even though you know another woman. Once
and for all, you will not deprive a girl of her unblemished character.
Indignation forbids me to write more, and bids me seek out men of
more worth, and to abandon you.

fol. 112^v

XLIX Iam felix valeas   letusque per omnia vivas,
       Pierides Muse   te largo sepius use!
       Ad nos deducto   iubilamus amore probato.
       Mercurius faciem   nobis monstraret herilem
    5 Si regis comites   non essent urbe frequentes.
       Hac causa vetite   trans aera desuper ire,
       Corde tibi canimus   melos quodcunque negamus.
       Ergo, pater, chere,   'salom lac' cui decet esse.

May you be happy now, may you live utterly in joy, while the
Muses visit you again and again in all your abundance! We rejoice

in the well-proven love that has been given us. Mercury would show us our master's face, if the king's courtiers were not assembled in town. Therefore as we cannot fly to you through the air, in our hearts we sing whatever song we fail to bring. So, dear father, welcome, you who deserve our 'Pax tecum'.

L Non constat verbis   dilectio, sed benefactis.
    Quod mihi te verbis   et amicam sentio factis,
    Si sospes vivam   benefactum par tibi reddam.

Love consists not in words but in gracious deeds. Because I feel you love me both in word and in deed, I shall if my life allows return an equal grace.

W: Wilhelm Wattenbach, *MSB* iii (1873), 710 ff. Wattenbach in his description of the MS. transcribed a large number of these fragments as well as other verse—elegies, satires, political and didactic pieces, misogynica. At times he also suggested useful emendations, but on the whole he did not attempt to edit or make sense of these verses, his purpose being to acquaint historians with the contents of the MS., not to establish a critical text. The difficulties in the way of a critical text are so exceptional in the case of this MS. (see above, p. 221) that the present edition of the love-verses must be regarded only as a first attempt.

I. 1 ff. Cf. Phaedrus, *Fab.* IV. 2.

II. 2 Proverbial (cf. A. C. Friend, *Mediæval Studies*, xvi (1954), 199, Proverb 40).
    3 = Ovid, *Am.* III. 11, 35 (and *CIL* IV. 1520, 2).
    4 MS. Ne

III. 1 This poem is preceded in the MS. by an outline of the stories of Phyllis and Demophoon, Meleager and Atalanta, Briseis and Achilles, ending

Briseis hanc epistolam victori suo direxit, deprecans ut illam reciperet. El*eiacus* (MS. Elios) sermo. Eleiacum carmen est miserabile. Quicquid flos flori . . . .

(Cf. Schol. Hor. Vind. *Ars*, 77: elegos id est versus de miseria factos).
    This suggests prima facie that the poem is meant to be the letter that Briseis wrote, a free variation on *Heroides*, III. But the chaos of this MS. makes it perfectly possible that the rubric once served to introduce Ovid's epistle, and that neither the definition of 'elegiac' nor the poem that follows has any connexion with Briseis. This is reinforced by line 3: 'Qui te pre cunctis   amat: excole nomen amantis', which indicates a man as the speaker. Admittedly it seems also to echo Briseis' challenge (*Her.* III. 26): 'I nunc et cupidi nomen

amantis habe'; but I am not sure that this echo would justify emending 3 *Qui* to 'Que'.

4 *sic* MS.　W effrenatius, amatis

8 *sic* MS.　Corr. tenuique?　[W timidaque]

9 MS. nimium. stabiles

10 MS. amor id ferus　[W amor furit]

17 MS. si plus [W mihi]

IV. 2 *sic* MS.　Corr. deformis, comis?

V. 3 sibi—for ei (choro).

X. 1 Two or three syllables short. MS. qui

XII. 1 MS. optat [R. M.] Does this line belong with the two that follow?

3 qui—*sic* MS.　W qua

XVII. 1 Cf. Ovid, *Metam.* xiv. 291–3:

> Pacifer huic dederat florem Cyllenius album:
> moly vocant superi, nigra radice tenetur;
> tutus eo monitisque simul caelestibus intrat . . .

and Boethius, *Cons.* iv, m. 3, 17 ff.　Mercurius ingeniosus—cf. the Carolingian inscription 'Mercurio Susurrioni' in the cathedral at Aachen (*CIL* xiii. iv. 12005). It is tempting to suppose that the writer of these verses, and her *magister* (who had probably grown up very near there—*v.* xxvii. 19 n.) had actually seen this inscription.

4–5 MS. in reverse order.

8 A subject such as 'chorus noster' must be understood, perhaps from a lost preceding line.

10 extrema . . . luna (for the expression, cf. Varro, *R.R.* i. 37)—i.e. just before the *interlunium*, so that those 'moulded' will benefit from the power of the waxing moon (cf., for instance, *Picatrix*, ii. 3 [transl. H. Ritter–M. Plessner, London, 1962, pp. 65–66]).

XVIII. 2 perpendiculum—'Ansa, Catena, qua quippiam pendet . . . illud unde lebetes feruntur et suspenduntur' (Du Cange, s.v.).

XX. 3 MS. quo　W quod

XXI. 2. MS. Ad te cum nostre concussunt　W concurrant　W printed these lines as a continuation of xx. 3–4. MS. has paragraph-sign only before *Fedus*.

XXII. 3 MS. continues:

> Nuper velate,　　domino vos sanctificate,
> Ne frustra sponsum　signaverit anulus illum.
> Velatas noviter　　vocat ad nova iura magister—
> Scilicet ut sapiant　et opus levitatis omittant.

W printed these lines as a part of XXII, which is by a woman, perhaps one of special rank or authority. These lines, on the other hand, are clearly by a priest.

XXIV. 1–2 Two separate lines from Ovid (*Her.* xx. 61 and xvi. 168) have been combined by the medieval writer to make a leonine couplet.

XXV. 9 MS. si ctomnis

XXVI. 2 MS. pro potuisti

7 MS. Ascendens (by confusion with *accessus* in 6?)

XXVII. 1* The poem is clearly fragmentary, and the first line corrupt (if indeed it belongs to the verses that follow).

5 Iusta—i.e. Iuxta.

9 MS. titubes [W –et]

10 Euprophoren (Εὐπροφόρην)—MS. Enprophonen palesgi—*sic* MS. (for *Pelasgi*) W palefg

11 Commoten—i.e. Κομμωτήν. MS. Commoce bonos que

12 Engialen (*Εγγυάλην)—from ἐγγυαλίζω? (used especially of the gifts given by gods, the honours they bestow, the labours they entrust to mortals—*v*. A. Bailly, *Dictionnaire*, s.v.). I have not found these daughters of Mercury and Philology recorded elsewhere.

13 MS. basithea

16 MS. vite

19 Unda calens patrie—as the birthplace of the *magister* is Liège (see XXXI. 6), W refers this to the springs near Aachen.

20 MS. amori

XXVIII. 8 MS. sic ignoscere

9 MS. late

XXIX. 3 *v*. Hyginus, *Fab.* 165.

7 MS. continues 'Tu me clamoso cornix . . .'. But these lines (printed by W as a part of XXIX) are unrelated.

XXX. 4 MS. solidaret [R. M.]

5 MS. laus ete (105ᵛ) laus etenim quam fert

6 MS. ēe

12 sobolem Mercurialem—i.e. this poem (cf. XXVIII. 5).

13 ff. Do these lines belong here? From 15 the text is corrupt and interpretation must remain tentative. What is clear is only that the alternative gift is expressed in words echoing Juno's in *Aen*. 1. 71 ff., where she promises Aeolus Deiopea, the loveliest of her nymphs. The problematic lines 15–16 seem to suggest that *sub involucro* another gift is intended. Do they conceal a private joke, or can we guess? It would seem to turn (if, following W, I have emended 17 correctly) on the meaning of the name Deiopea. Fulgentius (*Virg. Cont.* 148–9, ed. Helm, p. 91) gave the (absurd) explanation

Eolus enim Grece quasi Eonolus, id est saeculi interitus. . . . Nam vide quid etiam ipso Eolo promittatur. Deiopea in coniugium; demos enim Grece puplicum dicitur, iopa vero oculi vel visio; ergo nascentibus in mundo seculare est periculum; cui quidem perfectionis puplica a dea partus promittitur visio. (Cf. Bernardus Silvestris, *Commentarium in Aen*., ed. Riedel, p. 9—Deiopea serenitas, splendor aeris.)

This suggests that Deiopea is used as a figure of the prospect of perfect peace, which the women wish their *magister* to find in Italy, far from the *commotio* (18) in Germany.

17 MS. prestet omnia [W propter nomina]

18 MS. commoda [W commotio]

20 MS. qui [W quae]

21 MS. Esse

24 MS. nil in eis [R. M.]

XXXI. 1 Preceded by unrelated lines on the Muses, ending 'Grecos inlustres Muse quondam facientes. Est fedus cum matre Cupido.   Qui tibi spe vacua...'

18 MS. carnem [R. M.] (cf. l. 19 *quo*)

21 MS. Antodoto

25 MS. que   [W qui]

At this point the text becomes, in my opinion, too garbled to edit or interpret satisfactorily (though isolated sentences are still clear). Transcription in W (pp. 726–7); but note 40 MS. philosophiam 65–66 MS. (*sic*) Quas nosti per me. nil responsi. In quibus astute. facundia lingue.

XXXII. 1 ff. An example of the poetic greeting. Cf. the tenth-century St. Gall greetings (*Poetae*, IV. 315 ff.) and, more generally, Hans Walther, 'Tot-Quot: Mittelalterliche Liebesgrüße', *ZfdA* lxv (1928), 257 ff.

XXXIII. 7 MS. ... sorbet. Si puer est talis .... But the poem is clearly unfinished.

XXXIV. 1 puer—i.e. Amor.

8 MS. profert [R. M.]

9 MS. quemquam medio

11 MS. (in margin) .. cquid ames ni .. ium incautus .. utat utile .. mum. Cf. fol. 108ᵛ (prov.) Nequid agas nimium vehemens reor utile primum.

12–13 I take the words in quotation-marks to be an echo of her lover.

15 Possibly the lover had some such name as Hartman or Kuonrat.

18 MS. Habere potius   The context requires a name or adjective contrasting with 'fortis'.

20 In MS. follows 22

23 MS. rescripsi [R. M.]

24 Some lines probably missing here.

25 *sic* MS.   W protexit pectus

28 MS. qua

29 W Sclavo (i.e. Slav)—but this raises unnecessary difficulties, and in a context where the girl taunts her lover with cowardice 'slave' (*v.* Du Cange, s.v. *sclavus*) yields a far better sense.

31 MS. tua mihi

32 si componere scires—i.e. she assumes he is at a loss what to say because he has grown indifferent to her.

XXXV. 4 W Sclavi—see XXXIV. 29 n.

XXXVI. 1 Preceded by two (incomplete) distichs which appear not to belong to these lines:

Nomine quod resonat	tibi res feliciter addat:
Hoc mittens obtat	que bona cuique parat.
Cum scriptis oculos	subigat tua dextera nostros
Ne pigram me tibi	missa credas ....

4 MS. stolide   [W stolida]

8 MS. Agnus, dolet   [W Agnis, solet]

XXXVII. 4 MS. operam   [W opera]
  6 MS. quacumque [R. M.], serpentis   [W serpentes]
XXXVIII. 4 MS. Repellas

XXXIX. 2 MS. que   [W quia]

XL. 5 MS. Hos   [W Nos]
  8 MS. ferens
  9 MS. te   [W tibi diximus, abeunti]

XLI. 6 MS. iacet   [W iacit]

XLIII. 1 MS. Me [R. M.]
  3 MS. utilis [R. M.]
  6 MS. laute mea līmata (but cf. Tacitus, *Ann.* IV, 43). It was customary for nuns and other young women in convents to make or embroider vestments and other clothing for clercs whom they favoured (cf. Spanke's remarks, *ZffSL* lvi. 249 ff., on Hilarius Anglicus, whose poem *Ad Superbam* likewise mentions the gift of a *zona*; also see above, p. 211).

This girl, however, gives her present explicitly as a pledge of love to her *magister*. The last two lines are difficult, and probably incomplete. Do they mean: 'If only I had not merely skill in music, but also purity of heart'?

XLIV. 1 MS. nobis [R. M.]
  3 MS. Stant
  4 MS. Provulus
  5 MS. curvus. The fable is found in Ovid, *Metam.* II. 534 ff.

XLV. 1 MS. cara cara
  2–3 Cf. Hugh Primas, 'Idibus his Mai' (Langosch 19, Meyer VI):

> Turturis in morem, cui dat natura pudorem,
> Quod, simul uxorem tulerit mors seva priorem,
> Non sit iocundum thalamum temptare secundum . . .

Also *Physiologus*, 'De Turture' (*P.L.* 171, 1223).

XLVI. 1 ff. Clearly separate from XLV (though W printed these as one). A playfully extravagant compliment accompanying a gift of apples (compare Chap. IV. 2, pp. 203 ff.). The 'rex Palladiarum' is the *magister*, who 'rules' over his maidenly company. In 'doxa puellarum' the girl sending the gift and the verses must be echoing a compliment he had made her, and then going one better in the terms she uses to him. The last line is wittily ambiguous: he has conquered her heart, but, unlike Hercules with the Hesperian apples, he has shown *noblesse* in love, he has not taken everything at once.

XLVIII. 1 ff. The woman's reply to XLVII. Follows without break in MS.

  2 MS. agnoscens
  4 MS. vetit   [W vetat]

XLIX. 3 W deducito
  5 W in urbe
  8 chere—i.e. Gk. χαῖρε
  salom lac—i.e. Hebr. Shālōm lākh ('peace be to thee').   W saloni (correction pointed out to me by B. Bischoff).

METRICAL AND LEONINE VERSE

Roma, Vat. Reg. lat. 585, fol. 4ᵛ; Escorial, O. III. 2, fol.
98ʳ⁻ᵛ s. XII; s. XIV

Cuidam cotidie obiurganti, cotidie supplicanti

Ira quidem prodest, quia corda reformat amantum
    Cum nimia languet pace sepultus amor.
Dissolvit nubes aurora, vel aura favillas,
    Verius ut niteat et magis urat amor.
5 Obtusas acuit mundatque rubigine mentes,
    Pacemque obpugnans vincula pacis habet.
Accendit tepidos, titubantes firmat amores,
    Et quasi iam veteres parturit ira novos.
Hinc sibi provideat ne decipiatur amicus,
10   Nam que sepe iuvat, sepius ira nocet:
Affectus hebetat aciemque retundit amoris,
    Concipit invidiam tristiciamque parit.
Dividit hec socios et amoris federa rumpit,
    In lites linguas ducit, in arma manus;
15 Dissociat populos, urbes et menia solvit,
    Fecundat stigios mortis amica sinus.
Ira igitur tua, quisquis amas, sit rara brevisque:
    Ira frequens furor est et diuturna scelus;
Solvitur hac animos socians concordia morum
20   Et duplici socios gracia fune ligans.

To one who each day reproaches and each day implores:

Anger has its value, indeed: it revives the hearts of lovers when love lies languid, buried in too much peace. Dawn then scatters the clouds, or a breath of air the sparks, that love may more truly shine, more fiercely burn. It sharpens blunt minds, cleanses away their rust, and even in fighting peace holds bonds of peace. It kindles lukewarm, strengthens faltering loves, and as it were brings old loves to new birth.

But let the lover take care, lest he be deluded—for if anger often helps, more often it harms. It can deaden feeling, blunt the edge of love, bring envy to conception, grief to birth. It sunders friends and breaks up pacts of love, anger leads tongues to strife and hands to war. It severs peoples, consumes cities and citadels; a friend to death, fills Hades' teeming womb.

May your anger, then, you who love, be rare and brief: frequent anger is madness, long-lasting anger a crime. Through such is overthrown that harmony of behaviour which makes minds unite, that grace which binds friends with a double cord.

12 (follows 18 in both R and E)   RE stristiciamque

fol. 5ᵛ (fol. 101ʳ⁻ᵛ)

Ecce redit species et amoris grata voluptas,
     Et novus insolito surgit amore decor.
Crinibus atque genis croceum roseumque colorem
     Et sua luminibus spicula reddit amor.
5 Ad decus antiq[u]um rediens, invitat amantis
     Clara oculos species et caro pura manus.
Lux videat sua, noxque probet, superantque probata
     Luce oculos species et caro nocte manus;
Nec radii vultus paciuntur lumina figi
10   Nec glacies carnis lubrica stare manus.
Hec annos si ducta magis quam docta sequatur
     Et quo ducit amor *nec* docet usus eat,
Unius si lateri latus unaque membra reformans
     Ducat in alternas absque labore vices—

. . . .

15   Murmure grata suo tura favumque ferunt, ·
Guttura melle fovent, penetrant precordia, replent
     Pectora, rimantur viscera, corda traunt.
Alternant animas, laqueataque corpus in unum
     Corpora spiritibus pervia corda parant.
20 Corpora spirituum transfusio languida reddit,
     Dumque sibi moritur vivit uterque pari.

Look how beauty and the dear delight of love return, and a new grace rises with matchless love. Love gives back a golden colour to the hair, roses to the cheeks, little darts to the eyes. Radiant beauty, returning to its glory of old, beckons the lover's eyes, an innocent body lures his hands. Let his eye behold, let him touch at night— by day beauty, once known, will overcome his eyes, by night that body captivate his hands. The brightness of her face will not let the lover's eyes stay fixed, her ice-smooth body will not let his hands take hold. If, guided rather than taught, she follows her youth and goes as love leads, not as custom teaches, if, shaping her limbs and body to fit another's, she brings them into a rhythm that's effortless. . . .

In their murmuring they bring precious incense and honey, caress the throat with honey, pierce the heart's centre, fill the breast, tear at the reins, distract the heart. They exchange souls, and their entangled bodies, made into one body, make their hearts penetrable through the spirits; the transfusion of spirits makes their bodies languorous—each dying to itself lives in the other.

2 E in solito (rightly?)
12 RE non docet
13 RE si cui lateri
14 RE ducit
15 Probably more than one hexameter missing, perhaps three lines in all. The last will have contained the subj. for 15—*verba amoris*?
19 spiritibus—*v. supra*, Chap. III. 4, pp. 150 ff.

These two poems, out of a larger group that is probably the work of a single Anglo-Norman poet, show a rhetorical mastery of a kind best paralleled in the secular poems of Hildebert, with which they seem to be contemporary.

Oxford, Laud lat. 25, fol. 3ʳ s. XII

Musa iocosa veni, mihi carmina suggere vati
Fingere quo possim subsisto qui novitati!
Virgo decora nimis, laudabilis et generosa,
Quam peramabilis, atque decora sit, et speciosa!
5 Hec fulgore micat, facie prefulget honora,
Eius cesaries est certe nigricolora,

Libera frons splendet, multo preclara deco-
Lumina sub qua sunt vehementi compta nito-
Maxille radiant fulvo splendente colo-
10 Equalis nasus non parvo dignus hono-
Carnea labra rubent redolentia semper odo-
Sermonisque favus distillat ab illius o-
Eius et est sermo solummodo plenus amo-
Est et mens eius nullo detempta mero-
15 Prerutilat collum cum gutture candidio-
Emicat et pectus thesauro fulgidio-   re
Brachia prefulgent, candoris fulgida flo-
Palma, manus, digiti sunt lactis candida mo-
Corporis in specie cunctis nitet hec melio-
20 Sed quid dicemus de re laudabilio-
Cum nequeat dici de causa nobilio-
Que latet absconse casto precincta pudo-
Hic asstant coxe cum re peramabilio-
Crura quibus subsunt, magno repleta vigo-
25 Que siquidem nullo lassantur victa labo-
Cuncta pedes portant, fulgentes absque pedo-

Come, Muse of mirth, inspire songs in your bard, that I who
thrive on the unheard-of may be able to compose!

A maiden, very beautiful, praiseworthy, and noble—how very
lovable she must be, and—beautiful, and—lovely!

She gleams with brightness, shines with a face full of honour, her
hair, forsooth, is black in colour, her wide brow glistens, radiant
with great—splendour, her eyes beneath it graced with over-
powering—candour; her jaws shine with resplendent tawny—
colour, her even nose deserves no little—honour, her red plump lips
always give forth an—odour, the honey of speech drips from them
in a —shower, her speech is full of love, nothing else whatso—ever,
her mind is not weighed down by any—dolour. Her neck sparkles,
the throat is even—whiter, her breast gleams with a treasure even—
brighter, her arms effulge, fulgent with whiteness'—flower, palm,
hand and fingers are in the milk-white—manner, if women shine
in bodily beauty, she shines—better. But what to say of more

deserving—matter, when none may speak of that part which is—
nobler, hiding,—concealed,—girded with chaste de—meanour: here
there are hips, and something even—sweeter, below that, legs, full
of exceeding—vigour, which don't get tired with any amount of—
labour. The lot is based on feet, radiant without bad—odour.

1 ff. A remarkably early parody of the rhetorical *descriptio pulchritudinis* (*v.*
Chap. IV. 2, pp. 193 ff.). Probably prior to Matthew of Vendôme's famous set
piece on Helen (Faral, pp. 129 ff.), which likewise itemizes every feature in
order, from the hair downwards. Later variants include Hoccleve's 'La Com-
mendacion de ma Dame', and Shakespeare's Sonnet 130.

4 MS. peramabalis

7 ff. In the MS. there are lines drawn from the end of each verse to the letters
're'.

9–10 As the *vates* works systematically downwards, should *nasus* (10) come
before *maxille* and these two lines be reversed?

München, Clm 19488, pp. 128–30   s. XII ex.

      Profuit ignaris   aliquid nescisse: probaris
      Quedam nescire   melius quam singula scire.
      Unde probas esse   simul omnia scire necesse?
      Rectius ignoras   aliquid quam scire laboras.
 5 —'Plus id ego credam?   quod non ignoscere quedam
      Aut ignorare   melius possim reputare.'—
      Sepe recensentes   dicenda viri sapientes
      Hoc decrevere   melius quam multa: tacere.
      Nonne quiescendum   Iob iudicat atque silendum
10 Lege refutata,   cum legis significata
      In Christo vere   vult consummata docere?
      Nomen persone   Paulus tacet ex ratione
      Ne sermo veri   potuisset vilis haberi
      Nomine scribentis   prelato: verba docentis
15 Frivola pro certo   fierent auctore reperto.
      Quod taceo nomen   duplicem reddo rationem:
      Si me vestrorum   discretio iudiciorum
      Arguit erroris,   confusio nulla pudoris
      Imminet auctori   pro versu deteriori.
20 Rursus ad hoc cavi,   si delectacio pravi,
      Mentibus humanis   temptacio surgat inanis,

Lingua perita foris   commercia pensat amoris
Et stilus hec vota   describit imagine nota,
Vos insignate   quasi canonica gravitate
25 Dicta refuta*tis*,   ob dicta reum reputatis
Carminis auctorem.   Quis enim Venerem vel amorem
Aut Veneris puerum,   quis tela Cupidinis, arcum
Nominet in vobis,   ubi sunt scola castra pudoris?
†Ne contingenti   quid si[t] lascivia menti,
30 Ut commentetur   hec,† in tantum dominetur
Hic indignantis   furor: insultare parantis
Cum nomen nescit   reprehensio, cepta quiescit.

Scripta poetarum   divum probra sive dearum,
Et genus et mores,   vitam reserunt et amores.
35 Cum Iove Iunonem,   cum fratre coisse sororem,
Fertur amasse thorum   primus de gente deorum,
In dampnum matris   truncasse virilia patris.
Fedo natali   cum sanguine de genitali
Candida spuma *maris*   coit—hinc, Venus alma, crearis.
40 †Fertur amasse Iovis   connubia feda sororis.†
Quis lascivire,   scort*a*ri sive coire
Numina concedat?   superos quis denique credat
Hec exercere,   nuben*di* vota tenere?
Nec thalamos tantum   celi movet [ardor] amantum:
45 Ad terras pariter   migrans divinus adulter,
Expertus rite   mortalis crimina vite,
Nunc viciat Similen,   nunc decipit Amphitrionem,
Cuius in uxore   longo mor*a* tracta labore.
*Pass*a deum meta   maiore fit Hercule feta,
50 Et triduum totum   consumpsit amabile votum.
Continuata mora   tridui, prolixior hora
Debuit impendi,   quo gloria concipiendi
Maior haberetur,   semen celeste daretur
Ad tante molis,   tante primordia prolis.
55 Nec qui gesserunt   peccare dii potuerunt—
Aut monstravere   nobis ea facta licere.

At si que nobis   virtus dominatur amoris,
Igne sui teli   superavit numina celi.
Quid culpare soles   quod amat nunc carnea proles?
60 Et mortale genus   quid ob hoc culpare solemus?
Vos notat et clerum   tam mystica fabula rerum:
Abbatissarum   genus, et grex omnis earum
Sunt Pallas plane,   tria virginis ora Diane,
Iuno, Venus, Vesta,   Thetis—observantia vestra
65 Est expressa satis   cultu tante deitatis.
Vos notat istarum   genus et gens sacra dearum,
Nos ratione pari   divum deitate notari
Credimus, et cleri   typus illa videtur haberi
Inclita magnorum   series memorata deorum.
70 Nos qui virtutis   opus, ardua vota salutis,
Et canonum scita   sectamur celibe vita,
Cum deliramus,   ea numina significamus!
Militat in nobis   hic sepius ardor amoris,
Nos etiam superat,   in nobis sepe triumphat!
75 Cum rapit in peius   nos ardor et inpetus eius,
Virtus, maiestas,   gradus altus honoris, honestas
Miliciam Veneris   et castra secuntur Amoris.
Nonne deos cernas   sedes odisse supernas
Et commisceri   cum simile numina celi?

80 Qui mundum vicit,   superos delinquere fecit.
Vos etiam nostis   quam sepe domesticus hostis
Iste fores vestras   irruperit atque fenestras,
Vota pudicicie   quociens fedaverit ipse.
Traxit ad erroris   proclivia vota pudoris—
85 Cum Venus instigat,   cum membra libido fatigat,
Vix superest ulla   cuius caro sive medulla
Non sit adusta satis   his motibus improbitatis.—
Quando nos vobis   pacto sociamur amoris,
Hec sunt magnorum   connubia sacra deorum!
90 Quando personis   diverse condicionis
Iungimur, et vobis   miles, vel laica nobis

Femina miscetur,   Iovis hic migrasse videtur,
Et mortale genus   superis nupsisse videmus.
Frangunt magnorum   sublimia corda virorum
95 †Luxus,† Iuno, Venus,   Amor—h*i*c mutare videmus
Materiam superum   formas et corpora rerum.
Iupiter in taurum   fertur mutatus, et aurum:
Ut mutaretur   Amor hoc fecisse docetur;
Phillis mutata   sensit crudelia fata:
100 Sevus Amor *fingit*   quod Phillis amigdala gignit—
Phillis it in florem   per Demoph[o]ontis amorem!

Cum de mutatis   formis metaphora *v*atis
Hec commentatur,   opus et res magna paratur.
Cepto sermone   de mundi conditione,
105 Mundi nascentis   que forma, quis incipientis
Vultus Nature   scribit, docet omnia pure.
Condicio mundi   fluitabat more profundi,
Lis erat et rixa   pugna[n]t contraria mixta,
Quatuor exempta   mundum reddunt elementa—
110 Vim diversorum   Natura ligat mediorum.
Quomodo volvatur   celum, qua lege feratur
Axis uterque poli,   que sit progressio soli,
Sidera cum signis,   quidquid facit etheris ignis,
Corpora, naturas   hominum, genus atque figuras,
115 Orbis terrarum   situs et decursus aquarum
Quis sit, qua venti   regnant flatu vehementi,
Mores, etates   et regna, per omnia vates
Est commentatus.
                Orbis quia sit reparatus
Quondam deletus   ab aquis, cum coniuge letus
120 Deucalion reparat   hominum genus, omne reformat.
Dumque cupit credi   proles certissima Phebi
Pheton equos solis   et currus nomine prolis
Scandit. Quem cursum   visum teneat modo sursum,
Sol docet: 'A centro   rect*o* distare memento

125 Orbem signorum   medium; convexa polorum
   Molliter atque parum   contingat biga rotarum,
   Signa tibi cure   sint Elycis et Cinosure,
   Semita certa rotis   sint ardua signa Bootis.'
   Profuit illa parum   descripcio facta viarum:
130 Ille paternorum   malus arbiter officiorum,
   Vicinus celis   ab equis sublatus anhelis,
   Devia sectatus,   descendit precipitatus.
   Iam frenis laxis   auriga rotatur et axis
   Temperat ardores   mersus. Flevere sorores.
135 Flent et, mutate,   nunc arborea levitate
   Ramis utuntur: ita fratris fata loquntur.

   Miror cur vates   tot feda, tot improbitates
   Dicturus demum,   voluit primordia rerum,
   Celi vel terre,   subtiliter ante referre.
140 Iuxta Platonem   Nature condicionem,
   Post res mutatas,   rerum species variatas,
   Et mutatorum   scelus, impia stupra deorum
   Explicat—et quare?   Vult nobis significare
   Quantum Natura,   quondam sine crimine pura
145 Nunc degravata,   corrupta sit et viciata.
   Cum perscrutamur   celum, cum philosophamur
   De planetarum   cursu, sedes animarum
   In stellis esse,   nascentibus inde necesse
   Rebus prodire,   sic debita *fata* subire,
150 Huc se migrantes   in corpus et hic habitantes,
   Felice[s] anime   qua lege cubilia prime
   Nunc repetant sedis,   vel, cum moriendo recedis,
   Suppliciis dignis   commissa quis expiet ignis,
   Quo redeas purus,   perpes celo fruiturus—
155 Hec de virtute,   de vera verba salute
   Quando tractamus,   ad sidera mente volamus:
   Sic celum petimus,   non ut ferat Ossan Olimpus.
   Hunc habitum mentis   tum rursus ad impia sentis
   Prave mutari,   scortari, luxuriari.

160 Mortales actus   Iovis implet ad infima tractus,
    Mens vitio victa   pecca[t] virtute relicta.

    Est quod in illorum   discas deitate deorum,
    Nec sine doctrina   migrare feruntur ad ima.
    Vis elementorum,   concors operatio quorum
165 Rerum naturas   dat, rebus *ha*bere figuras,
    Et quid agat spera   celestis, et illa serena
    Sidera que ra*p*idi   cursum moderantur Olympi,
    Sol, Ven*u*s et Luna,   Mars et Mercurius una,
    Quinque simul zone   quit agant, et qua ratione
170 Sol elongatur,   nobis hiemes operatur,
    Rursus ad Arcturum   scandens, ver a*ere* purum
    Prestat et estatem,   dat terre fertilitatem,
    Quidquit in hoc mundo   crudeli sive secundo
    Sidere versantur,   et qui*c*quid in hec operantur,
175 Ex quibus omne genus   rerum constare videmus,
    Quod sapis et sentis,   quod ab his fit et est elementis—
    Hoc opus istorum   coitum dixere deorum.

    Multarum rerum   ratio mentes mulierum
    Et movet et temptat,   et questio multa frequentat,
180 Ocia servantes   et Amoris opus celebrantes.
    Istis commentis   vaga consultatio mentis
    Se consoletur,   mora temporis adbrevietur.
    Versibus inspectis,   repetitis, sepe relectis,
    Fiat longa mora   brevis, et prolixior hora
185 His commentatis   compendia det brevitatis.
    Si quid in his cartis   industria protulit artis
    Quod placet expresse,   quo sit laudare necesse
    Carminis auctorem,   non exigo laudis honorem;
    Si minus aut [m]ultum,   si quicquam denique stultum
190 Me reprehendetis   dixisse, quid hic facietis?
    Quando reum nescit   vindex, vindicta quiescit.

A certain amount of ignorance is worth having: you are better
thought of than if you know every single thing. Why do you hold

it necessary to know all at once? Better not know something than be over-anxious about it.—'Shall I really believe this? For I could not imagine that overlooking certain things or not knowing them is better (than knowing).'—Often wise men, considering what should be said, have thought silence even better. Did not Job judge silence best when the Law was done away with, wishing to show the meaning of the Law truly fulfilled in Christ? Paul rightly conceals his name, that no one should hold the truths worthless the writer's name being disclosed—the teacher's words would certainly carry no weight if the author were found out.

I give a twofold reason for concealing my name: if your discerning judgement convicts me of error, then the confusion and shame of having written poor verse would leave the author unscathed. Again, I have looked to this: if a delight in wickedness, a vain temptation arises in the human mind, (if) a skilled tongue from the outside world expounds affairs of love and a pen describes them by a vivid image, you who are endowed with almost canonical seriousness will reject such things, and hold the poem's author guilty. For who has ever mentioned Venus or love or Venus' son or Cupid's shafts and bow to you, whose school is a stronghold of chastity? †Lest to the mind that encounters these things anything should be wantonness as it ponders over them,† let the objector's anger be curbed thus far: when reprehension cannot abuse the author's name, she dies no sooner than begun.

The writings of poets reveal the immodesty of gods and goddesses, their race and behaviour, their life and their loves. We are told that Juno united with her brother Jove, that the highest of the gods loved a mistress, and that to thwart his mother he cut off his father's organs. When in polluted birth the white sea-spray united with the blood from the genitals, you, bountiful Venus, were created. †Jove is said to have loved the polluted marriage with his sister.† Who would admit that gods can wanton loosely, or make love? Who indeed would believe both that the gods do such things and that marriage vows are binding? What is more, the love-passion is stirred not only by heavenly unions, but the divine adulterer likewise comes to earth: duly experimenting with the faults of earthly life, he now corrupts Semele, now deceives Amphitryon, having with great effort planned to occupy his wife. Suffering the god's

embraces for a longer course (than normal), she becomes pregnant
with Hercules. The answer to the lover's prayer took three whole
days. When his visit had lasted three days, a longer time had to be
imposed, that the greater glory of conceiving might be realized,
that a heavenly seed might be implanted in the firstborn of such
might, of so great a race.

The gods who did such things could not have sinned—rather they
have shown us that these actions are right. If any power of love
prevails in us, it is that which has conquered the gods by its burning
shaft. Why do you ever censure the fact that now mankind also
loves? Why are we wont to blame the race of men for this? This
profound myth signifies you and us: clearly the abbesses and all
their flock are Pallas, the three aspects of Diana, Juno, Venus, Vesta,
Thetis—your rites find adequate expression in ceremonies of so
much divinity. You are figured in the sacred kind and race of these
goddesses, and similarly we believe ourselves figured in the nature of
the gods—that the glorious and famous assembly of great gods can
be considered as a figure of the clerc. In our celibate life we follow
the paths of virtue, of prayers for salvation, we follow the canonical
decrees—it is when we run riot that we signify the gods. Often this
passion of love is fierce in us, us too it overcomes, triumphs in us.
When its heat and force take us into a worse state, virtue, dignity,
reputation, and honour enlist in Venus' service and Amor's wars.
Do you not see the gods dislike their heavenly dwellings, and dislike
being joined with their own kind?

He who has conquered the world caused the gods to stray. You
too know how often this familiar foe has forced himself in through
your doors and windows, how often he has corrupted your resolutions to stay chaste. He has confronted such resolve with entice-
ments to wrong. When Venus rouses you, when desire wearies the
limbs, there is scarcely one whose body and inmost core are not
burned by these stirrings of abandon.—But when we are united
with you in love, these are the sacred unions of the great gods!
When we unite with persons of other estates, you with a knight or
we with a châtelaine, then Jove seems to have wandered to earth,
and we see the race of men wedded to gods. [. . .] Juno, Venus,
Amor strike the high hearts of great men—here we see matter of the
gods transform the forms and bodies of created things. Jupiter is
said to have been transformed into a bull, and into gold—Amor, we

are told, brought his transformations about. Phyllis, transformed, was aware of cruel fates: it was fierce Amor who made Phyllis bring forth almonds. Phyllis bursts into flower for love of Demophoon.

When the poet contemplates these things under the metaphor of transformations, a great theme and work are at hand. Beginning with an account of the nature of the universe, he tells us clearly what was the form of the world at its birth, how Natura looked as she began. The world was in flux like the ocean's depths, there was turmoil and the mingled opposites clashed in strife, the four elements, released, made the world appear—Natura conjoins the power of the various agents. Heaven's rotation, the support of heaven's axes, the sun's progression, the stars and constellations, the action of the ethereal fire, the bodies and natures of men, their kind and appearance, the position of the earth and the courses of the waters, the cause of the violent blast of winds, customs, ages, realms—the poet has taken all these into account.

Because the earth, once destroyed by floods, was restored, joyfully Deucalion and his wife restore the race of men—he reshapes everything. And wanting to be acknowledged with absolute certainty as Phoebus' son, Phaethon mounts the horses and chariots of the Sun in assertion of his race. The Sun instructs him: let him now keep to the course he has seen on high. 'Remember that the middle cycle of constellations is far from the true centre. Let the chariot-wheels graze gently past the arches of the Pole; observe the constellations of the Great Bear and the Little Bear; may your wheels find safe tracks in the glowing stars of Arcturus.' That description of the way was little use; he discharged his father's office badly. Borne almost as high as heaven by the panting horses, straying in his course he was hurled down. Now, the reins loose, the chariot is whirled about; the axletree, drowned, cools its flames. The Heliades begin to weep. They weep, and now, with the lightness of a tree they have grown branches—thus they bear witness to their brother's fate.

I wonder why the poet about to tell of so many monstrous and shameful things wished first to relate the beginnings of heaven and earth. Like Plato he gives a cosmology, and then explains the things that were changed, the varied species, the flaw in what is mutable, the unholy lewdness of the gods. Why does he do this? He wants to show us how much Natura, once guiltlessly pure, has been dragged down, seduced and defiled. When we contemplate heaven, when we philosophize about the planets' courses, (believing) that the dwelling of souls is in the stars, that they must proceed from there into whatever is born, submitting to their destiny, descending into a body and inhabiting it; when we discuss how blessed souls seek their first resting-place again, or else, departing in death, atone for their deeds in the just suffering of flames, by which you become pure again, destined to enjoy heaven for ever—when we expound such things about virtue and true salvation, in spirit we are flying to the stars. Thus do we (truly) seek heaven—this is not to pile Ossa on Olympus! Then again you feel this state of mind changing, turning to impiety, wantonness, and luxury. Jove, drawn deep down, fills human action, the mind sins, overcome by vice, casting virtue aside.

Yet there is something you can learn from the nature of these gods: it is not without significance that they are said to make their way to the depths. The power of the elements, whose concordant working determines the nature of the world and allows things to have their own forms; the activity of the heavenly sphere and of those bright stars that regulate the course of swift Olympus—Sol, Venus, Luna, Mars, and Mercury together; the function of the five zones of heaven; the reason why the sun withdraws and produces winter, and then again rising to Arcturus brings on the pure air of spring, brings summer and fertility to earth; whatever comes to pass in this world under a cruel or kindly star, whatever has influence on these, from which we see every created form established, whatever you know and feel, whatever is begotten and exists by virtue of these elements—all this men saw in the sexual unions of these gods!

When women have leisure and celebrate the rites of Love, an intellectual curiosity often comes over them, and their minds are stimulated and attracted by an account of many such things as these. I hope these theories may relieve the ranging mind and while away the time, that if you look at these verses, read them out and peruse them often, a long day will seem short, a lengthy hour pass quickly while reflecting on them. If my efforts in these pages have produced anything skilled to please you specially, so that you (feel you) must praise the poem's author, I do not ask for such an honour. But if you blame me for having said too little, or too much, for making any kind of faux pas—what will you do about it? When the avenger does not know who is guilty, revenge is left to lie in peace.

W: W. Wattenbach, *MSB* iii (1873), 695 ff.
2 MS. sincula
5–6 These difficult lines are perhaps best taken as an imaginary objection.
12 ex ratione—*sic* MS. W et
17 MS. Sic, disiecti   [W Si, discretio]
20 *sic* MS. W praxi
22–23 MS. in reverse order
24 insignate—*v*. Du Cange s.v. *insignare* (instruere, munire)   [W indignate]
25 MS. refutate (by confusion with the preceding rhymes)   [W –is]
27 W arcem
30 MS. cum mentetur   [W commentetur]
34 *sic* MS. W referunt
39 MS. matris
40 This line seems out of place. Is it an alternative for 36? Iovis is nom. (as in 92, 160).
41 MS. scortiri   [W scortari]
43 MS. nubenti   [W nubendi]   Is there a possible sense in the MS. reading?
—'Who will believe that the gods can do these things and (at the same time) keep their promises to one who marries?'
44 Inserted from foot of page. W thalamus, [ardor]
47 Similen—*sic* MS. (i.e. Semelê) W similem
48 MS. more
49 MS. Pñsa
59 MS. sol es
63 MS. hora   The second half-line is from Vergil, *Aen.* IV. 511.
71 MS. secta   [W scita]
82 MS. irrumperit
91 MS. Iugimus   [W Jungimur]
95 *Luxus* can hardly be right in this context, but I cannot suggest a plausible alternative. MS. hec   [W hic]
99 ff. *v*. Ovid, *Heroides*, II, and Servius, *in Ecl.* v. 10. The other mythological allusions are (as 102 indicates) to the *Metamorphoses*.
100 MS. fecit   amigdala—*sic* MS., made into –ola
102 MS. fatis   [W vatis] Cf. 149.
113 W Sidera cum signis quid, quid facit etheris ignis
123 visum—*sic* MS.   [W iussum]   MS. modo teneat
124 MS. rectus   Cf. Martianus Capella, *De Nupt.* 834–6.
127 Elycis—i.e. Helices.
144 MS. Quantum natura quantum (*quondam* in margin)
145 degravata—*sic* MS.   [W degradata]
149 MS. vata   [W fata] Cf. 102.
150 se migrantes—*sic* MS.   [W emigrantes]
155 Hec—*sic* MS. W hic [em. sic]
165 MS. (in the line) b̄aē (in margin) h̄are
167 MS. rabidi   [W rapidi]
168 MS. venais
171 MS. area   [W aere]

174 MS. quioquid   A new hand begins with this line.
187 quo sit—*sic* MS.   [W quod]
191 MS. Cum rerum   [W Quando reum]

Note

Lines 36, 40, 55–60, 100–1 of this poem, and numerous half-lines and phrases
from it, recur in a verse-letter to a nun, (unpublished, inc. 'Non honor ac-
ceptus, gradus altus honoris adeptus'), in another twelfth-century MS. from
Tegernsee, Clm 18580, fols. 59ʳ–64ʳ. The author is one Otto, as appears from
some lines (185–7) in the poem itself:

Scis, non ignoras	quis ego: si scire laboras,
Si simul aptata	fuerint O.T. geminata,
Nomen mittentis	apparet in his elementis.

Otto's epistle is duller and more diffuse than 'Profuit ignaris', of which I am
convinced it is an adaptation, not a source. It is in 591 leonine hexameters
('Profuit ignaris' has 191). I add a brief outline of its contents.

The letter begins with moral *sententiae*, and passes swiftly into a recollection of former love. Fearing that in her cloister the nun he had loved may have
come to regret her love and regard it as sinful, Otto argues that what is lawful
for the gods is lawful for mankind. Then, fearing her reproaches for his
having neglected her, he speaks of Dido's death and of Phyllis losing her former
nature, and says, You have not suffered as they have done; but if you should be
in a mood of repenting love, I shall give you an exemplum. There follows a
long allegory of the three ointments used by the Magdalen to anoint Christ's
feet, which passes over into an account of the wonders of creation. The creation
of the angels and of the elements leads the poet to an account of the first Paradise, which reminds him of the coming of spring and love to earth each year
and carries him into a new invitation to love.

Commentary (on 'Profuit ignaris'): Ch. IV. 3, pp. 232 ff.

München, Clm 19411, fol. 70ᵛ   s. XII²

    Ubere multarum,   carissima, deliciarum,
    Ecce, tua facie   castigas me sine fine.
    O dulcedo mea,   tota dulcedine plena,
    O quam pulchra meis   oculis et honesta videris!
5 In cono capitis   auro tu consimilaris,
    Effulgent oculi   tibi sicut radius auri,
    Aurea cesaries,   dimissaque lactea cervix,
    Guttur habes lepidum,   cuncta dulcedine plenum,
    Testudo manuum,   tornatilis, talis ut aurum.
10 Immo te solam   plus cunctis dico decoram—
    Censeo te pulchram   maculam quia non habes ullam.

In the fullness of your many allurements, dearest one, see how with your looks you reprove me endlessly. O my sweetest, utterly full of sweetness, how beautiful, how virtuous you stand before my eyes! Your head is crowned with gold, it seems, your eyes are radiant as a golden beam, golden your hair, your milk-white neck free-flowing, your throat enchanting, full of every sweetness; the lyre of your hands is wrought like gold. Indeed I call you fair, you alone more than all others—I find you beautiful because you have no blemish.

2 castigas me—on the theme of the 'reproachful beloved', see Ch. II, pp. 91 ff.
8 Is this line (taken verbally from Maximianus, *Eleg.* 1. 93) an interpolation?
9 MS. tona, tilis *superscript*

fol. 72^v

    Iam satis et nimis est quod litera nostra moratur
    Inter nos, †et iacet et iacet et nihil† operatur.
    Evigilet, mentemque meam tibi deliciose
    Pandat, amabiliter canat, exprimat officiose!
5   Quid tamen est quod noster amor tepuisse videtur?
    Non tepuit sed delituit—sic sepe tenetur
    Nube iubar solis, et celat cornua luna,
    Cum tamen eius vis sine vel cum nube sit una.
    Sic tacitis nobis non splenduit ignis amoris
10 Et tacitis nobis caluit tamen ignis amoris.
    Pone supercilium, ne me tibi crede minor[em]—
    Equa lance meum tibi compensabis amorem.

It is enough, it is too much that a letter (that passes) between us makes delay, †and lies there, lies there and accomplishes nothing†. If it could come alive, delicately reveal my mind to you, sing to you lovingly, speak with courtesy! But why is it that our love seems to have grown lukewarm? Not lukewarm, hidden away rather—as often the sun's brightness is covered by a cloud, or the moon hides her horns, though with or without the cloud her power is the same. So too when we were silent love's fire did not shine, yet, when we were silent, love's fire remained warm. Don't be proud, don't think I am less devoted to you—you will weigh my love for you on a just scale.

2 I do not know how to emend this line. *Inter nos* is written between ll. 1 and 2; MS. may read *et tacet et iacet*.

7 MS. zelat

11 Pone supercilium—cf. Martial, 1. 5, 2.

Oxford, Rawlinson G. 109   *c.* 1200

p. 44

> Tela, Cupido, tene, quoniam non ille *nec* illa
>   Sustinet esse meus, vel mea.—Tela tene,
> Tela tene!—Quid amo?—Quod amat. Non absit.—*At*
>   *huius*
>   Quod fugit, huius ero? Non ero.—Tela tene,
> Tela tene—quia non teneo quod amo tenuisse.
>   An dixi quod amo? Non amo!—tela tene,
> Tela tene—vel tange parem. Ne feceris imo—
>   Dico tibi, sine!—vel tange, Cupido, parem.

Keep back your shafts, Cupid: neither he nor she consents to be mine. Keep back, keep back your shafts! What do I love?—One that loves. Let her not go.—But am I to belong to one who flees? I'll not belong—keep back, keep back your shafts!—for I cannot keep her whom I'd have loved to keep. Did I say love? I'm not in love! Keep back, keep back your shafts—or try them on your own kind. Don't do this! Stop, I say! Or try them, Cupido, on your own kind.

1 MS. sed
3 MS. sed [R. M.]
Quod amat—gender is deliberately left undetermined throughout, but this becomes awkward in translation.

p. 66

> Constat et apparet   quod amo—nec Amor mihi paret.
> Flore iuventa caret,   caro defluit, et cutis aret.
>
> Impedior loris   vix expediendus Amoris;
> Causaque meroris,   thalamos exosa Licoris
>
> 5 Non didicit flecti,   sed haborret nectere, necti—
> Oscula dilecti   fastidit et ocia lecti!

Plus fera virgo feris,   que non miseris misereris,
Quid mihi bella geris?   quid victum vincere queris?

Quis modus aut finis,   que te seduxit Erinis?
10 Finem pone minis;   ruditatem linque Sabinis!

It is plainly evident that I am in love, but Amor does not help me. The flower of my youth is gone, my body wastes away and my skin grows dry. I am almost inescapably held in by Amor's reins. The cause of my grief, touch-me-not Lycoris, has never let herself be persuaded to yield, she detests embracing and being embraced, she disdains her lover's kisses and the delights of bed. Girl wilder than wild creatures, who take no pity on the wretched, what battles are you waging against me? Why seek to vanquish one already vanquished? What means or end, what Fury has led you astray? Make an end of threats—leave such harshness to the Sabines!

4 Licoris—*v. supra,* p. 377.
6 MS. delicti

p. 67

Cur infirmaris? cur palles? cur maceraris?
    Queris consilium, Candide, iure meum.
Ni tibi plus iusto formosa Corina placeret,
    Nulla foret morbi, Candide, causa tui.
5 Sepe cohis—cohitum morbus maciesque sequntur
    Ex quibus assiduus pallor inesse solet.

Why are you weak and pale, why are you wasted? You are right to seek my counsel, Candidus. If the lovely Corinna did not allure you over-much, there'd be no reason, Candidus, for being unwell. You often make love—sickness and thinness stem from the act of love, and these regularly bring about a perpetual pallor.

1 ff. On the medical symptoms of love, see Nardi, art. cit., *supra,* p. 309 n.
2 Candide—cf. Martial, II. 24, 43; III. 26, 46; XII. 38. The verses are in the manner of Martial's epigrams, though medievalized by the leonine rhymes in 1, 2, and 4.

München, Clm 17212, fol. 22ᵛ   s. XIII

    O utinam nobis servetur fedus Amoris—
    Nam quamvis illum comitentur plurima dura
    Ipse tamen letus, et amabilis est sua cura.
    Utile, dampna, minas promissaque, tristia, leta,
5 Aspera, blanda, preces, terrores, mota, quieta,
    Mellea, fellea, spemque, timorem, mollia, dura
    Equo fert animo; presentia sive futura—
    Omnia sunt eius—insomnia, somnia, somnus.
    Leges et reges sine lege regit, quasi domnus.
10 Cuncta iubet cunctis incunctanter facienda:
    'Nemo "suus" dicet. Mihi non sunt hec patienda.'

Oh would that we might hold to Amor's law—for though he is surrounded by many adverse things, he himself is joyous and full of loving care. Profit and loss, threat and promise, sadness and joy, harshness, sweetness, prayers and terrors, things disturbed and at rest, honeyed and galled, hope and fear, soft things and hard—he bears them all serenely; present or future, all is his—nightmares, dreams, and sleep. Without law he rules laws and kings, like a master. He commands all things to be done by all without demur: 'Let none speak of "his own"—I will not have it.'

    4 ff. On the topos 'Love's contraries', see *MÆ* xxxii (1964) 50 ff.
    8 insomnia—oppressive, deluding dreams. *V.* Macrobius, *in Somn.* I. 3, 5–6, who cites *Aen.* VI. 897 and the opening of *Aen.* IV. John of Salisbury (*Polycraticus*, II. 15) adds 'Unde et male sanis amantium mentibus insomnia nunquam desunt.' Cf. also V. Ussani, *Insomnia* (Roma, 1955), esp. pp. 58 ff.

fol. 24ᵛ

    Horula non hora qua te vidi reputatur,
        Vidi tamque brevi, te periisse piget.
    Sed perii potius, tu tantum delituisti—
        Disparere tuum sane perire meum:
5 Perdita me perdis, et reddita me mihi reddis.
        Reddere!—sic certe restitues mihi me.
    Irritamentum prestat libare parumper
        Et degustatum si rapis ore cibum.

It seems an 'hourlet', not an hour, in which I saw you, and saw you so swiftly, it grieves me you are lost. I was lost rather—you only hid yourself; but in your vanishing I lost myself. Gone, you destroy me, returning take me back to me.—Come! only thus will you bring me to myself again. It is only provocation to offer food a moment, and snatch it, barely tasted, from the lips.

fol. 25ᵛ

> Cum duo sint quos unus amor conformet in unum,
> Illos unus amor non sinit esse duos.
> Est in amore fides: duo sint—si tercius assit,
> Nulla tribus, nam vix ulla duobus erit.
> 5 Secreto stat amor, ad se vocat, et facit unum:
> Ipse duos unit; tercius, exit amor.
> Nil amor est aliud quam mens connexa duorum,
> Sed dum vivat amans, non moriatur amor.
> Si quis amor carus sit primo, denique vilis,
> 10 Non amor, immo dolus; non dolus, immo dolor.
> Ergo suo sit uterque suus;—sed erit meus ille
> Nunquam qui semper incipit esse meus!

When there are two whom a single love has joined, one love does not allow them to be two. In love is faith: let there be two lovers— if there's a third, there's no faith among three, hardly any will remain even for two. Love remains secret, calls lovers to itself, and makes them one. Love itself unites two lovers—if a third comes, love goes. Love is nothing but the joined mind of two—as long as the lover lives, let love not die. If any love is first held dear and then disprized, it is not love but fraud—no, not fraud, anguish rather. So let each be the other's own;—but he'll never be mine, this man who always merely begins to be mine!

fol. 26ʳ⁻ᵛ

> Celitus artifici res elimata paratu,
> Cui Natura 'Meum sis, Thai,' dixit 'opus'—
> Ei mihi plus nimio ferrumque lapisque roganti!
> Esto minus ferrum, queso, minusque lapis.

5 Cur, cum Pirra suo mollivit saxa rotatu,
   Non movit saxum pectore Pirra tuo?
Ne pudeat lesos vite sibi complacuisse
   Teque sibi speculum composuisse deos—
Cui Phebus crines, oculos Venus, ora Cupido,
10   Quodque minus laudo, Mars sua corda dedit.
Tolle tuum Martem demissum numen ab astris:
   Mutuus alterna pace tuetur amor.

Creature perfected by the skill of heaven's artificer, you to whom
Natura said 'Thais, be my masterpiece'—more like iron and stone,
alas, to me who so beseech you—be less iron, less stone, I beg of you!
Why, when Pyrrha softened stones by throwing them, did she not
move the stone within your breast? Do not be embarrassed because
the gods, smitten, determined to make of you a mirror for themselves—you to whom Phoebus gave his locks, Venus her eyes, Cupid
his lips and Mars (this I commend less) his heart. Take away that
Mars of yours, that god sent down from the stars: mutual love is
secured by spells of peace.

2 Cf. pp. 212, 219.
5 *v*. Ovid, *Metam*. I. 490 ff.

Bern 211, fol. 160ᵛ–161ʳ   s. XV

Feminei sex[us] decor et decus hec Heloyssa
   Mole sub hac lapidum clauditur ante dies.
Illa suo Petro par sensu, moribus, arte,
   Scripturas omnes noverat absque *pare*.
5 Os, virtus, formam, famam, fulgore, valore,
   Que sunt rara satis, perpetuavit ei.
Iunius implevit septemque decemque Kal*e*ndas,
   Hoc facto cursu tempore dixit [ave].

Héloïse, the beauty and glory of womankind, lies closed beneath
this mass of stones, before her time. She was a match for her Peter
in feeling, deed, and thought; she had a matchless knowledge of all
writings. With her radiance, with her excellence, her face, her virtue,
perpetuated her beauty, her renown—these being rare indeed. May

completed sixteen of his days, then, having run thus far, bade her [farewell].

4 MS. fere

Scripturas—possibly.'Scriptures'; but it is the breadth of her literary knowledge for which Héloïse was celebrated ('per abundantiam litterarum erat suprema', *P.L.* 178, 127A).

6 MS. implent, kalandas XVII Kal. Iun.= 16 May.

These lines show affinities with two epitaphs for Abelard. I give the first (Zürich C 58/275, s. XII, fol. 5ᵛ), from Werner, *Beiträge*, p. 24:

> Epitaphium Petri Baiolardi a semet compositum.
>
> 'Servi animam servans ancillis redde cadaver!'
>> Hanc tibi fundo, deus, nocte dieque precem.
>> Una fuere caro, tumulus quos continet unus,
>> Nec minus amborum spiritus intus erat.
> 5 Nunc quoque communem dat bene terra thorum.
>> Habaelardus hic est; hec illius est Heloysa,
>> Imo utrosque tuos, Christe, fuisse scias.   Amen.

and the second (Z ibid., Werner, loc. cit.) corrected with the help of Bern 211, where it immediately precedes the lines for Héloïse:

> Est satis in titulo: Petrus hic iacet Habaelardus,
>> Dilectumque tenens huic Heloisa latus.
> V[enereum] studium coniunxit philosophie:
>> Huic soli patuit *scibile* quicquid *erat.*
> 5 Unus nunc tumulus, sicut et ante thorus,
>> Unum propositum viteque professio sacre,
>> Una perennis eis sit super astra domus.   Amen.

3 Werner, V. . . . My completion assumes a metrical irregularity (cf. Vēneris, Vēnus, *infra* pp. 523 ff. ll. 11, 44, 126, 155, etc.).

B has the superscription: Aliud quod est insculptum in libro quem ymago sua supra tumulum tenet. Then only one distich, consisting of 1 and 4 (*titulo* in 1 written as correction over *tumulo*). The value of B lies in establishing 4 (where Z has the unintelligible and unscannable 'quicquid risibile fuit'), showing that these verses also had two pentameters aligned.[1]

[1] The life of Abelard in the *Hist. litt. de la France* (XII. 86 ff.) claims that this tomb still survived in the seventeenth century and was engraved as follows:

> Est satis in tumulo, Petrus hic iacet Abaelardus,
>> Cui soli patuit scibile quidquid erat.

This may be based only on hearsay, but again it may offer independent confirmation. It may even be that the lines in Z are an elaboration of an original distich on Abelard's monument.

The epitaph for Héloïse is probably either by the same author as the two for Abelard or a copy (or source) of one or both of these. Despite the 'a semet compositum' in Z, it is hard to imagine that Abelard himself should have written any of these epitaphs. Nonetheless they are early—the Zürich MS., itself inaccurate and derivative, was written before 1200. The significance of the epitaphs seems to me to lie in the fact that within a few decades of Abelard's death (1142), and in the years immediately following Héloïse's (1163), their legend should result in such verses. Even more that, in the two for Abelard, the outer form of a conventional epitaph should be filled with a remarkable conception of the two lovers, of a love-union holding through life and beyond life. More explicitly than any medieval romance of love and death these epitaphs suggest that the fulfilment of such a union is attained in God. This is also the keynote of the often printed song 'Requiescat a labore', which claims to be the dirge of Héloïse and her nuns over the dead Abelard. Does it also belong to the beginning of the legend? or is it a Renaissance forgery? (Does it even exist in manuscript?—none of its editors has ever referred to one!)

LOVE-LETTERS

I Amico amica.

S. suo dilecto,
omnium cognatorum sibi dulcissimo,
H. fidem
et dilectionem.
5 O utinam, mi dilecte,
si tu posses scire
que et quanta mala
postquam a te discessi sum perpessa!
quia die et nocte
10 tuus delectabilis vultus est mihi in mente,
et hoc iure,
quia nullus cognatorum meorum tam amicabiliter suscepit
me
colloquio et munere.
Ergo, omnium diligendorum dulciscime,
15 dignis digna repende,
diligentem te ex corde dilige;
nec ulla de me tibi sit reprobatio,
quia in me prorsus non est simulata neque ficta dilectio;
quod multum facilius potest aurum in stagnum converti
20 quam mens mea de tuo amore evelli.
Ideo nulla
sit tibi mora
quin venias ad me.
Vale, vale.

The beloved to her lover. To her beloved S——, sweetest of all
her kinsmen, H—— sends her trust and love. If only you could know,
my beloved, how great is the distress I have been through since
leaving you! Day and night your face, that gives me such joy, is in

my mind, as it must be, for none of my kinsmen has ever welcomed
me so affectionately, with words or with gifts. So, sweetest of lovable
men, return grace for grace, and love one who loves you from her
heart. You shall never have a reproach from me, because the love in
me is utterly unfeigned, unsimulated. Gold can more easily be
turned to tin than my mind be torn away from love of you. So do
not delay, but come to me. Farewell, farewell.

II Amico amica derelicta.

H. quondam carissimo,
nunc autem perfidissimo,
N. mercede digna
secundum opera sua.
5 Anima mea consummabitur dolore et merore repleta,
quia a memoria tua funditus videor deleta,
que fidem et dilectionem
semper a te sperabam, usque ad vite consummationem.
Que est enim, H, fortitudo mea, ut sustineam pacienter
10 et non defleam nunc et semper?
Numquid caro mea est enea,
aut mens mea saxea,
aut oculi mei lapidei,
ut non doleam malum infortunii mei?
15 Quid feci? quid feci?
Numquid prior te abieci?
In quo invenior rea?
Vere abiecta sum absque culpa mea.
Si culpam queris,
20 ipse, ipse, culpabilis haberis!
Nam sepe et sepissime
meam ad te   direxi legationem,
sed nunquam in maximo
vel in minimo   verborum tuorum percepi
consolationem.
25 Ideo mortales cuncti discedant,
fidem et dilectionem a me ulterius non querant!

Cave diligentius,
ne tercius
interveniat oculus.
30 Vale, vale,
meliora sectare.

The beloved, abandoned, to her lover. To H——, once her dearest,
but now her most perjured one, from N——, who deserves mercy
because of all she has done. My soul will be destroyed by pain and
filled brimful with grief, because I seem to have been utterly wiped
out of your memory, I who always hoped for constancy and love
from you, even to the end of my life. What strength have I, H——,
to bear this patiently, and not to weep now and for ever? Do you
think my body is of bronze, my mind like rock, or my eyes stony,
that I should not mourn the harshness of my misfortune? What have
I done? what have I done? Did I reject you first? In what am I found
guilty? Indeed I am cast off for no fault of my own. If you look for
a fault, you, you yourself are at fault!—for I have often, again and
again, sent messages to you, yet never have I received even the least
word of solace from you. Let men now stay away from me, let
none ever again ask me for love or constancy! Be very careful that
no other eye light upon (this letter). Farewell, farewell—and mend
your ways.

III

Accipe scriptorum,   o fidelis, responsa tuorum.
Quid dignum digno
valeam scribere ignoro—
presertim cum doctoris aures pudor sit inculto sermone
    interpellare,
5 et nefas sit silentio preterire;
tamen prout potero
tibi respondebo.
Durum mihi videtur ac difficile
quod conaris a me inpetrare,
10 scilicet integritatem mee fidei,
quam nulli unquam mortalium promisi.

Attamen si sciero me casto amore a te adamandam,
et pignus pudicicie mee inviolandum,
non recuso laborem
15 vel amorem.
—Si consistat absque dolore,
non potest dici amor,
unde constat maximus labor.—
Cave ne quis videat ista dicta,
20 quia non sunt ex autoritate scripta.

My loyal friend, accept this answer to your letter. I do not know
if I can write anything worthy of you. If it is a shame to intrude
my uncultivated language on a scholar's ears, it would be a crime to
pass it by in silence; so I'll reply to you as best I can. It seems a
troubling, difficult thing you are trying to win from me—my complete trust, which I have never yet promised to any man. Yet if I
know I shall be loved by you in a pure love, and my pledge of
innocence is not to be violated, I do not refuse you the hardship, or
the love.—If it exists without pain, it cannot be called love, to which
the greatest hardship belongs.—Take care that no one sees this
letter—it was not written with permission.

IV

Affamina salutationis
quibus deberet appellari magnitudo tue dilectionis
haut apparent mee indagini meditationis.
Gaudium etenim mihi est super numerum harene maris
5 si omni prosperitate sustentaris.
Litteras tue melliflue dulcedinis
redolentes aromata summe caritatis
gratissimas suscepi,
sed desideranter perlegens aliquantulum defeci,
10 quia durum tibi esse ac difficile quod a te quero in his inveni.
Quid plura? Qualiacumque mihi rescripseris vel dixeris,
me quasi captivum et vinctum tuo amore sub tua potestate
                                        habebis.

Vale, vale.
Quod celum stellas   retinet, quod pontus harenas,
15 Tot laudes vite   tu promerearis adire.

The words of salutation which should hail the greatness of your love are not forthcoming as my thoughts grope for them. Indeed I have joys beyond the number of the sea's sands if all your happiness holds. I received your most delightful letter, mellifluously sweet, scented with the perfume of great love, but reading it through with longing I was a little disheartened, because I saw from it that what I am asking of you is troublesome and difficult for you. What more shall I say? Whatever you reply or say to me, you will hold me like a captive bound by your love within your power. Farewell, farewell —may you gain as many praises for your life as heaven has stars and the ocean sands.

V

C. Cara karissime,
dulcissime
dulcis, omne quod excellit
totum quod est et quod erit—
5 quamvis nos disiungant maxima intervalla locorum,
tamen coniungit nos equanimitas animorum,
et vera amicicia, que non est ficta,
sed cordi meo infixa.
Quia in somnis astas quasi Philosophia,
10 prebebis verba consolatoria et pia.
Mori vellem si liceret,
ut nemo sub hac luce ulterius me videret,
quod tua optata non fruor visione,
que fide repleta es et dilectione!
15 Quis dabit mihi genus volatile,
ut volitem more aquile,
ut ad te veniam
et leticiam
cordis sumam aliquam?
20 quia pre omni sexu in animum te recepi seorsum,

si nunquam suasione alicuius abis retrorsum;
et hoc volo stabilire,
si simili mihi occurris fide.
Quid amplius? Te amare volo
25 quousque luna cadat de polo,
quia ante omnes qui sunt in mundo
cordis mei fixa es profundo.
Vale—dormiendo quasi vigilando
non cesso tibi bona optando.
30 Valeas, cupio,
et prosis velut Io!
O dulcedo mea,
veniant tibi gaudia plena.
Munus do dignum
35 non, sed fidei tibi signum.
Salutat te, dulcis margarita, et conventus iuvencularum.

C——, most dearly dear, most sweetly sweet one, all that surpasses all that is and shall be—though the greatest distances of space
keep us asunder, serenity of minds holds us together, and true friendship, which is not feigned but impressed within my heart. As you
are present in my slumbers like Philosophia, you will grant me words
of solace and devotion. If it were lawful I'd wish to die, that no one
see me again by this heavenly light unless I am blessed with the
longed-for sight of you, you who are filled with constancy and love.
Who will give me the power of wings, that I may fly like an eagle,
that I may come to you and take some of my heart's joy?—for
beyond all your sex I have given you a place apart in my mind, if
you never desert it at anyone's persuasion. This is what I desire to
hold fast, if you meet me with equal loyalty. What more can I say?
I would love you till the moon falls from the sky, because beyond
all others in the world you are fixed in the depths of my heart. Farewell—in sleeping as in waking, I never cease to think of you with
love. I long for your well-being—may you be blessed like Io! O my
sweet love, may the fullness of joy come upon you. I am not sending an offering worthy of you, only this token of my constancy.
The convent of young women also greets you, my precious pearl.

VI

C. super mel et favum dulciori,
B. quidquid amor amori.
O unica et specialis,
cur tamdiu in longinquo moraris?
5 Cur unicam tuam perire vis,
que anima et corpore te diligit, ut ipsa scis?
et que more avicule esurientis
te suspirat omnibus horis atque momentis.
Ex quo enim dulcissima tua presentia contigit me carere,
10 nolui hominem ulterius audire nec videre,
sed quasi turtur, perdito masculo,
semper in arido residet ramusculo,
ita lamentor sine fine
donec iterum fruar tua fide.
15 Circumspicio et non invenio amantem,
nec in uno verbo me consolantem.
Dum enim iocundissime
allocutionis ac visionis tue
dulcedinem revolvo in animo,
20 dolore comprimor nimio,
nam nil invenio tale
quod velim tue dilectioni comparare,
que super mel et favum dulcescit
et in cuius comparatione auri et argenti nitor vilescit.
25 Quid ultra? In te omnis suavitas et virtus:
iccirco de absentia tua meus semper languet spiritus.
Omnis perfidie cares felle,
dulcior es lacte et melle,
electa es ex milibus,
30 te diligo pre omnibus,
tu sola amor et desiderium,
du dulce animi mei refrigerium,
nil mihi absque te iocundi
in latitudine tocius mundi.
Omne quod tecum erat suave

sine te laboriosum est et grave.
Unde dicere volo veraciter,
si fieri posset quod vite precio te emerem—non segniter,
quia sola es quam elegi secundum cor meum.
40 Iccirco semper obsecro deum
ne prius me mors preveniat amara
quam visione tua fruar optata et cara.
Vale—
omnia que sunt fidei et dilectionis de me habe.
45 Quem transmitto accipe stilum,
et adhuc animum meum fidum.

    To C——, sweeter than honey or honeycomb, B—— sends all
the love there is to her love. You who are unique and special, why
do you make delay so long, so far away? Why do you want your
only one to die, who, as you know, loves you with soul and body,
who sighs for you at every hour, at every moment, like a hungry
little bird. Since I've had to be without your sweetest presence, I
have not wished to hear or see any other human being, but as the
turtle-dove, having lost its mate, perches forever on its little dried-
up branch, so I lament endlessly till I shall enjoy your trust again.
I look about and do not find my lover—she does not comfort me
even with a single word. Indeed when I reflect on the loveliness of
your most joyful speech and aspect, I am utterly depressed, for I
find nothing now that I could compare with your love, sweet
beyond honey and honeycomb, compared with which the brightness of gold and silver is tarnished. What more? In you is all gentleness, all perfection, so my spirit languishes perpetually by your
absence. You are devoid of the gall of any faithlessness, you are
sweeter than milk and honey, you are peerless among thousands, I
love you more than any. You alone are my love and longing, you
the sweet cooling of my mind, no joy for me anywhere without
you. All that was delightful with you is wearisome and heavy without you. So I truly want to tell you, if I could buy your life for the
price of mine, (I'd do it) instantly, for you are the only woman I
have chosen according to my heart. Therefore I always beseech God
that bitter death may not come to me before I enjoy the dearly
desired sight of you again. Farewell. Have of me all the faith and
love there is. Accept the writing I send, and with it my constant
mind.

VII

G. unice sue rose,
A. vinculum dilectionis preciose.
Que est fortitudo mea, ut sustineam,
ut in tuo discessu pacientiam habeam?
5 Numquid fortitudo mea fortitudo est lapidum,
ut tuum exspectem reditum?
que nocte et die non cesso dolere,
velut qui caret manu et pede.
Omne quod iocundum est et delectabile
10 absque te habetur ut lutum pedum calcabile,
pro gaudere duco fletus,
nunquam animus meus apparet letus.
Dum recordor que dedisti oscula,
et quam iocundis verbis refrigerasti pectuscula,
15 mori libet
quod te videre non licet.
Quid faciam miserrima?
Quo me vertam pauperrima?
O si corpus meum terre fuisset creditum
20 usque ad optatum tuum reditum,
aut si translatio mihi concederetur Abacuc,
ut semel venissem illuc,
ut vultum amantis inspexissem,
et tunc non curarem si ipsa hora mortua fuissem!
25 Nam in mundo non est nata
que tam amabilis sit et grata,
et que sine simulatione
tam intima me diligat dilectione.
Unde sine fine non cesso dolere
30 donec te merear videre.
Revera iuxta quendam sapientem magna miseria est hominis,
  cum illo non esse
sine quo non potest esse.
Dum constat orbis,

numquam deleberis de medio mei cordis.
35 Quid multis moror?
Redi, dulcis amor!
Noli iter tuum longius differre,
scias me absentiam tuam diutius non posse sufferre.
Vale,
40 meique memorare.

To G——, her one-and-only rose, from A—— the bond of precious love. What strength have I, that I may bear it, that I may have patience while you are gone? Is my strength that of stones that I should wait for your return, I who do not cease to ache night and day, like one who lacks both hand and foot? Without you all that's joyous and delightful becomes like mud trodden underfoot, instead of rejoicing I shed tears, my spirit never appears joyful. When I remember the kisses you gave, and with what words of joy you caressed my little breasts, I want to die as I am not allowed to see you. What shall I, unhappiest, do? where shall I, the poorest, turn? Oh if my body had been consigned to the earth till your longed-for return, or if Habakkuk's trance-journey were granted me, that I might once come to see my lover's face—then I'd not care if in that hour I should die! For in the world there is no woman born so lovable, so dear, one who loves me without feigning, with such deep love. So I shall not cease to feel the endless pain till I win the sight of you again. Indeed, as a certain wise man says, it is a great misery for a man not to be with that without which he cannot be. While the world lasts you'll never be effaced from the centre of my heart. Why say more? Return, sweet love! Do not delay your journey longer, know that I cannot bear your absence longer. Farewell, remember me.

I. 12 MS. ullus
    15 MS. reprende   Cf. Regensburg, XXII. 2.
    16 MS. diligente

II. 3 MS. dignam mercedem
IV. 14–15 Quod=quot. For the uses of such formulae, *v.* Hans Walther, art. cit., *supra,* p. 446.
V. 9–10 *v.* Boethius, *Cons.* I. 1 ff.; also Chap. II, pp. 91 ff.
    10 MS. preberis
    15 ff. Cf. *Psal.* LIV. 7, *Deut.* XXXII. 11.
    24–25 Cf. *supra,* p. 41 n.
    31 Cf. Hyginus, *Fab.* CXLV: 'Iovis . . . deam Aegyptiorum [Ionem] esse fecit.'

36 dulcis margarita—could also possibly be nom., not voc.

VI. 1 (and 23–24) Cf. *Psal.* XVIII. 11.

11 Cf. note on Regensburg XLV. 2–3.

32 du—*sic* MS.

VII. 1 G.—here a hook has been added to make the G unmistakable; but in V. 1 and VI. 1 the initial letter, though without hook, may also be G, not C.

21 *V. Dan.* XIV. 35. The episode is dramatized in the Beauvais *Danielis Ludus.* Cf. also *supra,* p. 198.

As I have argued elsewhere (*RF* LXXII (1960), 223 ff., especially 230–5), it is often impossible to demarcate the 'artificial' from the 'natural' in medieval letters. The astonishing passages of rhymed prose in Héloïse's letters to Abelard are not stylistic exercises—they express torrents of emotion in a mode which she had made 'second nature'. While the letters in Clm 19411 can hardly be compared with Héloïse's, with which they are probably contemporary, I think that despite all their attempted artifice they too were never meant for a model *epistolarium.* They are often clumsy, often repetitive, they vary considerably in manner and quality. The first and fourth scarcely go beyond the topoi of Christian *amicitia* (*v.* Chap. IV. 2, pp. 195 ff.), the fierceness of the second and the shyness of the third strike different notes. The third has parallels in the Regensburg verses—here too the *doctor* (4) could be the girl's teacher—but there is something more melancholy too. 'Non recuso laborem, vel amorem' is less a commonplace of love's anxieties than a recognition that, under the only conditions in which a man and woman in orders can ever know it, love will not be easy. In this letter the rhymes and assonances almost disappear from view, and neither III nor IV has the rhythmically balanced phrases which emphasize the rhymes, and which are most marked in the last three letters. VI and VII are remarkable in being love-letters of women to women (in V there is no indication of the writer's sex). All three are too long and aimless, but contain some striking phrases (e.g. V. 9, 31; VI. 7; VII. 19 ff.), and VII seems to presuppose a passionate physical relationship. While it is difficult to single out what goes beyond the traditional hyperboles of *amicitia* discussed in Chap. IV. 2, I think a *recollection* such as 'Dum recordor que dedisti oscula' is not quite parallel to the extravagant *anticipations* of meeting, such as the Alcuin passage discussed *supra,* pp. 198 ff., or Anselm's 'Anhelat ad oscula vestra os meum' (*Epist.* II. 28, 120), recently discussed by R. W. Southern (*Saint Anselm and his Biographer* (Cambridge, 1963), pp. 72 ff.).

Paris, B.N. lat. 8654, fol. 22ʳ

(from the *Epistolarium* of Boncompagno)

De uxore formosa que revocat virum litterarum studio
insudantem.

Ultra bienium, promisionis federe penitus violato, fecisti
moram in scolis, nec quod sim femina et iuvenis recordaris;
unde cotidie ingemisco, quoniam in meum agrum ros vel
pluvia non descendit. Sed nunc arescat digitus qui potiri
coniugali annulo non procurat! Sed scio quod legis in Codice
alieno; unde si mora postposita non redieris, studere disposui
aliquantulum in Digesto.

From a beautiful wife, calling back her man, who is swotting at
his literary studies.

You have lingered on in the Schools for more than two years,
flagrantly breaking the promise you made. You seem to forget that
I am a woman, and young, so that every day I get depressed, because rain and dew never light upon my field. If your finger is ill-at-
ease wearing a wedding-ring, I wish it would shrivel up! I know
you must be poring over a different sort of Codex; so if you don't
come back without delay, I've been thinking of studying the Digest
a little myself.

fol. 22ᵛ

De muliere que amicum suum revocare intendit.

Sedens more turturis in ramusculo sico, gemo assidue,
turbans potum cum bibo, et mecum voce flebili colloquens
pertraho suspiria dolorosa: quia scire non possum ubi sit quem
diligit anima mea, imo illum cuius corpori anima [mea] est
unita.

Ille nimirum est qui tenet vite mee claves, sine quo vivere
mori esse puto, quia spiritus est amoris qui precordia mea
vivificando regirat, et cum deest non sum, et donec sum
deesse non potest—

Quia per voluntatem et ineffabile desiderium illum appre-
hendi et in memoriali meo secrecius teneo circumclusum; ac
ipsum velut mirre fasciculum sub quodam spei remedio inter
ubera mea brachiis peroptabilis dilectionis astringo.

Spes enim est quoddam refugium ymaginarium que multos
in calamitate positos refocillat, ex eo quod anima in dubiis
rebus frequencius exitum felicem expectat, nec refrenat corpus,
licet terminum ignoret quesitum.

Sed audite, filie Grecorum et adolescentule regni Tyronensis:
Vos forte putatis dilectum et desiderabilem meum inter brachia
retinere.

Sed fallimini! Quia semper cum sopori sum dedita intrat per
hostia thalami, ponit levam sub capite meo, dextra suavius
tangit renes et pectus, et conpressis labellis me dulcius osculatur.
Transfert me super ulnas in pomerium florigerum in quo
suavior est rivulorum decursus. In eodem phylomene ac
diversa genera volucrum dulciter modulantur, sunt ibidem
omnia genera odoramentorum; sicque amplexibus et colloquiis peroptatis diucius adinvicem fruimur in tam desiderabili
paradiso. Et istud inenarrabile mihi gaudium in omni sopore
occurrit.

Cur ergo illum revocare optarem ex quo tam desiderabiliter
me non desinit visitare?—presertim cum scientia quod sine me
vivere non poterit neque mori.

Translation and commentary: Chap. IV. 4, pp. 251 ff.

Roma, Vat. lat. 1599, fol. II^r   s. XV

> O decus, o splendor, vultu generosa benigno,
> O roseis redimita genis, o pectus eburnum,
> O tu cui radiant nivea duo sidera fronte,
> Quando michi misero, tanto quem langor amore
> 5 Detinet, occurres, et brachia lucida collo,
> Brachia iam cinges? dignabere quando moveri
> His lacrimis, dillecta, meis? dignabere quando

Affari miserum, tantasque repelere curas
In quibus exardet mens hec agitata furore,
10 Crudel*is* nimium? Pietas te ducat amoris,
Et Veneris iam castra colas. Venus ipsa medulas
Sauciat heu nostras—tu, tu, miseresce parumper!

O beauty, splendour, noble one, gracious in your aspect, you who are blessed with rosy cheeks and ivory breast, you from whose snowy front twin stars shed light, when will you come to me, to one woeful and languishing in love? When will you throw your radiant arms about my neck? when, beloved, deign to be moved by these my tears? when deign to speak to an unhappy man, and drive out the great cares burning within a mind wrought, far too cruel one, to madness? May love's devotion guide you, may you now come to dwell in Venus' camp. Venus herself, alas, pierces my inmost being —but you, can you not show a little mercy?

10 MS. Crudelius

These lines are superscribed 'Epistola misa per quemdam iuvenem sue amaxie' [*sic*]. They may be humanist verse, though several Latin verses on this fly-leaf of Vat. lat. 1599—fragments, proverbs, mnemonics—can be traced back to the twelfth and thirteenth centuries.

FRAGMENTS AND EPIGRAMS

Roma, Vat. lat. 3251, fol. 178ᵛ s. XIIˡ

ecce filia[m] regis audierunt . . . . . . animo
[vo]lucres silvarum bestie delphines et omne genus aquatile.
[anime que] dulce decantant pulsanti pectine. O amice
nobilis tu cunctis prevales voce et cithare

. . . Behold, they heard the king's daughter . . . in mind . . . birds
in the forests, creatures, dolphins and every water-race. . . . spirits
that enchant sweetly when the lyre is struck. O my lover . . . noble
one, you surpass all in song, even the lute [. . .]

> 1 ff. The legible words are arranged as in the MS., with readings not wholly
> certain in square brackets. It is hard to ascertain the margin, but probably four
> or five words are missing before 'ecce', and at least one or two before each of
> the other three lines. There is space for about six letters between 'audierunt'
> and 'animo'.
> 3 MS. plectine—by confusion with *plectrum*?

These lines are immediately above the mutilated Vatican text of
'Foebus abierat' (*supra*, pp. 335 ff.). Like it they are probably a
fragment of a short lyrical narrative, and even the words that survive
hint that this had beauty and imagination. Possibly here too there
was a theme of *féerie*. The enamoured king's daughter occurs also in
two other poems of the 'Foebus abierat' group (*supra*, loc. cit.). It is
difficult to conjecture about the verse-form, but there seem to be a
number of rhyming six-syllabled lines ('silvarum bestie, genus
aquatile, pulsanti pectine, voce et cithare'), alternating with unrhymed ones of a different rhythm ('delphínes et ómne, que dúlce
decántant, tu cúnctis preváles').

Paris, B.N. lat. 11867, fol. 216ʳ s. XIII²

Langueo—	sed pereo,
dum amoris—	sed furoris,
saucior—	sed crucior,
telo—	sed tormento.

I am languishing, no, dying, as I am wounded, no, tormented, by the shaft of love, no, by the rack of madness.

E: M. Esposito, *EHR* xxx (1915), 456.

3 MS. sauctior   E sanctior
4 E celo sum
MS. continues:

> Inopes divicias
> admonet ne sicias
>   Crassi mors tam nota.
> Quod casus sit facilis
> testatur volubilis
>   Ixionis rota.

E printed this as part of the love-verses—mistakenly, for it is clearly separated from these by a sign in the MS. 'Inopes divicias' is probably a fragment of a didactic lyric such as those in *CB* 1. 1, made to be sung to the same melody as 'Langueo—sed pereo'. This I take to be not a fragment but a self-sufficient *ritornello* of the type discussed in Chap. I, pp. 27 ff. and Chap. V, pp. 276 ff., though it shows its scholastic origin in the use of *vers rapportés*. It is formally unlike any other verse in the MS., and was presumably copied from an original where it indicated the melody for 'Inopes divicias'.

fol. 218ᵛ

Arent assiduo tenuata labella labore
  Totque exhausta apibus oscula mella negant.

The lips grow dry, weakened with so much passionate effort—so many kisses drained dry leave no honey over for bees.

1 *v*. Bibliography, pp. 574, 578 (Vat. Reg. lat. 585).

Aspectu leni veniens, pectus michi leni.
  Nil michi rescribas—attamen ipsa veni!

Come with gentle look, make my heart serene. No, do not write to me—but come, oh come!

2 Cf. Ovid, *Her.* 1. 2; Walter of Châtillon, 'Eliconis rivulo', st. 16.

Tu michi leso les   vulnus; gemini tibi soles
  Sunt oculi; sol es;   cuique placere soles.

You efface the wound for me who was hurt: your eyes are twin suns, you yourself a sun; your wont is to give joy to everyone.

Que dicis de me?   Dic si bona, si mala, deme!
Diligo te pre me—   queque nociva preme!

How do you speak of me? If well, tell me, if ill, leave off! I love you more than myself—restrain all your cruelty!

München, Clm 17210, fol. 40ᵛ; Clm 12725, fol. 16ʳ

s. XIII; s. XV

Visus et alloquium,   tactus, post oscula factum.
Ni fugias tactus,   vix evitabitur actus:
Post visum, risum,   post risum transit in usum,
Post usum tactus,   post tactum transit in actus.

Looking, addressing, touching, kissing, then love. Unless you shun touching, the act of love is bound to follow: looking gives rise to laughter, laughter to being familiar, familiarity to touching, touching to love itself.

This is one of the many variations on the topos of the *quinque lineae amoris*, which from its origins in Ovid and in the grammarians Donatus and Porphyry became a favourite device in Medieval Latin, and passed into vernacular literatures, above all into French, where it continued to be widely used in the Renaissance. For detailed discussion, see H. Unger, *De Ovidiana in Carminibus Buranis quae dicuntur imitatione* (Strasbourg, 1914), pp. 16 ff.; Curtius, pp. 512 ff.; Peter Dronke, *Classica et Mediaevalia*, xx (1959), 167 ff. To the passages cited in these I can now add two others: John of Salisbury, *Polycraticus*, VI. 23—

Cum fabulationibus et conviviis se totis viribus immiscet Venus, cuius qui prima missilia libenter admittit, quin posterioribus gravius vulneretur vix evadit.

Visus et alloquium, contactus et oscula, factum,

sicut se praecedunt ordine, ita ex necessitate doloris inferunt partum. Voluptatis siquidem finis penitentia est.

And an unpublished distich in Paris, B.N. Nouv. Acq. lat. 1544, s. xv, fol. 108ᵛ:

Visus et adloquium, contactus, basia, risus—
hec faciunt cohitus continuare vices.

Webb in his edition of the *Polycraticus* (loc. cit.) noted that the verse 'Visus et alloquium, tactus, post oscula, factum' occurs in old glosses to Justinian's *Digesta*, XLVIII. 5, 23. This presumably is the point of departure of the verses in the two München MSS. These vary the device by *gradatio per inflexionem* (Geoffrey of Vinsauf, *Summa de Coloribus Rhetoricis*, Faral p. 323), a figure parodied by Shakespeare in Polonius's 'declension' of Hamlet's six stages of love-madness (*Hamlet*, II. 2, 146 ff.).

Cambridge, Trinity O. 2. 45, p. 362   c. 1250

> Candidior stella   me diligit una puella!
> Non est in villa   virgo formosior illa.

A girl more radiant than a star is in love with me! In all the town there's none more beautiful than she.*

The first line of this couplet is one that rings through Medieval Latin love-poetry. To rhyme *stella* with *puella* is to 'couple but "love" and "dove"'. The ultimate source is Ovid, *A.A.* I. 59. Compare, in the later eleventh century, Marbod's *Ad virginem devotam* (*P.L.* 171, 1654), which begins 'Splendidior stella, simplex et munda puella', and Wido's *Versus Eporedienses*, 259, 'Lucifer ut stellis, sic es prelata puellis'. In the twelfth century this line recurs in a poem in the Zürich miscellany, 'Dulcis amica mea, speciosior es Galatea' (Werner, 49, 14); later in the same collection (Werner, 117, 2) we have 'Lucifer ut stellas superatve Diana puellas'. (Cf. also Werner, 92.) In the Viennese MS. CV 2521, s. XII, fol. 138ʳ, the following verses *Ad amicam* are attributed to Ulrich of Bamberg (†1147):

> Lilia ceu flores,   sic vincis, amica, sorores,
> Utque nitens aurum   supereminet omne metallum,
> Et quasi sol stellas,   sic vincis, amica, puellas.

* For variants and MSS., *v.* Walther, *Initia* 2354, 18533; *Proverbia* 2283, 13987, 30241. In the Cambridge MS. follows:

> Si superarum   turba dearum   tota choisset,
> Omnibus illis   sola Matillis   prevaluisset!

Other love-verses in the MS. are: Walther, *Initia* 3800, 11032, 13729, 17138; *Proverbia* 6518, 7264, 7267, 18843a, 19230, 23293a, 26198, 29744a, 34030a.

(Text, in J. G. Eckhardt, *Corpus Historicum Medii Aevi* (Lipsiae, 1723), II. 4). The *Ovidius puellarum* (36) has 'Splendidior stella fuerat michi visa puella' (*Comédie*, II. 143), and the *anoním enamorat* of the Ripoll MS. (d'Olwer, 45) has a poem beginning 'Luna velut stellas, sic vincis, amica, puellas'. The couplet that I print above may be later than any of these instances. In the Laurenziana MS. Libri 1545, however, it is found in the midst of epigrams of Hugh Primas (*v. NE* xxxII. 1, 68), and it is quite possibly his.

München, Clm 6911, fol. 128ʳ   s. XIII–XIV

In te Natura   —que pulchrior omnibus una
Es—nil peccavit,   nisi quod mortale creavit.

In creating you—who alone are more beautiful than all—Natura has been faultless, save that she made you mortal.

Vite dulcedo,   mihi te da, nam tibi me do!
Sim dea tuque deus: sim tua tuque meus.

Joy of my life, give yourself to me, for I give myself to you. Let me be goddess, you the god—let me be yours and you be mine.

2 Sim dea tuque deus—cf. Otte von Bottenlouben, XII. 2, 1–2 (*DLD* I. 314).

sim tua tuque meus—for the uses of this phrase in Medieval Latin, *v.* H. Walther, 'Zur Geschichte eines mittelalterlichen Topos (Me tibi teque mihi)', *Liber Floridus*, pp. 153 ff.

Oxford, Bodley 315, fol. 268ʳ   s. XV in.

Ite, pares pariter paribus suadete medullis!
Convict*us* vestros non vincant oscula conche,
Brachia non edere, nec oscula blanda columbc.
Vivite vos similes insimul absque dolo!

Go, each urge on the other with mutual ardours! Let not the close-pressed lips of the oyster-shell or the arms of ivy or the soft kisses of doves surpass your own embraces. Live like (these) in accord, without deceit!

Written in the margin in the same hand (presumably in jest): 'hoc illustris ille Iulius cesar'.

2 MS. Convictos

Verses for an epithalamium, perhaps fragmentary. The irregular use of pentameters was not infrequent in the twelfth century—compare the epitaphs for Abelard (printed *supra*, p. 470), or other pieces in Zürich C 58/275 (e.g. Werner, 48, 49, 116). Godfrey of Viterbo regularly used pairs of end-rhymed hexameters followed by a pentameter (*v. SLP* II. 165–6).

Braunschweig 103, fol. 46ʳ   s. XVⁱ

> Amor almus, ardens affectus alacris animi, amenitas
>   appetibilis,
> Exultatio extatica, estimatio expedientis elemosinalis
>   eucaristie,
> Iocunditas, inflammans iubilatio intentionis indulgencie
>   impetrative.

Gracious love, ardent affection of the joyful mind, desirable loveliness, ecstatic exultation, preciousness of the liberating, mercy-giving sacrament, joy, kindling jubilation of the thought of tenderness won.

These lines are set to music. Two further lines, of words beginning with 'o' and 'u', are missing. For details of the device (παρόμοιον) of series of words beginning with the same letter, a device which extends from Ennius, through late Antiquity and the Middle Ages, as far as the Renaissance, see Curtius, pp. 283 ff. Compare also Marner's 'Iam dudum estivalia' (Schmeller, 95, and *WSB* liv [1866], 319), which has seven rhymes on each of the five vowels, and its German source, Walther von der Vogelweide, 75, 25.

Many Medieval Latin verses are epigrammatic 'definitions of love': *v.* Walther, *Initia*, 1434b, 4393, 5549, 5578, 5580, 5581, 11740, 11741, 15693, 15787, 17923, as well as the trilingual 'Amor est quedam mentis insania' in the Oxford MS. Douce 139 (*v.* Bibliography, p. 570). Again, there are lyrical poems defining human love, such as *CB* 87 and Walter of Châtillon's magnificent 'Dulcis aure temperies' (Saint-Omer, 25), and others defining divine love, such as 'Amor sponte cor afficit' (Walther, 931). What is remarkable about the fragmentary song in the Braunschweig MS. is that human and divine love seem to be invoked simultaneously.

In the songbook Montpellier 196 (*v.* Bibliography, p. 559), 'Amor qui cor vulnerat' distinguishes between human and divine love, but the motet on fols. 378^v–379^r seems to be concerned with an ideal of human love that is both *courtois* and Christian:

Triple	*Double*
Amor potest conqueri	Ad amorem sequitur
videns se nunc deprimi,	et concomitatur
quia cepit minui	fides et constancia,
fides et constancia,	nam in hiis fundatur;
que sibi restitui	hiis duobus igitur
peritum iudicii	amor dum privatur,
petit cum instancia.	totus perit penitus
	et adnichilatur.

SERLONIAN VERSE*

In bivio ponor,   binas amo, ducere conor
  Unam—vel neutram—   nec mihi constat utram.
Hec satis, illa satis,   nimis utraque pulcra notatis
  Vultibus. Hac uror,   hac mihi corde furor.
5 Hec Venus, illa Thetis;   hec comibus, illa facetis
  Prevalet. Hec clamat   'Sis meus', hec sat amat.
Fallit que sat amat,   spernit que talia clamat—
  Spernetur clamans,   decipietur amans!
Hanc plus, hanc amo plus!—   neutram plus. Sic mihi
                                                duplus
10   Est amor: his suplex   sum quasi corde duplex.
Sic utramque volo,   quod utramque dari mihi nolo,
  Nolo, quid, imo volo—   spes vacat ista dolo.
Malo carere mea   quam ferre dolosa trophea:
  Fraude magis quavis   fraus in amante gravis.
15 Quis certus dubitat?   ego solus. Quis sua vitat
  Gaudia? solus ego.   Me sine mente rego.
Dum gravor a binis   gravior me vexat Herinis,
  Plus vereor, finis   quod mihi non sit in his.
Quid precer?—ignoro.   Scio quod nequit esse quod
                                                oro,
20   Nescio solamen   querere, quero tamen.
Quid deceat nosco,   quod non decet hoc mihi posco.

---

* From the MS. analysis in Jan Öberg's new edition of Serlo of Wilton
(Stockholm, 1965) it is clear that the love-verses printed below on pp. 493–509
are by Serlo himself (only the distich *Si tibi sum cordi* is less certain), but that
there are no good grounds for attributing to Serlo the brief pieces on pp. 510–
12. Nevertheless, they may stand here, as having distinct 'Serlonian' affinities.

Quis me fallit? ego.　　Fallor, idemque nego.
Una mihi detur,　　sic altera decipietur;
　　Utraque ducatur—　　sic mihi nulla datur.
25 Pono quod in me sint　　duo, sive quod una due sint—
　　Sanor. An illud erit?　　Non. Amor ergo perit.
Non perit, imo furit:　　furor est qui taliter urit.
　　Illum quis sanet?　　Quis perit adque manet?
Sum quasi mansurus　　dum sic amo; sum periturus
30 　Dum frustra spero:　　sic ero, sic nec ero.
Queque dee, quique　　dent dii, coiturus utrique
　　Iungar! Quid pocius?　　Quid precer ulterius?

I am in a dilemma: I love two women; I try to win either—or neither—and cannot make up my mind which. She and she are passing fair, each has an excellent fair face. For her I burn, for her I rave in heart. She is Venus, she Thetis; she excels in courtesy, and she in elegance. One cries 'Be mine!', the other fondly loves. The fond one deceives, the crying one resists; she'll be resisted, and the other deceived! I love her more, no her!—neither more. So love for me is double: I have as it were a two-faced heart as I entreat them. I so desire both that I don't want *both* given me, indeed not, why, but I do—this hope's free of deceit. I'd rather be without my lady than win a cheating triumph; fraud in a lover is the worst of all. Who is certain and in doubt? Only I. Who avoids what is his joy? Only I. I rule myself without a mind. When I'm oppressed by (the thought of) both, an even more oppressive Fury vexes me, and all the more I fear lest for me it should end like this! What should I pray, then? I don't know. I know that what I pray for cannot be; I don't know how to seek for solace—yet I seek. I know what is comme-il-faut, and want the opposite. Who is deceiving me? I myself. I am deceived—yet I deny this too. If one becomes mine then the other will feel cheated, if both are won, then neither can be mine. Suppose there are two of me, or that the two women are one—then I am cured. But will this ever be? No. Therefore love dies. No, not dies, raves—it is madness burns like this. Who could cure it? Who dies and stays alive? I survive, as it were, when I love like this, I'm at the point of death when I hope in vain—thus I am and am not. May every goddess, every god allow me to possess both! What better, what more should I ask?

H: B. Hauréau, *NE* 1. 305.

6 H Illa sat amat
9 H si mihi duplus
10 H sum mihi corde
17 MS. g^(ra)u̅r (*graviter*, Öberg)   Herinis—i.e. Erinys.

Illas aut illos de cunctis elige mille:
Vincet eas vel eos mea vel meus, illa vel ille!

Choose a thousand girls or boys from among all—my one, she or he, will surpass them all!

fol. 58^r

  Te voco Naida,
   sentio Taida,
    scireque nolo!

  Quod prece nequeo,
5 te mihi mulceo
   munere solo.

  Te domo munere
  cogoque dicere
   'Pamfile!' rursum;

10 Si nego premia,
  nil nisi 'Birria!'
   nil nisi 'sursum!'

> Gaudia mutua,
> sive magis tua,
> 15   vendis amanti.

> Me pete, non mea!
> Gratia postea
> sit mihi danti.

I call you a Naiad, but feel you're a Thais—I don't want to know! I cannot make you yield by pleas, only by gifts. With a gift I make you tame, make you say 'Pamphilus!' once again; if I bring nothing, there's nothing but 'Birria!'—nothing but 'Go away!' Our mutual joys, or rather your own joys—you sell them to your lover. Look to me, not to what's mine: then let the thanks come to me, the giver.

2 Taida—the name's associations derive principally from (1) Ovid (*A.A.* III. 604, 'liberior Thaide'; *Rem.* 385, 'Thais in arte mea est'); (2) Terence—Thais is the leading lady in the *Eunuchus*; (3) the legend of Thais the converted courtesan in the *Vitae Patrum*, the subject of Hrotsvitha's play *Pafnutius*. But the name need not always suggest a *meretrix*—compare the verses 'Celitus artifici res elimata paratu', *supra*, p. 468.

9–11 Pamfile, Birria—the contrast is between 'My lover!' and 'Scurvy knave!' The helpless young lover and his crafty servant (types almost unaltered from Plautus and Terence) occur in most of the twelfth-century *Comoediae*, several times with the names Pamphilus and Birria. One (*Comédie*, II. 93 ff.) is even called *Pamphilus, Gliscerium et Birria*.

12 MS. may read *fur sum* (Öberg).

fol. 58ᵛ

> Si mavis perdi lucro quam perdere lucrum,
> Dum captas lucrum captus es ipse lucro.
> Que sua sunt Fortuna tibi committere non vult,
> Non sua ne dicas sed tua que sua sunt.
> 5 Excubias timet illa tuas oculosque manusque:
> Hos quia non claudis, has quia non aperis.
> Hoc ea iuris habet quamvis sine iure feratur:
> 'Cuncta petas, nil do. Nil pete, cuncta dabo.'
> Quisquis Fortunam non novit, Thaida noscat:

10   Eius more venit spreta, rogata fugit.
    Si satis ergo sapis, cum te delectet habere,
      Parcius affecta, largius illa dabit.

If you would rather be lost by wealth than lose it, while you seize hold of wealth it seizes you. Fortuna does not wish to entrust what's hers to you, lest you deny her what is hers and say it's yours. She fears your spying, fears your eyes and hands—eyes which let nothing past, hands which let nothing slip. This device is hers by right, though she wears it wrongfully: 'Seek all and I give nothing; seek nothing, I'll give all.' If anyone has not met Fortuna, let him meet Thais: like her, she comes when spurned, and flees, being desired. So if you are wise, when you feel it's bliss to possess her, pretend to be less keen—she'll give you more.

7 MS. quodvis

fol. 59ʳ⁻ᵛ

    Cipre, timent dii te: tu fortior es Iove dite.
    Que tua sors? que vis?   tibi res obnoxia quevis?
    Nulla premit te lis—   validis premis omnia telis.
    Cur tua sic se vis   probat in me? cur ita sevis?
5 Quid timeas de me?   pacem peto. Spicula deme!
    Castam non amo rem,   quia nil amo preter amorem.
    Speque *t*uique metu   trahis et tollis mihi me tu—
    Parcius, oro, tume;   que cuncta regis, rege tu me!
    Cui vix par es tu,   me, virgo, tuo premis estu.
10 Qua mea mens arsit   huic nota Cupidinis ars sit.
    Cur Amor huic parsit?   Mihi fac ut vulnere par sit.
    Dis equans es se—   precium nequit illius esse.
    Hanc in spem fer me   sine qua sum me sine ferme.
    Cur mea meque darem?   —mea si foret, hanc·mihi da
                               rem!
15 Summa salus hac re   mihi vel vulnus datur acre,
    Nam mihi si se dat   per eam data vulnera sedat,
    Huic male si res stat,   non spes sed mors mihi restat.
    Regno nec sub dis,   Venus, istam si mihi subdis.

O mea, me cures. O lux mea, mors mea cur es?
20 O mihi spes vite, Veneris sequor et colo vi te,
Sicque Venus iussit; Veneris tibi non leve ius sit!
Nosti que sua vis— non hostibus illa suavis.
His testem do te: nemo tuus est sine dote;
Ius quibus hoc dandi, si te dant, omnia dant dii.
Dotes queque date tibi sunt dabis omnia. Da te!
Me mihi das; te da; tua Palladis est mihi teda.
Non sequeris fas tu si non vivis sine fastu.
Vivere me tedet nisi vita mihi mea te det—
Vel te non mete dent dii, vel non sine me te!
30 Si te gusto semel, gustandum dat mihi se mel.
Transgrediar tute Sirtes, comitem dato tu te.
Sum tibi non parvi: vix Hector erit mihi par vi,
Vi supero Resum si qua carus tibi re sum—
Quisque mihi dispar, si sis mea, sic ego dis par,
35 Nam superis par tu, supero vel es edita partu;
Efficeris par dis si sis pia—si fera, pardis.
Si gemis aut meres, que restituet mihi me res?
Me sine fine teres si nulle dant mihi te res.
Que retrahit res te? Veneris trahor ad iuga reste.
40 Qua teneam re te? Veneris vis fallere rete?
Concilii vi—ve tibi, ne moriar—mihi vive!
Ut placeam dive dent, queso, dee mihi dii ve.
Ha, nil me reris quia dis placuisse mereris—
Hac miser in parte videor, qui non amo par te.

45 Absentant sedi Iovis ad mortalia se dii.
Per iuga, per sepes Iovis egit ad oscula se pes,
Europam sumsit, dixitque 'Suus, mea, sum, sit!'
Cum puero pes te tulit, o Venus, haud sine peste.
Mens mea se nescit, in me dolor iste senescit.
50 Cur spiro? cur sum? non tendo quo volo cursum.
Si pereo, rea tu, si sanor, es absque reatu.
Cur in amore tepes? maneat qui fert retro te pes—
Res procul amote tristes, si dicis 'Amo te'.

Hac male re mota,   longe sors fausta remota,
55 Nec valeo nec sum   si non vis quem volo nexum.
Cordi nulla sedet   mihi sors, mea ni mihi se det.
Partho seu Medo   similem—mea—non tibi me do.
Dulce sapit ver te.   Luctus in gaudia verte!
Hoc mihi det ver se,   sortes mihi nam bene verse.
60 Prona mihi fac sis,   maiorem me Iove faxis—
Tu mitem fac te,   Parce mites mihi facte.
Quale mihi cor dii   tibi dent, si diis ego cordi?
O faustum ter me   si me socient tibi terme,
O faustam te ter   si non animus tibi teter!
65 Tango lire cordas,   tu discordans mihi cor das.
Duc melius redas,   mea sors—mihi spem sine re das.
Siqua mihi fert his   ratio, dii, spem mihi fertis.
Dii, mihi spem ferte!   Quid dii? Mea, tu mihi fer te!
Ni mihi te prodis   facilem, iam nil ego pro diis.
70 Vix stips, vix as sum,   nisi dicis cum precor 'assum.'
Hoc in corde reses,   rerum pulcerrima res es.
Iure queror de diis   si frustra *te mihi* dedis.
Spes mihi sunt curte—   cur me tollis mihi? cur te?
Placo deos thure,   sed qua placabere tu re?
75 Nescio qua vi sum   tuus, an superis ita visum?

Perdere me cur vis?   vis recta refellere curvis?
Tu mea lora tene—   trahor in Stiga! qua duce? tene?
Tristi mergor aqua: non 'a quo' quere, sed 'a qua?'!
In Stige qua no vi?   tua vis—ea quam bene novi.
80 Fel mihi triste seres,   male si vertit mea se res.
Spes rata me rexit.   'Rex Serlo' dic—ita rex sit.
Te duce cur, o spes,   vagor eger, ut exul, ut hospes?
Digna viro vir ago   si te colo, summa virago.
Fausta dies luxit   mihi, quam peto si mea lux sit,
Quas rogo sic he res   mihi sint, et ero Iovis heres.
Parca tibi dixit   'Hic maior erit Iove.' Dic 'Sit'!
Nam bene qu*i* vixit   carus tibi, qui sine, vix sit.
Cerbereo dente   teneor—qui dii mihi dent te!

Que mihi spes, que res   mea, si me perdere queres?
90 Me prior es. Me vis?   —sed destituit mea me vis.
Inveniam ver bis: minus acribus utere verbis,
Nec mihi me nec te   tolles, Veneris iuga necte,
Da mihi que sperem,   vel quam peto da sine spe rem—
Quas mihi si ferres   rex dicerer, has mihi fer res!
Vincunt qui dant es   alias, non te mihi dantes.
Spe dapis et mense   qua vivo, fovet mea mens se.

Dii, mites estis!   Iam finis, iam modus est his!
His moveo divos,   his mites sentio, di, vos.
Vobis thus, dii, do.   Redimi me vult mea Dido!
100 Sum felix, o dii: quod amo stat, abitque quod odi.
Liberor a morte!   Mea, iam meus urit amor te.
Mors retrahit morsum: quia dicis 'Non tibi mors', sum.
Qui meus est, noster   sit amor. Beat hoc ita nos ter.
Summo digna statu,   tibi sum, tibi sto—mihi sta tu!
105 Fer vaga sic rota te—   di, sic mea fata rotate!
Hac una sta re,   si scis, Ramnusia, stare.

Aphrodite, the gods fear you—you are mightier than great Jove. What is your part, your power? Is everything at your mercy? You are not afflicted by mutiny—you afflict all with your forceful shafts. Why does your power test itself so much on me? Why are you so fierce? What could you fear from me? I'm all for peace. Take those darts away! I don't love anything chaste, I'm in love only with love. With hope and fear of you, you draw me and take me from myself. Not so many outbursts, I beseech you—control me, you who control all! You afflict me with an ardour, maiden, to which (even) you are scarcely equal. Let her by whom my thoughts are kindled come to know Cupid's craft! Why has he spared her? Let her wound be equal to mine. You liken her to the gods—her worth cannot be told. Lead me to that hope without which I am almost beside myself. Why should I surrender myself and what is mine?—if she were mine, give me but that! In this I shall be given my fullest salvation, or else a piercing wound: for if she gives herself to me she stills the wound she has given, if it's against her will no hope but death remains. If you make her yield to me, Venus, I'll reign above the gods.

Think of me, my only one. O my light, why are you my death? O hope of my life, with the force of love I follow you and worship you—this is Venus' behest, do not take it lightly. You know how powerful she is, she is not gentle with enemies. To them I give you as a witness: no one is yours without a gift; if the gods, in whom this law of giving rests, give you, then they give all. You give out all the gifts with which you were endowed—then give yourself! You give myself to me, so give yourself—your Vestal torch is mine. You are not living rightly if you don't give up disdain. It wearies me to live unless my life brings me you. May the gods not bring you to your end, at least not you without me! If once I taste you, an irresistible honey becomes mine. When you are my companion, the Syrtes (themselves) will be safely crossed by me. You'll not find me a man of no account: Hector will scarcely be my equal in strength, I'll be stronger than Rhesus if I am at all dear to you. No man will be my equal if you are mine—I'll be the equal of the gods. For you are their equal, or else divinely begotten: you are made godlike if you are gentle, panther-like if fierce. If you sigh or moan, what will restore me to myself? You will exhaust me without end if nothing gives me you. What is it holds you back? I am dragged to Love's yoke by a rope. With what shall I hold you? Do you want to evade Venus' net? By the power of our bond—live for me; woe to you if I die. May the goddesses or the gods grant, I pray, that I please my goddess. Ah you think me naught because you manage to please gods—in this respect I seem the hapless one, I who love none but you.

The gods absent themselves from the throne of Jove to go to mortals. Jove's foot went through yokes, through fences for the sake of kisses, he took Europa, saying 'I am hers, let her be mine!' You went your way with a boy, Venus, not without harm. My mind does not know itself, this pain grows old in me. Why do I breathe? why exist? I cannot take the course I wish. If I die, you are guilty, if I am healed you are cleared. Why are you lukewarm in love? Stay your backward step, all that's sad is banished if you say 'I love you'. If it should go amiss, good fortune is drawn far away, I shall have no strength, no being, if you do not wish the bond that I wish. I care for no fate unless she who is mine gives herself to me. I do not offer myself, my beloved, like a Mede or Parthian. Sweet spring has the scent of you; transform grief into joy! May this spring yield to me, as fortune is on my side. Let yourself incline to me, you will make me greater than Jove. Make yourself gentle—the Parcae themselves have become gentle for me. Tell me, what kind of heart may the gods give you, if I am dear to the gods? Thrice-happy I if we could bathe together; you too thrice-happy if your mind took no offence. I play chords on the lyre, you set discords in my heart. O my fate, guide those wagon-wheels better, you are giving me hope without substance. If reason tells me anything in this, you are bringing me hope, you gods. Gods bring me that hope! Why gods? My own one, bring me yourself! Unless you show yourself yielding, by the gods I am naught. Scarcely a farthing, a copper, unless you say when I beseech you 'I am here'. Abiding in this heart, you are the loveliest creature of creatures. I'll rightly complain of the gods if you're only pretending to yield. My hopes are broken; why take me—or yourself—from me? With incense I soften the gods, with what shall I soften you? I know not by what power I am yours—did it seem so to the gods?

Why do you wish to destroy me, to refute what is straight by curves? Rein me in, I'm being dragged into Styx! Who is leading me? You? I am drowned in a desolate pool—don't ask 'By him?' but 'By her?' Through what power do I swim in the Styx? Your power, which I know so well. You will produce bitter gall in me if my effort turns out ill. A fixed hope has ruled me: say 'Let Serlo be king'—and he will be. Why then, my hope, if you guide me, do I wander distraught, an exile and a stranger? Being a man, I do what behoves a man if I worship you, greatest of heroines. A lucky day grows light for me if the light I desire is mine. If the things I so ask for are mine, I'll be Jove's heir. The Fate has told you 'This man will be greater than Jove.' Say 'Let him be so.' For he who has lived beloved by you has lived well, he who has lived without you has scarcely lived.

I am transfixed by Cerberus' bite; may the gods give you to me! What is my hope, my possession, if you seek to ruin me? You are of more worth than I. Do you want me?—but see, my strength is leaving me. May I find a second spring: don't use such harsh words, take neither myself nor yourself away from me, bind Venus' yoke, give me what I hope—or what I seek without hope. If you give me that I'd be called king—oh give it to me! Those who give money win other women—yet they cannot give me you. My mind consoles itself in the hope of a table and a feast, for which I live.

You gods, you are kind! now the end, the goal of all this is here! In this I am moving the gods, in this, you gods, I feel you are good. I give you incense, gods. My Dido wants me to be redeemed! O gods, I am happy: what I love survives, what I hate is gone. I am freed from death! Now, my own, my love burns you. Death draws back her sting: because you say 'No death for you', I live. May the love that's mine be ours both—then we are thrice-blessed by it. You who are worthy of the highest place, I am yours, I dwell in you, dwell in me too! This is your course, my wheel—you gods, revolve my fate thus!—Nemesis, stay still in this alone, if you know how.

1 ff. dii te, dite—it is impossible to find an English equivalent for this device, except perhaps in a completely free version. Thus a literal translation (attempted only for the sake of clarity) cannot in any way suggest the special quality of these verses, which lies in the incongruity between the seeming seriousness of the lover's *planctus* and the outrageous word-play which ends each line.

7 MS. cuique

9 virgo—for the figure of 'Venus virgo' or 'Venus caelestis' in the Latin tradition, see (apart from *Aen.* I. 319-20) Apuleius, *Metam.* x. 31 and *Apol.* XII; Martianus Capella, *De Nupt.* 85 ff.; Mythographus Tertius XI. 18; Alanus, *De Planctu Naturae* (*P.L.* 210) 454A ff.; Chap. V, *supra*, pp. 324 ff.

18 (and 31-34, 60, 85-87, 94). Cf. Chap. V, pp. 297 ff.

41 MS. Concilio

44 MS. q

45 Cf. 'Profuit ignaris' 33 ff. (*supra*, p. 453), and commentary in Chap. IV. 3, pp. 233 ff.

69 MS. Si

72 MS. me tibi dedis

77 In MS. follows 79

85 MS. Quam

87 MS. quis vixit

91 MS. Invideam

92 MS. Hoc

Between lines 10 and 11 (in margin): Reges hac (MS. hec) avi, tuti sat ab arte, sat a vi? Between 35 and 36 (in margin): Dic 'Serlo pro me perit' et, quam sis pia, prome. (Öberg, pp. 97-8; only the extreme edge of these letters is visible on my microfilm of the MS.).

fol. 59[v]

Pronus erat Veneri Naso, sed ego mage pronus,
Pronus erat Gallus, sed mage pronus ego.

Nasoni, Gallo placuere Corinna, Liquoris—
Queque mihi; nec me cuique placere putem:
5 Unus me coitus vincit, non mille puellas—
Unum qui vix do, quomodo mille dabo?
Opto placere tamen mihi dum placet ulla, sed a me
Nondum tacta placet—tacta, placere placet.
Spe tantum primi coitus amo, spe satiatus
10   Ultra quid sperem? Spe nichil ulterius.
Infestare quidem non cessat oves lupus, hostes
Miles, aves nisus, dentibus, ense, pede.
Non lupus esuriens una satiabitur agna,
Non eques hoste ferus, non ave nisus atrox.
15 Taliter in multis meus heret amor, nec ab ulla
Cessat: plus habita semper habenda placet.
Diligo dum spernor, dilectus sperno; faventes
Odi, dum cupiam quamque favere tamen.

Ovid was inclined to love, but I am more inclined; Gallus was inclined to love, but I am even more. Ovid's flame was Corinna, Gallus's was Lycoris—mine is any girl at all. Not that I think I'd satisfy every girl: I'm done for with one act, girls can cope with a thousand; I can hardly do one completely, how should I do a thousand? But as long as any girl's attractive, I'll make a bid for her —though only if I've not yet taken her—and then my aim is to pleasure her. I fall in love only in the hope of that first act; what else should I hope for when that hope is satisfied? There's nothing else.— Indeed a wolf, a knight, a sparrow-hawk never cease to plague lambs, enemies, or birds with tooth or sword or talon: a hungry wolf's not satisfied with one lamb, a fierce knight with one foe, a grim hawk with one bird. So too my love cleaves to many, not stopping at one: the one to be possessed lures more than the possessed. I love when I'm rejected, and, being loved, reject; I hate women that woo, but long to woo each one.

H: B. Hauréau, *NE* I. 313.

4 H Quamque mihi, non me
8 H Nundum
11 ff. Cf. Geoffrey of Vinsauf (Faral, p. 322): '*Articulus* est quando singula

verba, singulis intervallis, distinguntur caesa oratione.' For an illuminating recent discussion of *vers rapportés*, see Dámaso Alonso's 'Tradition or Polygenesis?' (*Modern Humanities Research Association*, November 1960).

Flos floris flori: 'Florem—flos, flore liquori
Es nitor equalis—   mihi das, mihi plus specialis.
Ver veris veri,   vero, ver, vere videri
Vis, mea. Flos, pares!   Spumis rutilas; mage clares.'

A flower says to the flower of flowers: 'O flower, in your flowering you are a brightness rivalling the ocean; you give your flower to me, my very own. Spring of true spring, you, my spring, my beloved, want to appear in a true spring. O flower, you are here! You sparkle in the foam, you outshine it.'

1 *v*. 'Flos florum', *supra*, p. 181.
4 The last image is that of Venus Anadyomene.

The lines remain a conundrum; the paraphrase is only one possible indication towards a solution.

fol. 63ʳ

Quadam nocte, loco quodam, cum virgine quadam
    Solus eram, soli sola maligna fuit.
Talibus allexi verbis suspiria—vultum
    Finxit Amor, fictis verba dedere fidem—
5 'Aspera, quem refugis? non hostis ego, sed amicus;
    Non Ciclops, sed Achis; non meus, imo tuus.
Cunctas finge meas—volo nullam, diligo nullas.
    Te volo, te solam, quam volo, velle velim.
In te turpe nichil, nisi quod nil diligis. Illam
10   Credo valere nichil que scit amare nichil.
Cerne, precor, quis sim, quid sis, quid utrumque deceret,
    Quid sibi poscat Amor, quod sine teste locus.
Cur probitas maribus, cur virginibus data forma?—
    Ut valor [h]os illis, ut decor has det eis.
15 Qui nescit quid mel sapiat, non mel probat, imo
    Qui semel hoc tetigit tangere sepe velit.
Nosti quid sit amor?—sic non desistis amare.
    Nescis?—sic acidus. Incipe, dulcis erit!

Quod Natura iubet fieri, scelus hoc renuisse:
20   Quicquid agis vite vel scelus est vel amor.'
Nec renuit, nec paret. Utrumque veretur: amorem
    Casta fugit, simplex horret inire scelus.
Infero vim dubie, complector et osculor, arcet
    Nunc leviter collum dextera, leva femur.
25 Cirma levo tunice, verbis nocet illa manuque,
    Vi tamen invite sublevo pube tenus.
Restat adhuc femorum nexus, dissolvere carnem
    Sentio, que sensu pene carere facit.
Excitat illa nates, crissari pene putares,
30   Pectora non motus, cetera motus habet.
Dum se sic agitat, dum sic evadere sperat,
    Quo magis intus amo, gaudia libo foris.
O nova simplicitas—tanquam querenda sit extra
    Virginitas! Hac se stulta carere putat.

One night in a certain place I was alone with a girl—though alone with me, she was obstinate. I sighed, and said to her (Love gave me fair-semblance, and in dissembling my words carried conviction)—'Cruel one, whom are you fleeing? I am not foe but friend, not Cyclops but Acis, not my own but yours. Suppose all women were mine, I desire none of them, love none. It is you I desire, you alone, wishing you'd wish as I do. There is no fault in you, save that you do not love. I think a woman who cannot love has no true worth. I beseech you, think who I am, who you are, what is right for us both, what Love demands—and that this place is secret. Why is prowess given to men, beauty to girls? That excellence and loveliness may give each to each. Whoever does not know the taste of honey cannot praise it, but one who has tried it once would often try. Do you know what love is?—then you'd never cease loving. Do you not know? That's why it's bitter. Begin, it will be sweet! It is a crime to refuse that which Natura bids: whatever life you choose, it is crime or love.'

She neither consents nor refuses. Fears both. Chaste, she flees love; innocent, trembles to commit a crime. To compel her to decide I embrace her and kiss her; now my right hand gently enfolds her neck, my left her thigh. I lift the train of her dress, she struggles with words, with her hands, but though she resists I whisk her last covering away. Nothing remains but the knot of her thighs, I feel the flesh dissolving, that makes the senses almost fail. Her little bottom's quivering so you'd think her hips were soliciting, her breast is calm, the movement's all below. She so excites herself in trying to escape, the more I instil love within, the more I cull its joys without. What new silly idea!—as if one needed innocence as well as all this! How foolish she is to think she misses it!

H: B. Hauréau, *NE* I. 323 (lines 1–26 only).
6 H Athis   Achis—i.e. Acis (*v. Metam.* XIII. 750 ff.).
11 H Cerne, precor, quid sim, quid utrumque deceret
12 H quid sine teste
13 H quid virginibus
24 MS. levo
25 Cirma—i.e. syrma.

> Dum studeo,
>   dum solus eo,
>   tres cerno puellas.
>
> Opstupeo,
>   studioque meo
>   res addo novellas.

As I go alone, full of thoughts, I behold three girls. I marvel, and receive new matter for my thoughts.

Fragment or epigram?

We can find *tres puellas* in many places—in ballads, in popular songs (the most remarkable perhaps being 'Tres morillas me enamoran'—*v.* Julián Ribera, *La música de las Cantigas*, pp. 86 ff.), but also in the Greek Anthology (IX. 16), in the pseudo-Ovidian *De Tribus Puellis* (*Comédie*, II. 232 ff.), and in Dante's profound canzone 'Tre donne intorno al cor mi son venute'.

fol. 63ᵛ

> Thaydis in ceno
> tenuit mea vota Celeno,
>   que qu*asi* centeno
> me polluit ydra veneno.

5 Ictu me pleno
rapuit Venus, 'Huncque cateno'
 dixit. 'Sit leno,
sit amoris coctus aeno.
 Non Stige sed Reno
10 fluvio duceris ameno—
 non comes Alpeno,
nostroque fruere Caleno.'
 Sic dea terreno,
sic callida mentis egeno
15 prefuit, et ceno
pede me tulit absque sereno.
 Pardo sic Peno
par agnus, parque Ruteno
 Maurus, par Zeno
20 Bacuo, Mars*us* Cluvieno.
 Iam sua mens Heleno,
de sicco fit rosa feno.
 Iam bene me freno,
iam sum meus ex alieno.

Celaeno, who poisoned me like a hydra a hundredfold, held my desires bound in the mire of Thais. Venus caught hold of me with all her force. She said 'I am chaining this man. Let him be a debauchee, stewed in the brazen pot of love. You shall be led along a delightful river—not the Styx but the Rhine, not as in Alpinus' company; and you'll enjoy our wine.' So the goddess prevailed over the mortal, the crafty one over the weak-minded, and dragged me by the foot, not serenely, in the mire. Thus the lamb becomes like the Punic pard, the Blackamoor like the (blonde) Rutenian, Zeno like Bacchus, poet like poetaster. But now Helenus is returning to his senses, out of the dry grass a rose is born; now indeed I restrain myself, now I who was another am my own again.

1 Thaydis—*v. supra*, p. 496.
2 Celeno—i.e. Celaeno, the Harpy in *Aen.* III (211, 245, 365).
3 MS. Que que [R. M.]
 11 i.e., as Öberg notes, not like the turgid poet Alpinus (Horace, *Sat.* i. 10, 36 ff.).

12 Caleno—cf. Juvenal, I. 69.
17 ff. Images of 'the world upside down' (cf. Curtius, pp. 94 ff.).
18 Ruteno—cf. Lucan, I. 402.
19 Zeno—the founder of the Stoic school.
20 MS. Mars par   Cf. Walter Map, *De Nugis* IV. 2: 'Dormiat cum
Homero Maro, cum Catullo Marsus, vigilent et dictent Cherulus et Cluvienus.' Cluvienus is 'insipidus et ydiota scriptor' (ibid. I. 25, from Juvenal,
I. 80). Alternatively, 'Maro par Cluvieno' (communicated by D. Schaller).
21 Helenus—a metonymy for *vates*?

> Parce, Cupido!
>   lora tibi do,
>   me minus ure!
>
> Quo feror, o di?—
> 5   que prius odi
>   sunt mihi cure.
>
> Que probo, sperno,
>   que mihi cerno
>   noxia, quero:
>
> 10   Hunc gero morem,
>   qui timeo rem
>   quam fore spero.

Spare me, Lord Cupid! I'll give you the reins, but do not lash me
so! O gods, where am I being led? The things I hated once are now
my dearest care. What I approve I now despise, what I see will hurt
me I now seek. This is my way of life, mine who fear that which I
hope will come.

2–3 lora . . . ure—cf. Horace, *Epist.* I. 16, 47.
11 MS. q

fol. 66ʳ

> Si tibi sum cordi,   foveant tua fata precor dii.
>   Si spernor, stamen   sors tua rumpat! Amen!

If I am dear to you, may the gods cherish your destiny. If I am
spurned, may your fate break your life-thread! Amen!

814346.2   N

fols. 60ᵛ, 66ʳ

> Pauper amator agit risu verbisque iocosis;
> Nil quia nil habuit pauper amator agit.

The poor lover proceeds with a smile and amusing talk; because he has nothing, the poor lover proceeds to—nothing.

   2 MS. (fol. 66ʳ) Nil que nil tribuit

fol. 61ʳ

> Nescio quid sit amor, sed amoris sentio nodum;
> Hoc scio—si quis amat, nescit habere modum.

I do not know what love is, yet I feel love's knot; this I do know— if one loves, one does not know how to have measure.

For other, and expanded, versions of these lines in later MSS., cf. Walther 11740, 11741.

Oxford, Digby 53, fol. 11ᵛ   s. XII ex.

> Dulce malum Venus est, et opertum melle venenum,
> Viribus indomitos sepe iuvando domans.
> Ille minus peccat qui caute peccat, et ampla
> Est virtus vicium scire tacere suum.

Venus is a sweet hurt and a poison coated with honey, often taming those whose strength is untamed, by gratifying. Whoever sins circumspectly sins less, and it is virtue enough to know how to conceal one's vice.

1 These verses, above all the first line, come close to the 'definitions of love' referred to above, p. 491. They are written here as one poem, but should probably be read as two separate couplets: the second occurs alone in Oxford Bodley 570, fol. 120ʳ.

fol. 13ʳ

> Alteritas sexus quos alterat, unio mentis
>   Omniter unificans vix sinit esse duos.
> Sic duo non duo sunt, sic alter vivit utrumque,
>   Mortuus alteruter cogit utrumque mori.

Beyond the difference of sex, oneness of mind, bringing absolute union, scarcely allows (lovers) to be two. Thus two are not two, thus each lives both, and the death of either compels both to die.

fol. 13ᵛ

> Dulcis amica vale, sine te procul hinc habiturus
> Anxius abscedo, quia non cito sum rediturus.
> Non discedo tamen totus, remanet quia tecum
> Mens mea corque meum. Discedo vix ego mecum.

Sweet beloved, farewell. I must go far away without you; I depart full of care, for I cannot return soon. Yet I do not wholly depart, for my mind and my heart remain with you. I hardly take myself away at all.

fol. 15ᵛ

> In qua delectant   illam mea lumina spectant,
> Mente quod affecto   mentis quoque lumine specto.
> Qui †tenet omni te   vico ducunt oculi te,
> Lumina spectant te   quicumque loci teneant te;
> 5 In *me* ducent te   *que* lumina fixa vident te.

My eyes look upon her in whom they take delight, and the eye of my mind looks at my mind's affection. My eyes that fix on you in every street invite you, whatever places hold you, my eyes behold you; the unwavering eyes which see you will lead you into me.

3 tenet—*sic* MS. I cannot suggest a metrically possible correction.

5 MS. In te ducunt te vie   If my emendation is right, it is the neoplatonic image of the beloved 'contracted' into the eyes of her lover.

Dr. A. C. Friend (*Med. Studies*, xvi (1954), 215) printed an even more awkward text of this from Dublin Trin. B. 3. 5, s. xv, fol. 273ᵛ, with the English verse epigraph 'Euir is min eye i þe wode leie' (cf. *Ancrene Wisse*, EETS, p. 52): 1 In quam, illic; 2 quo lumine; 3 omitted; 5 In te ducente me lumina fixa vidente te.

SAPIENTIAL VERSE★

Paris, B.N. lat. 3110, fol. 63ᵛ   s. XI ex.

Mater materne   rationis, adesto superne!
Matrem devote   filius audio te.
    Ecce, lyram recit*o*:

Quantum gauderet   si se semel ire deceret
5 Imantop*o*da gens,   poplitibus peragens
    Cursus retrograda—

A*l*ysinus quantum   miratur flumine cantum,
Aut antropophagus   quam cupit or*e* vagus
    Cognato pasci—

10 Quam gaudetque mori   cui mors est mixta sopori
Postquam dens hip*n*ale   †fixit amara male,†
    Vulnera seminet ei—

Gressibus innatis   quam *s*cenopoda quoque latis
Et quam ventilabris   alce popella labris
15   Congaudet paribus—

Quam letusque bonus   solet hic fons esse Gelonus
Cum replet haut gravidas   aut relevet gravidas
    Germine feminulas—

Corvus quam gaudet   quia solus ab omnibus audet
20 Seva camelonis   ferre venena bonis
    Unguibus incolomis—

★The four poems in this section illustrate some further ranges of the 'Sapiential' language discussed in Chaps. II and V, pp. 87, 268 ff. The first poem uses an invocation to Sapientia for a brilliant burlesque. The next is a variation on the Song of Songs, an epithalamium for the wedding of Christus and Ecclesia (perhaps liturgically for the anniversary of the dedication of a church). The third is a scholar's invocation to the Boethian Philosophia, who already in the *Consolatio* has certain obvious affinities to the lover's 'sovereign lady'. The last, from the same manuscript, shows an attempt to transform a secular love-poem into a sacred one.

Tam sum gavisus,　　isto michi tempore visus,
　Propter quod merui　　dogmatis, alma, tui
　　Pocula melliflua.

Mother of mother-wit, be present on high! I, your son, hear you devoutly, mother. See, I recite my canticle:

As greatly as the bandy-legged tribe would rejoice if for once it were able to walk, the Himantopodoi marching backwards on their knees—

As much as the Alisian marvels at the song in the river, as much as the wandering anthropophage longs to chew his blood-relative—

And as he rejoices to die whose death is mingled with drowsiness, because the Hypnalian tooth †has brought about bitter woe (and)† inflicts wounds upon him—

As the tent-foot man rejoices when (the power to take) huge steps is born, and as a little herd of elk rejoice when their lips (that flap like) winnowing-fans are of equal size—

As the Gelonian fountain is wont to be joyous and good as it fills girls who aren't pregnant, or relieves the pregnant of their seed—

As the crow rejoices because he alone dares to endure the chameleon's savage poison, undamaged to the tips of his fine claws—

So I rejoiced at this time, bountiful one, because I seemed to deserve the honey-dropping goblets of your doctrine.

3 MS. recita　　lyram—Alcuin, citing *Prov.* IX. 1, interpreted the seven columns of Sapientia's dwelling as the seven Liberal Arts. Martianus Capella had fixed their number at seven when making them Philologia's bridesmaids. It is probably more than coincidence that here the invocation to Sapientia, the *lyra*, is a sevenfold one, in seven stanzas.

5 MS. imantopada　Cf. the pseudo-Ovidian *De Mirabilibus Mundi* (ed. M. R. James, *Essays and Studies presented to William Ridgeway* (Cambridge, 1913), pp. 290 ff.) 16: Hymantopoda—

　　　　Hoc genus ire nequit,　　sed flexo *poplite* repit.

Also (verbally less close) Pliny, *Nat. Hist.* v. 46; Solinus, *Coll.* 31; Martianus Capella, *De Nupt.* 674.

6 Corr. retrogrados? [R. M.]

7 MS. Artysinus (by confusion with Pliny's description, v. 142, of the stream that rises 'in stagno Artynia'?)　Cf. *De M.M.* 41–42: Tibicen, fons Alisinus—

　　　　Hic fons pauper aquis　　cum perflat tibia flabris
　　　　Admirans odas　　transcendit litoris oras.

and (verbally less close) Solinus 5.

8 antropophagus—cf. Pliny, VII. 12, Solinus 15, *De M.M.* 17–18. MS. ora

11 MS. hiphale Cf. *De M.M.* 80–81: Hypnale—

> Hec stirps serpentis   quem ledit acumine dentis
> Illi dulce *mori*,   quia *mors est mixta sopori.*

Solinus (27) claims that Cleopatra was sent into her death-sleep by an *hypnale*.

13 MS. cenopodas Cf. *De M.M.* 85: Scenopoda—

> Hic pedis obiectu   sese defendit ab estu.

14 alce—cf. Pliny, VIII. 39: 'alcen iuvenco similem . . . labrum ei superius pergrande'. Also Solinus 20, and (this time less relevant) *De M.M.* 70–71.

16–18 Cf. *De M.M.* 57–58: Fons gelonius—

> Exstat huic liquido   diversa potentia rivo;
> Nam steriles gravidat,   fecundas *germine* privat.

Also Solinus 5 (two different fountains, not one).

19–21 Cf. *De M.M.* 82–84: Cameleon, Corvus, Laurus—

> Extimuere meum   volucresque fereque *venenum*
> Sed *corvo soli*   cessit victoria nostri,
> Cui contra virus   prestat medicamina laurus.

Also Pliny, VIII. 101, Solinus 40 (*corax*, not *corvus*).

In the MS., the poem is written in stanzas. The form, a leonine elegiac couplet followed by an hemiepes, is one I have not found elsewhere. Seven of the lines have a marginal gloss, and the first three stanzas interlinear notes. Unfortunately neither notes nor glosses are the slightest help towards a commentary.

The poem is a comic fantasia upon 'encyclopedic' knowledge, with particular reference, it seems, to the *De Mirabilibus Mundi*, with which it has a number of words (including half a line) in common. These words do not occur in the parallel passages in Pliny or Solinus, or in the late eleventh-century adaptation of Solinus by Thierry of Saint-Trond (v. *Latomus* VI. 363), which must be at least a little younger than the cycle of Sapiential verse in B.N. lat. 3110. I have italicized the verbal coincidences with the *De M.M.* in my quotations.

Cambridge, Trinity B. I. 16, fol. 2ʳ   s. XII

1a [E]pithalamia
decantans dulcia,

1b Chorus hic canticis
assit in musicis.

2a Cristus factus hodie
sponsus est Ecclesie,
cuius flagrans pignore
clamat omni tempore:

2b 'Oris sui osculo
delectari cupio!
Removeri nequeo
hoc a desiderio.

3a 'Eius nomen itaque
       redolet ut oleum,

3b 'Omne pellit citius
       quod latet vipereum.

4a 'Vos adolescentule,
       mecum concinite!

4b 'Cui coniungi cupio
       hunc et diligite!

5a 'Quamvis nigra videar
       solis ex ardoribus,
     sum formosa variis
       virtutum coloribus.

5b 'Filie Iherusalem,
       fulcite me floribus
     Et stipate languidam
       pomorum odoribus!

6a 'Languor hic donat
                ardorem,

6b 'Ardor incendit amorem.

7a 'Dilectus meus candidus,
       elegi quem ex milibus,

7b 'Armillis me splendificat
       perpulcris et monilibus.

8a 'Luce fruor gaudio,
       noctibus suspirio;

8b 'Mesta que sum tenebris
       luce fio celebris.

9a 'En per montes saliens
       et colles transiliens

9b 'Venit quem optaveram,
       michi loqui cupiens.

10a 'Per fenestras et cancellos

       me videre voluit;

10b 'Ad contactum manus
                          sue
       venter meus tremuit.

11a 'Vox dilecti sonuit,
       favo michi dulcior,

11b 'Cuius sole facies
       est claro preclarior:

12a ' "Columba mea nitida,
       amica mea splendida,

12b ' "Surge! veni! propera!
       postponendo vetera.

13a ' "Gressus tui quam sunt
                          pulchri,
       principis o filia!
     Violarum flores pulchros
       excedis et lilia.

13b ' "Sponsa mea, veni, veni,

       surge, veni, propera!
     Inber abit et recedit,
       cedit hiemps aspera.

14a ' "Tibi dabo munera—   14b ' "Mecum tanges
                                        ethera!" '

Let the dancers come with their tuneful songs, sweetly singing
epithalamia.

Today Christ is made the bridegroom of Ecclesia, and constantly
she, perfumed by his promise, cries: 'I long for the delight of the
kiss of his mouth, I cannot be shaken from this desire.

'His name indeed has a scent like oil, swiftly it drives out all that
hides serpent-like.

'Sing with me, all you maidens! Love him too, him to whom I
long to be joined!

'Though I seem dark because of the sun's blaze, in the many colours
of perfections 1 am fair. You daughters of Jerusalem, rest me on
flowers, fill my languor with apple-scents.

'Here languor begets passion, and passion kindles love.

'My shining lover, whom I chose from thousands, makes me
resplendent with bracelets and the loveliest necklaces.

'By day I take joy, by night I sigh; I who am sad in the dark in
the light become renowned.

'Look! he whom I'd been wanting so is bounding over moun-
tains, leaping over hills, longing to speak to me.

'He wanted to see me through windows, through railings; my
womb trembled at the touch of his hand.

'The voice of my lover rang out, sweeter than honey to me, his
face was brighter than the bright sun itself:

' "My shining dove, my resplendent beloved, arise! come, make
haste! leave all that's old behind.

' "How lovely is your walk, my king's daughter—you are fairer
than violet-blossoms and lilies. Come, my bride, come rise, come
swiftly! The shower has passed and gone, harsh winter is departing.

' "I shall requite you—with me you will touch heaven!" '

13a. 4 excedis—ex (et?) deleted, almost illegible.
14b tanges—reading not wholly certain.

München, Clm 19411, fol. 68ᵛ   s. XII–XIII

Nobilis, apta, pia,   semper letare, Sophia!
Floribus ornaris;   mea nunc ancilla vocaris.

'Hinc acus et fusus   nostros habeatur in usus—
Hoc tibi commendo,   tibi mando precipiendo.'

·5 Multiplici laude,   dominarum gloria, gaude!
Digne laudaris—   merito Comitissa vocaris.
Tu formosa satis,   speculum tu nobilitatis.

Noble, benign, and virtuous one, Sophia, may you always be in joy! You are decked with flowers; now I call you my helpmate. 'Then use your needle and spindle to my advantage—this I commend to you, I trust you with this commitment.' Most glorious mistress, rejoice in endless praise! Praise you deserve—it behoves that I call you my Countess. You are excellently fair, you are the mirror of nobility.

3 Cf. Boethius, *Cons.* I. pr. 1: 'Vestes . . . suis manibus ipsa texuerat.'
6 MS. coma.

fol. 70ᵛ

Ad dei genitricem Mariam

Instar solis, ave!   tocius luminis atque—
Ut flos cum lauro,   sicut christallus in auro,
Sic luces forte   mulierum sola cohorte.
Sol superat lunam,   mulierum tuque figuram.
·5 Hinc tuus aspectus   succendit denique pectus
Sic in amore tuo,   quod nil intendere curo
Preter te solam,   *post Christum patris Sophiam.*
Corpore nunc absum,   tibi sensu sedulus assum;
Non vetat hora cibi   me sepe tui reminisci.
10 Hoc tacitus dicam   quando considero vitam:
'Eia! si nobis   iam iam locus esset amoris!'
Optans gaudebo,   sed quod nequit esse dolebo.

Hail, image of the sun and of all light! Like a flower in the midst of laurel, like a crystal set in gold, you alone shed radiant light among a legion of women. Sun surpasses moon—and you surpass woman's form. Indeed your presence so inflames my heart with love that I cannot aspire to any but you, *you who after Christ are the Sophia of the Father.* I am not with you now in body, yet in my senses with you ardently; even in the moment of eating I often think of you. When I contemplate life I shall say silently, 'Ah if only this moment we had a place for love!' In desiring it I shall take joy— and grieve for what cannot be.

Title: added in the margin, by a fourteenth-century hand.

7 The original second half of this line has been deleted, and these words added by the fourteenth-century hand.

8 MS. Corpore nunc assum   Marginal note in the fourteenth-century hand: *scilicet in celo*.

10 MS. Hac

11 Marginal note in the fourteenth-century hand: *scilicet in celo*.

12 MS. (superscript) probably f; The fourteenth century-hand adds 'Ubere multarum etc. vide in proxima columpna': this is the poem ed. *supra* p. 463. It begins with a large capital. Unlike H. Plechl (*Deutsches Archiv*, XVIII. 497), I am convinced this poem was never a continuation of 'Instar solis, ave'.

Lines 1–4 and 8 (reading correctly 'Corpore nunc absum') occur also in Zürich C 58/275, s. XII, fol. 6ʳ (Werner, p. 27), followed by some wholly unrelated unrhymed elegiac couplets, which Werner printed as a part of the same poem. The twelve verses as they stand in Clm 19411 are remarkable for their evidence of censorship and 'emendation' in the fourteenth century. By adding a pious title, deleting and rewriting only one half-line, and supplying two crude marginal glosses, the censor has 'spiritualized' the poem. Sacred or profane, the language of love can at times remain virtually a constant (*v.* Chap. II, pp. 58 ff.).

NARRATIVES

Quando tellus renovatur
in aprilis tempore
Lacrimarum pane satur
sedebam sub arbore;
5 Ibi corpus refovebam
spoliatum robore,
Sed in mente mea flebam
manens sine Nestore.

Dum hac cruce cruciarer,
10   repellens accidiam
Ut me solum consolarer
assunsi materiam.
Deus ori det virtutem
ponatque custodiam,
15 Ut lectoris ad salutem
opus hoc perficiam. Amen.

Rex insignis et famosus
erat in Yspania,
Cunctis bonis copiosus,
20   magna pollens gloria.
Sed que mundum interfecit
serpentis invidia
In cor huius telum iecit
incendens precordia.

25 Totus sue rex ardebat
in amore filie,
Nec iam color apparebat
in amantis facie:

Foris corpus egrotabat
30   tenuatum macie,
Et mens intus vigilabat
   rei tam nefarie.

Sed quid moror? Excecatur
   et potitur virgine,
35 Cuius alvus inpregnatur
   inmundo genimine.
Hoc ut pater intuetur,
   privatur solamine,
Timens ne diffamaretur
40   pro tam turpi crimine.

Mentem suam rex dolebat,
   horum memor scelerum,
Et singultus emittebat,
   inculcans 'me miserum!'
45 Contra natam cogitavit
   grande nefas iterum,
Nam post partum imperavit
   absorberi puerum.

Tamen nato suo mater
50   natura compatitur,
Et quod sibi dedit pater
   mandatum transgreditur.
Iussu suo purpuratus
   in vase reponitur

· · · · ·

In April, at the time the earth is renewed, I was sitting beneath a tree, sated with the bread of tears; I was comforting my body, deprived of strength, but weeping inwardly, being masterless.

Tormented by this cross, to drive away listlessness, I took up a subject to console me in my loneliness. May God give my lips the strength (to speak), may he watch over me that I may complete this work to the reader's profit. Amen.

Once there was a most distinguished king in Spain, abounding in all good things, possessing great glory. But the serpent whose envy ruined the world assailed his heart and set his breast afire with a shaft.

The king was all ablaze with love for his daughter. There was no longer any colour in the lover's face: his body, lean and hungry, wasted away, and the mind within was scheming so infamous a deed.

In short, the king is blinded and possesses the girl. In her womb she conceives a sullied child. As the father sees this, he is comfortless, fearing to be disgraced by such a wicked act;

he is afflicted at his own state of mind, constantly recalling his misdeeds, and he sobs, stifling the cry 'Unhappy that I am!' Once more he contemplates a great wrong towards his daughter—he commands the little boy to be drowned after his birth.

Yet by nature a mother has compassion on her son; she disobeys her father's command. At her bidding (the child), wrapped in purple, is placed in a vessel. . . .

3 Cf. *Psal.* LXXIX. 6, XLI. 4.

The motif of a king's daughter wronged by incest has many ramifications. The stories where the incest between father and daughter actually takes place, and a son is born and exposed, include the ancient story of Thyestes and his daughter Pelopia (Hyginus, *Fab.* 87) and the medieval Italian *Leggenda di Vergogna* (ed. A. D'Ancona, Bologna, 1869). In this type of story, to which the present fragment seems to belong, the interest is soon transferred to the destiny of the son, who always finds a rescuer. (Compare also the Gregorius legend, on which Hartmann von Aue based his romance —though there the boy's parents are brother and sister.) In another type of story (including the *Vitae duorum Offarum*, *La belle Hélène*, and *Émaré*) the daughter resists incest and her father exiles or attempts to kill her. Here the interest centres on the daughter and her adventures. This type of story has been studied in detail, most comprehensively by Margaret Schlauch (*Chaucer's Constance and Accused Queens*, New York, 1927). Other important versions of the incest between father and daughter include the Biblical story of the daughters of Lot (*Gen.* XIX. 31 ff.) and the Ovidian one of Cinyras and Myrrha (*Metam.* X. 298 ff.), in each of which it is the father who is seduced, and the opening episode of the *Apollonius*. The fragment printed above is remarkable as the only surviving testimony of stanzaic romances in Medieval Latin.

Escorial T. II. 16, fols. 68ᵛ–73ʳ   s. XV.

    [C]antica conponam nunc in me tristia narrans:
    Sum sic convictus quod psallere suficit arti.
    Per longum tempus sum de correntibus unus,
    Amplius vulnera porto, lassus plurima sperno.
5   Numquid vilius extat?—[quo] modo decipit ignis,
    Semper spernunt sidera parte dulciter acta.
    [O]mnia quidem videns pro nunc flebilis exto
    Dictando iam carmina; factis turpiter ago.
    O deus, actor Veneris artis, suscipe laudem.
10 Quomodo fugit gloria! leto cecidit a me.
    En ego qui fueram sic tunc peramantibus esca
    Obvior in campestribus; ergo plangite mecum!
    Amor dissipat, irruit, destruit org[a]na cordis
    Et lassat multum miseros in delectione prava.
15 Ergo parcens tu michi, Veneris accipe laudem,
    Et placeat tibi, lingua, pro nunc gaudia ferre.

    [D]umque talia intra me vaticinarem, propter solis radiorum exclusionem, occuli mei quasi erant [. . .] palpebreque mee super ocellos cadentes; non eram valens somnolentis resistere
20 voluntati. Dum vero recitarem, in sompnis vidi regem quendam miriffice adornatum, coronam auream abentem in quapite et torques in collo, et in pectore margaritam splendentem tenebat. Erat etenim digniter indutus, preciossisimus vestibus ad modum magni regis. Forma autem faciei et aspectus erat pulcerima
25 multum nimis. Titulum vero in manu dextera tenebat, scriptum literis hec aureys continentem: 'Omnes amatores, venite ad me et reficiam vos.' In pectore namque erat scriptum:

'Deus sum amoris'; et vertens dulciter occulos suos erga me
ayt:

30   '[Q]uid me clamas, tu puer? En ego dulcia mitam.
          Sum deus enim Veneris, illum concitas ardens.'

[Ga]udio quidem hiis audit*is* repletus tam cito ipse fui,
quoniam meis nunciatum fuit corporis potenciis habere
iudicem veritatis, qui omnia michi eventa in hiis verbis fin*ita*
35 som*ni*avi.

          '[S]peciosus multum, iam tibi nunc famulus sum!
          Si tua nobilitas michi petita dederit ante—
          Candida cum rubra fuit—et nunc virgo puella
          Dulciter hec capta fuit a me. Carmina mitens
40   †Crucior hic, me totus cum sit ca[n]didus Amor
          Inspiciens.† Morior desertus sor*dibus* ist*is*
          En ego, cum nunc video malos pessima dantes,
          Cantica psallentes factis mis opprobriorum.
          Consilium mihi, tu deus adhuc Veneris abtus,
45   Ut possim vindictam ducere fortiter illi*s*!'

'[Q]uid est,' ayt ille, 'de quo dicis terribiles hos sermones?
Numquid si malum pro malo reddideris laborum tuorum
accipies porcionem? Et dic, que est causa meroris tui? Perdidisti
amasiam tuam.—Quid me vocas? Aud quid responde[s]? Si
50 enim perdidisti, letare, quoniam tot tibi tamque dabit formosas
Roma puellas. Hec habet, ut dicas, quidquid in orbe fuit. Si
autem tantummodo Didimus, epistolam ordina illi, narrando
omnia nece tui. Ero insuper paranimphus.' Tunc ego certe:

          '[C]artula componet pro nunc narrando puelle
55   Ut minuat iam penas detque solacia luce.'

Cum debito honore ac reverencia, flexis genibus perorando,
Sue domine humiliter porrigantur:

[O] dulcis domina, precantis gretissima, si ego dulius
tuus studi*am* armariol*um* inveni*en*di, in alico non haberem
60 ocupatum preterquam in te. Aduc, gretissima, pulcritudin*i* tue

nequirem aliquam ferre comparacionem, quoniam dum re-
spicio aut respicere volo formam venustis[sime] tue faciei,
occuli mei obscurantur pre fulgore et claritate. Splendens
margarita es, velut Lucifer matutinus. Corde nitido—diu est—
65 te servivi absque versura falerata. Verumtamen nunquam votis
meis assentire voluisti. At ubi temporis advenit plenitudo, et
omnino me remisisti, et accepisti quos volebant te sed sperne-
bant: super hoc, soror, doleo, quoniam brevis est fama tua.
Responde nunc similiter colloquiis dulcirrosis.

70   [C]um vidisset, clamans ista iuvencula plancxit,
    Vilia cantans, prorrumpens in lacrimas ayt:
    'Omnibus est stulticia ferre iuvenibus hostem—
    Cespitat in planis mulier nunc gaudia sculpans.
    Verumtamen ducam pro nunc aspera verba
75   Et notum faciam tibi quod tu cautius ibis.'

    Suo preterito dilecto conferantur:

    Cape, iuvenis, de prudencia que apud te in tuo videtur esse
corpore perorata. Numquid in vulgari dicitur quod fatua est
mulier vere que puerum vult amare, et Facetus: 'Queque fiant
80 suo tempore. . .'? Tu autem dicta istorum sprevisti. Consilium
igitur tibi do quod mihi d[e] cetero nichil dicas. Nam 'Qui
propria culpa sibi placidam perdit amicam, perpetuo doleat sui
rusticitate'—hoc Facetus. Ego modo alios habeo amatores, quos
diligo plus quam te. Scito igitur te in vanum laborasse. Frustra
85 baccaris. Que poteris adversum me cogita mala omni tempore.

    [N]unc ego clamans iam suspiria misi,
    Respondendo vili cernens talia scripsi:

    Sue noverce porrigantur:

    [N]on tua miretur cordis cogitatio, si tibi non mitto [. . .]
quoniam nequeo illas dare; me namque omnino pretexti tu
privasti. Fuisti semper in scrinio mei cordis, per speculum in
enigmate figurata. Scis namque quod vias tuas sequebar
languens, pertorridus et estuatus; dapibus quoque et poculis

dum tuam faciem contemplabam satiabar. Eras michi sola
95 virgo. Nunc vero facta es duplex. Attende iterum et audi!
Michi unica eras, sed omnino renuisti: dixisti enim 'Non ego
cum uno sed cum pluribus esse volo.' Et sic fornicata es cum
amatoribus multis. Servivi enim tibi, et pro mercede me dimi-
sisti. Parce, parce, parce! Satis me vides consternatum. Finem
100 habeat ira tua. Veni ad me et adhuc suscipiam te. Responsum
tribue, ut curentur vulnera mei cordis.

Suo hosti presententur:

[B]one iuvenis, tuam noviter legi cartulam ex parte tui michi
missam, et video quod tu me ganeam extimas et corruptam.
105 Votum autem tuum ignoro. Sed si est ideo, quia tua non
sum facis et dicis que in te occultantur. Numquid quia votis
tuis assensum non dedi omnia ista sunt in me que dixisti?
Absit. Sed animadverte, quoniam si tenuisses consilium summi
magistri in hac arte Ovidii, necnon et Faceti, tua nunch forem.
110 Ex quibus infero aporisma, quod dignus es nomen amatoris
totaliter perdere sine mora, neque dignus es in eorum consilio
introduci, quoniam nisi habeat *sua*sorium modum, nulli con-
venit commisceri in numero amatorum. Attende igitur et
audi: quia tu mecum multociens fuisti solus, et nunquam que,
115 ut dicis, cupiebas accipere voluisti—propter quod existimavi te
meum non esse philocaptum, sed poscius exploratorem. Ego
autem iuvenem trementem sperno, sed virum audacem per-
quiro. Dic enim Veneri quod tibi faciat iusticiam competentem,
non enim timeo illum. Captet que potue*r*it iam directe—sui
120 enim non sum iuris; si sic, appello Iovem. Tu autem confortare,
et esto robustus. Satis, satis, satis de me habuisti et possedisti!
Finem igitur ducendo nostris colloquiis, Venus [vel] quem fore
dicis deum amoris respondeat nostre littere.

[G]audio non repletus, tunc ego corpore nudo,
125 Sed prorumpens Veneri talia lacrimas ay[o]:
†'Veneris in quid es tu regens omnia corda?†
Nobilis et prudens es, dasque iuvenibus artem;

Audias, ergo, precor: cantans dulcia verba
Et dominam properans duc pulcras cedulas illi.'

130 Peracta quidem suplicacione, Rex ille Veneris est ista *con-victus* oda: 'Video enim te iuvenem adolescentem impuberem istius artis et lactantem, ideo compasciens te dulciter protegam et deffendam. Indignatio mea erit super illam. Stulte se habuit ac locuta est adversum te, atque malum fecit omni tempore.

135 'Primitus enim ducam verbum pessime tue,
Corripiendo nece mitam pessima verba:

'Pro salute *sint* tibi dolores, quoniam lingua tua sagitta vulnerans et archus versucie, qui videtur mittere lanceas toxicatas adversus fratrem suum. Tu autem inique operata es,
140 et ocellos tui clientuli fecisti in lacrimas prorumpere amarissi-mas. Idcirco quia iniuste hoc egisti, dolor tuus erit super dolorem suum cunctis diebus vite tue. Meos etenim sprevisti sermones absque deliberacione, et dixisti "Non tantum unum sed plures quero", et sic pelix facta es super illos. Ubi est
145 virginitas tua? Ecce dies veniunt, et dicent "Ista est fatua que sprevit deprecacionem pauperis!" Propter omnia ista et †quia appellans es mel†, indignacio mea erit super te in brevi tem-pore. Omnes autem amatores tui longe ducam a te ach tribulabo, et proiciam te de rota cum ipsis *in* inferiorem partem, preter
150 istum, cui dabo munera magna, quoniam vere et fideliter te amavit. Dabo namque ei virginem gratissimam atque pulcram.'

Tamcito in terram postrans mea ienua iunxi,
Et sic dignas laudes tancito cum suis egi:
'Gracias in primis tibi viribus offero cordis,
155 Venus—de te fingam dulcia carmina modo.'

Post autem gratiarum actiones ecce a sompno fui subito excitatus. Iam enim *Titan* suos rubiculos sparserat radios per montium cacumina altiora. Et quasi stupefactus cecidi super faciem meam rigando omnia mea lacrimis fluctuosis,
160 maxime cum animadverterem verba comeat*oris*. Sed confisus de promissione, me surgente a terra, finem dedi gemitibus et

suspiriis. Demum autem gratias et laudes summo deo vero filioque unigenito suo atque spiritui sancto optuli prout decet.

> I'll now compose a song telling all my grief—
> I am so overcome, I can do no more than sing.
> For a long time I've been one who runs the race,
> Wounded more than the rest, yet too worn-out to care.
> What else is humbled so? How ever love's fire deceives,
> The stars' contempt remains when the sweet part is done.
> Seeing it all, I stand at this moment in tears
> Making my song—though my part's an unworthy one.
> O God, mover of Venus' art, accept my praise.
> How has the glory fled?—fallen from me who had joy.
> I who had known joy have become a decoy for lovers,
> Exposed in the open fields; lament with me!
> Love ravages, overwhelms, breaks the heart's mechanism,
> And greatly wearies men grown wretched in abandon.
> But spare me, Love—receive my praise of love;
> Now force yourself, my tongue, to tell its joys!

While I spoke such verses to myself, because the sun's rays had darkened, my eyes were like [. . .] and my eyelids falling over my eyes—I had no power to resist the will to sleep. And indeed, even while I read aloud, in dreams I beheld a king who was adorned wondrously, wearing a golden crown on his head, torques about his neck, and a resplendent pearl upon his breast. He was admirably dressed, most precious in his clothes, in the manner of a great king. The look of his face and bearing was beautiful to excess. In his right hand he held a scroll written in golden letters, saying 'Come to me, all you who are lovers, and I will refresh you.' On his breast was written 'I am the god of love.' Gently turning his eyes to me he said:

> 'My child, why do you call me? I'll give you all that's sweet.
> I am the god of Love; you rouse him by your passion.'

When I heard this I was at once filled with joy, because my faculties perceived I would have a judge of truth, I who dreamed that in these words all that had befallen me was at an end.

> 'Beautiful one, I shall serve you from this moment!
> If your noble nature had granted my wish before—

She was red and white—and now this innocent girl
Has deftly been taken from me. Sending my songs
I torment †myself here, though an all-radiant Love
Looks on.† Abandoned in this vile state I die,
I die, seeing myself injured by wicked men
Who make up songs in mockery of my love.
Lend me your counsel now, shrewd god of Love—
That I may take my fill of revenge on them!'

'What do you mean by saying such terrible things?' he replied.
'If you render evil for evil, will you not be requited for your deeds?
Tell me, what is the real cause of your grief? You have lost your
beloved.—Why are you calling me? Can you not answer? If you
have lost her, cheer up: Rome will give you many girls who are just
as pretty. Rome, you will admit, has all that the world can show.
But if you're such a Doubting Thomas, write her a letter, telling her
every phase in your undoing. What's more, I'll be your second.'
Then at last I said:

'A letter shall make peace between us, telling my love
To cause me less anguish, to solace me in the light.'

With due honour and reverence, imploring on bended knee,
(your servant) offers these words humbly—to his lady:

Sweet lady, most beloved of him who beseeches you, if I your
slave were to ransack imagination's treasure-chest, I should find
nothing, nothing but you. Even now, most beloved, I could make
no comparison to your beauty, for when I look, or want to look, at
the loveliness of your face, my eyes are darkened by its flashing
radiance. You are a resplendent pearl, you are like the Lucifer of the
dawn. I have long served you with shining heart, not with vain
twirling flourishes. Yet you never wanted to accept my dedication.
But when the fullness of time came, and you dismissed me entirely,
and received those who desired you but really despised you—this is
what I grieve over, beloved, because your reputation is short-lived.
Now give me a fitting answer, with your fragrant speech.

When she saw this, the girl cried out, lamented,
Sang out base injuries, burst into tears, then said:
'It's foolish to make enemies of all young men—

A woman bent on joy can trip even on level ground.
And yet for the moment I shall use harsh words
To show you that you must walk more warily.'

To her former lover:

Get back some sense, young man—judging by your words, there's
none left in your body. Isn't there a popular saying that a woman is
silly to love a mere boy? Doesn't Facetus say 'Let each thing be
done in its due time . . .' You have taken no notice of such words,
so I advise you to say nothing more. And as Facetus says, 'Whoever
loses a gentle beloved through his own fault, may he suffer no end
for his own churlishness!' I have other lovers now, whom I love
better than you. Then know that you have laboured in vain—your
raving is useless. Think of me as badly as you can whenever you like.

       Then it was I who cried out and sighed.
       I decided to write, answering that wretched one,

To his beldam:

Let your heart's thought not wonder if I do not send you [gentle
words], for I cannot give them: you have utterly deprived me of
such a pretext. You were always in my heart's casket, figured by
a glass, darkly. Indeed you know that wherever you went I followed
languishing, ablaze with love and scorched. Even at banquets, when
over the glasses I beheld your face, I was filled to the brim. You
were my only love. Now you are full of duplicity. Hear me out
once more! You were my one-and-only, but you resisted this out-
right. You said 'I want to be with many, not with one.' And so you
played the wanton with a host of lovers. I served you, and as my
reward you dismissed me. Spare, spare, spare me! You see my panic
—don't be angry any more. Come to me and even now I'll take
you back. Give me an answer, that the wounds of my heart may
be healed.

To her enemy:

My dear lad, I have just read the letter you sent, and see you think
me debauched and corrupt. But I take no notice of your protesta-
tions. If that is so, it is because I am not yours that you unleash these
things that you kept hidden. Isn't it because I have not consented

that I am all the things you say? No more of that. But remember this: if you had taken the advice of Ovid, the highest authority in this art, and of Facetus, I should now be yours. From all this I draw the conclusion that forthwith you should be wholly deprived of the name of lover, for you are not worthy to enter their conclave. No one can rightly join the society of lovers unless he has a persuasive manner. Now listen carefully. Because you were so often alone with me and yet never wanted to receive the favour for which you say you longed—because of this I thought you were no passionate lover, only an 'explorer'. I can't respect a trembling boy— I need a man who'll dare. Tell Love to give you the justice you deserve—I'm not afraid of him. Let him lay hands on what he can—I am not his subject; I call on Jove to say if this is so. As for you, take comfort and be strong. You've had and possessed enough of me—enough, enough, enough! To make an end to our exchanges, may Venus [or] he whom you call the god of Love answer my letter.

Joyless, naked, shedding tears I then said to Love
'†To what purpose do you rule over all hearts Venus claims†?'
You are noble and wise, you give the young love's skill,
Then hear me, I beseech you: with your sweet songs
Go swiftly to my lady, bring her fair messages!'

When my plea was done, the king of Love was won over by my song. 'I see you are still very young, an unweaned child in the art of love, so I shall take pity on you and with all gentleness protect you and defend you. My anger will descend on her. She has behaved and spoken foolishly to you, and done wrong continually.

'First I shall have a word with your cruellest one,
Cruellest words, to chastise her mortally.

'May sorrows be your greeting, because your tongue is a wounding arrow and a bow of cunning that seems to let poisoned shafts fly at its brother. You have done a shameful thing, and you have made the eyes of your devotee burst into bitterest tears. Because you have done this unjustly, your grief will be greater than his all the days of your life. Heedlessly you scorned my pronouncements, saying "I want many men, not just one", and so you prostituted yourself to them. Where is your innocence? Behold, the days are coming when men will say, "She is that vain creature who spurned the prayers of a poor man". Because of all this, and because †you are a pleasure-seeker,† my anger will descend on you before long. I shall lead all your lovers far away from you and plague them, and fling you from the wheel into a lower region, and your lovers too, except for this one, whom I shall give great rewards, because he loved you faithfully and truly. I shall give him a most lovable, beautiful girl.'

> At once I fell to the ground and knelt.
> At once with his devotees I sang his praise:
> 'With all the strength of my heart I give you thanks—
> Love, I'll now write of you, make songs of joy.'

But after this thanksgiving I was suddenly roused from sleep. Titan had already touched the higher mountain-tops with his red spray of light. And as if in a stupor I fell on my face, shedding torrents of tears all about me, above all when I thought of the words of my messenger. But trusting in his promise I arose and made an end of sighs and groans. Then at last I offered thanks and praise to the highest, true God, and to his only-begotten Son, and to the Holy Spirit, as is right.

The MS. distinguishes the verse passages from the prose. The text is often badly corrupt, and there are many eccentricities of spelling. In the verse passages more than half of the fifty hexameters are in some way metrically irregular. Though certain passages remain unsatisfactory, I have emended as little as possible. For the present I wish only to draw attention to this unusual text—an edition with full discussion must follow later.

5 MS. deci[p] . . . . . . decipit

11 MS. ergo

17 [D]umque . . . vaticinarem—this is written as the last line of verse, but (unless corrupt) belongs to the prose section.

18 MS. que me super

23 Corr. preciosissimis?

24 MS. (probably) faciey, pulyerima

26 Cf. *Matt.* XI. 28. As in 'Si linguis angelicis', the Biblical echoes here and later cannot be adequately described as parodistic or ironic (cf. my discussion in Chap. V, p. 318).

28 MS. dulcitur

31 illum concitas ardens—i.e. by your passionate complaints you move the god to help you. Corr. ill*am* conci*tus* ardens ('when stirred, I make Love blaze') would be metrically preferable.

32 MS. auditos

34 MS. finito sominavi [R. M.]

37–38 Is the broken speech deliberate, or is a line missing here?

41 MS. sorbidus ista

44 abtus—for *aptus*? Corr. *aptes*? *optes*? Or read *adduc* for *adhuc*?

45 MS. illi

47 Cf. 1 *Thes.* v. 15; *Rom.* XII. 17; 1 *Pet.* III. 9 etc.

50–51 Ovid, *A.A.* I. 55–56.

52 Corr. didimas? Du Cange gives *didimare* (=dubitare).

56 MS. honorore

58 MS. letter(s) before *precantis* doubtful; possibly a deletion.

59 MS. studium armorioli invenientis (or possibly, *mee mentis*).

60 MS. pulcritudine

62 MS. venustis, (probably) faciey.

64 Lucifer matutinus—the phrase occurs in the Roman liturgy, Sabbato Sancto, *Praefatio.*

66 MS. Sed at   Cf. *Galat.* IV. 4.

69 MS. silit3 [R. M.]

73 MS. Sespitat, scultans   An echo of the first line of John of Garland's *Cornutus* ('Cespitat in phaleris . . .')? [R. M.]

76 Written as if a line of verse (cf. 17 n.)

79 *Facetus* (ed. A. Morel-Fatio, *Romania*, XV, 1886, 224 ff.), 106 ('Sed tamen haec fiant tempore quoque [corr. queque?] suo').

81–83 Ibid. 319–20 ('placidam sibi . . . rusticitate sua').

86 The line is one foot short.

88 MS. purgantur

89 MS. non micto Quoniam (*sic*)

90 MS. pretexate

91 Cf. 1 *Cor.* XIII. 12.

92 MS. figuratā

95 MS. facta est

97–101 Cf. *Jer.* III. 1: 'Tu autem fornicata es cum amatoribus multis; tamen revertere ad me, dicit Dominus, et ego suscipiam te.'

110 aporisma—*v.* Du Cange, s.v.

112 MS. ausorium

116 philocaptum—*v.* Du Cange, s.v. poscius—i.e. potius (cf. 132 compasciens).

119 illum—did the copyist take Venus to be a man (cf. *infra*, 123, and Curtius, p. 406)? The poet himself does not always distinguish clearly between Love, the god of Love, and Venus.
   MS. potuerat [R. M.]

122 MS. Venus quem fore (*v.* 119 n.)

126 I do not know how to emend this line.

129 cedulas—i.e. schedulas (*v.* Du Cange, s.v.).

130 MS. emictens

137 MS fuit

144 MS. illas

145 Cf. *Is.* XIII. 9; *Ez.* VII. 10, etc.

146 quia appellans es mel—lit. because you ask (only) for honey? Or is the line corrupt?

149 rota—for the conception of the Rota Veneris, *v.* Chap. V, pp. 318 ff.
MS. infimiori parte
152 MS. Tamacito I preserve the MS. spellings of *prostrans* and *genua.*
157 MS. Iam enim iram [R. M.]
rubiculos—I have not found this (adj.) form elsewhere, but cf. Juvenal,
VI. 425 ('rubicundula').
160 MS. comeati

Gent, Archive de la Cathédrale 12 s. XV²

RHYMUS DE IUDITIO PARIDIS

Constans erat Thetidem parituram natum
Cui patri fuerat prevalere datum.
Dei disposuerant et erat fatatum:
Quod ita disponitur decet esse ratum.

5 [C]omperit hoc Iupiter et comperto credit,
Dignam Iovis thalamo Peleo concedit,
Quo concessu maxime voluntatem ledit,
Sed Fatis resistere nolens, eis cedit.

Gaudet sponsa Peleus, congaudetur ei,
10 Operam dant nuptiis, invitantur dei,
Tanta est iocunditas ibi tante rei,
Velut hora labitur spatium diei.

[N]uptias Discordia corde fert molesto:
Eo quod non interest nuptiali festo
15 Festi pacem impetit ausu tam infesto
Quod in brevi terminat leta fine mesto.

Facit unde doleant dives et egenus,
Multos lesa paululum ledit corde tenus;
Locum quem elegerant Iuno, Pallas, Venus
20 Petit. Tunc effunditur novum doli genus.

[I]nter eas pomulum iacit quo notarat
'Istud habe pulchrior, iam sit quod optarat'—
Nam quid et quampluribus per hoc mali parat
Rei miserabilis exitus declarat.

25 [I]am pacis tranquillitas prorsus est amota,
Lis succedit, usque tunc superis ignota,
Non pro pomi pretio sed pro pomi nota;
Rixa minas parturit, domus fremit tota.

Iuno stat in medio parum vago crine
30 Et vix manus continet, postponuntur mine.
Dee quod interserunt non sapit divine—
Due parum deferunt superum regine.

[S]ed si diligentius prenotent futura
Acquirendi pomulum iam cessabit cura,
35 Nam videre poterunt qualis et quam dura
Huius iactum pomuli sequitur iactura.

Ex hoc causa prodiit ordine fatali
Que subtraxit Helenam thoro maritali,
Et hinc fluxit, proh dolor! fons tocius mali
40 Quod Troes absorbuit, morsu dicam quali.

[Q]ueque sibi iudicat pomulum deberi;
Querunt a qua potius debeat haberi.
Sic obtusos fecerat omnes virtus meri,
Non est ibi super hoc quisquam certus veri.

45 Ergo quem in talibus noverant discretum
Ut si*t* iudex super hoc Paris est decretum;
Et ut hoc quod iudices flectit sit deletum,
Dicunt, non considerant dona, preces, metum.

[Dee:]

Tres sumus, ecce! dee. Forma se quelibet effert.
50 Hoc in discidio volumus, Paris, arbiter esto:
Cui pomum dederis, tytulum simul ipse referto.

Iuno:

Sceptrorum sublimis honor fascesque tremendi
Divitieque mei iuris. Te iudice palmam
Si tuleri*m*, regno per me donabere summo.

Pallas:

55 Que celum, que terra regit, que pontus et orbis,
Legibus astringo certis. Nil me sine rectum.
Te si me sequeris non abstrahet invius error.

Venus:

Plectra sonora, ioci, plausus, lasciva voluptas—
Hec mea. Si reliquis me prefers, ipsa puellam
60 Pro mercede dabo qua non formosior ulla.

Paris:

Grata michi tua forma, Venus, tua munera grata.
Plus aliis michi mente sedes. Certaminis, ecce,
Pignus habe, victrix, auri spectabile malum.

Poeta:

Hac in lite triplex hominum mellita poesis
65 Depinxit studium, quorum datur optio cunctis.
Falluntur tamen optando plerique: sequaces
Luxus habet multos, honor et sapientia paucos.

Thetis was destined to give birth to a son to whom it was given to outstrip his father. The gods had determined this, it was decreed by fate: it is right for a thing thus determined to be fulfilled.

Jupiter perceives this and assents: he gives a bride worthy of his own bed to Peleus. He grants this very much against his will, but, not wishing to resist the Fates, acquiesces.

Peleus takes joy in his bride, and others share his joy. They attend to the wedding, the gods are invited—there is such joy in so great an event, a whole day flies past as if it were an hour.

The wedding rankles in Discordia's heart. Because she was not invited to the wedding-feast, she disturbs its peacefulness with dangerous boldness, soon crowning joy with a dismal end.

She brings about something to cause grief in rich and poor; feeling a little wounded, she wounds many deep in their hearts. She makes for the place Juno, Pallas, and Venus had chosen. Then a new kind of evil cunning is unleashed.

She throws into their midst a little apple on which she had written 'This is for the fairest; may it fulfil her desire.' The unhappy consequences show what evil she was plotting in this, how many people were afflicted.

Now the serenity of peace is utterly gone, strife enters, till then unknown among the gods—not for the apple itself, but for what was written on it. From quarrelling come threats, heaven's house trembles all over.

Juno stands in the centre, her hair a little awry. She goes further than threatening, she can scarcely restrain her hands. The goddesses' exchanges have no air of divinity, the other two show scant deference to the queen of the gods.

Yet if they looked more carefully into the future, their passion to acquire the apple would cease. For they would be able to see how bitter a loss comes from the throwing of this little apple.

From this inexorably came the pretext by which Helen was taken from her marriage-bed. From this, alas, flowed the fountain of all the ills that engulfed the Trojans—I shall tell you with what pain.

Each goddess thinks the apple is her due; they try to find out who deserves it most. The strength of the wine had made all the guests so dull-witted that no one there could any longer tell for sure.

So Paris, whom they knew to be an expert in beauty, was appointed to judge the matter. And so as to avoid what biases a judge, the goddesses say they will refrain from bribes, pleas, and threats.

[Goddesses:] You see, we are three goddesses, each of us proud of her beauty. We want you, Paris, to judge in our disagreement. Whomever you give the apple, award her the inscription also.

Juno: The sceptre's high renown, awe-inspiring office and wealth are ruled by me. If in your view I win the prize, I shall give you the greatest of kingdoms.

Pallas: With inviolable laws I govern the contents of heaven and earth and sea and land. Without me there is no order. If you follow me, the most impenetrable error will leave you untouched.

Venus: The harmonies of lutes, sports, revels, blissful dalliance— all these are mine. If you like me best, I myself shall give you a girl whose beauty is unmatched by any.

Paris: Venus, I love your beauty and I love your gifts. You fill my mind more than the others. You are the victor in this contest: come take the lovely golden apple as my pledge.

Poet: In this contest sweet poetry depicts the threefold aims of men, the choice of which is given to all. Most men, however, are deceived in their choice: sensual delight has many followers, honour and wisdom few.

1 ff. This poem is probably contemporary with the other mythological narratives in rhymed stanzaic verse of the later twelfth century, such as those on Ganymede and Helen (*ZfdA* vi [1875], 14 ff.), Jupiter and Danae (ibid. 457 ff.), and Leda (*ZfdA* xxxviii [1908], 289 ff.). Though it has affinities with these poems, it is more serious-minded, and lacks their flair for the piquant.

40 morsu dicam quali—i.e. I shall tell you how. The poet tells the cause of the Trojan war in the episode that follows; I do not think this line implies that he intended to describe the fall of Troy itself.

46 MS. sis

49 ff. The hexameters occur alone in an inferior text in B.M. Lansdowne 762, s. xv–xvi, fol. 17ʳ (*v. PLM* v. 394 for variant readings; l. 12 [here l. 57] MS. Te, *not* Et).

52–63 In the Gent MS. these are written on scrolls given to the goddesses and Paris in the illustration. I adopt the order of speaking suggested by l. 19 in the poem—Juno, Pallas, Venus—which is also the traditional ancient order. In the Lansdowne MS. Venus is the first to speak.

54 MS. tuleri

58 A traditional list of things over which Venus has power, well known from classic astrological texts such as Albumasar's *Introductorium* and Alcabitius' *Isagoge*.

BIBLIOGRAPHY

I. GENERAL NOTE

CHAPTERS I AND 3

On the origins of the poetry of *amour courtois*: writings before 1937 have been given an excellent bibliography and discussion in Käthe Axhausen, *Die Theorien über den Ursprung der provenzalischen Lyrik* (Marburg, 1937). The *Literatur-* and the *Autorenverzeichnis* in Felix Schlösser's *Andreas Capellanus* (Bonn, 1960), and the bibliography in Klaus Heger's *Die bisher veröffentlichten Harğas und ihre Deutungen* (Tübingen, 1960), taken together, cover nearly all the more important work on this topic until 1960.

Of particular interest among more recent work, in my opinion, are the two essays of Theodor Frings (ch. 1, p. 7 n.), with their wide range of illustration, especially from popular poetry; the writings of Ramón Menéndez Pidal (p. 52 n.), Emilio García Gómez, and Aurelio Roncaglia (*v.* Heger, pp. xi–xii, xvi) on possible links with Arabic poetry (cf. my discussion *supra*, pp. 50 ff.); the last studies of Hans Spanke (*Marcabrustudien, GA* 1940, 24; *Deutsche und französische Dichtung des Mittelalters* (Stuttgart–Berlin, 1943); 'La teoría árabe', *Anuario musical*, i (1946), 5 ff.; 'Die Metrik der *Cantigas*', in H. Anglés' *La música de las Cantigas* III. i, 189 ff.) with their special attention to relations between Latin and vernacular poetry and music (Käthe Axhausen gives detailed references to Spanke's earlier work). On the approaches to the problems of *amour courtois* in Reto R. Bezzola's *Les origines et la formation de la littérature courtoise en occident* (Paris, 1944 ff.), in A. J. Denomy's essays (*v.* Heger, p. x) and in Felix Schlösser's book I have made some observations elsewhere (*RF* lxxiii (1961), 327 ff.; *MÆ* xxxii (1963), 56 ff.). Among very recent studies on concepts of *courtoisie* I would mention Moshé Lazar's 'Les éléments constitutifs de la *cortezia*', *Studi mediolatini e volgari*, vi–vii (1959), 66 ff., A. Viscardi's 'Le origini della letteratura cortese', *ZfrP* lxxviii (1962), 269 ff., and Erich Köhler's *Trobadorlyrik und höfischer Roman* (Berlin, 1962).

Love-lyrics in the European vernaculars. The following bibliographies and collections of texts are particularly important:

Provençal

A. Pillet, H. Carstens, *Bibliographie der Troubadours* (Halle, 1933).
C. A. F. Mahn, *Gedichte der Troubadours in provenzalischer Sprache* (4 vols., Berlin, 1856–73).

F. Gennrich, *Der musikalische Nachlass der Troubadours* (3 vols., Darmstadt, 1958 ff.).

Old French

R. Bossuat, *Manuel bibliographique de la littérature française du Moyen Âge* (Melun, 1951), pp. 199-223; *Suppléments* (Paris, 1955, 1961).

G. Raynaud, *Bibliographie des altfranzösischen Liedes, neu bearb. u. erg. von Hans Spanke*, i (Leiden, 1955).

F. Gennrich, *Bibliographie der ältesten französischen u. lateinischen Motetten* (Darmstadt, 1958).

K. Bartsch, *Altfranzösische Romanzen und Pastourellen* (Leipzig, 1870).

G. Raynaud, *Recueil de motets français* (2 vols., Paris, 1881-3).

F. Gennrich, *Rondeaux, Virelais und Balladen* (2 vols., Dresden, 1921, Göttingen, 1927).

Italian

B. Panvini, *La scuola poetica siciliana* (2 vols., Firenze, 1962-4).

G. Contini, *Poeti del Duecento* (2 vols., Milano-Napoli, 1960).

Galician-Portuguese

J. J. Nunes, *Cantigas d'amigo* (3 vols., Coimbra, 1928).

— *Cantigas d'amor* (Coimbra, 1932).

C. Michaëlis de Vasconcellos, *Cancioneiro da Ajuda* (2 vols., Halle, 1904).

Icelandic

L. M. Hollander, *A Bibliography of Skaldic Studies* (Copenhagen, 1958).

F. Jónsson, *Den norsk-íslandske Skjaldedigtning* (4 vols., Copenhagen, 1908-15) —includes love-poetry by Kormákr, Hallfreðr, Hallbjǫrn Oddsson, Björn breiðvíkingakappi, Gunnlaugr.

Middle High German

Bibliographie der deutschen Literaturwissenschaft (Frankfurt am Main, 1957 ff.).

C. von Kraus, *Minnesangs Frühling* (Leipzig, 1944).

— *Deutsche Liederdichter des 13. Jahrhunderts* (2 vols., Tübingen, 1952-8).

K. Bartsch, *Die schweizerischen Minnesänger* (Frauenfeld-Leipzig, 1886).

Middle English

J. E. Wells, *A Manual of the Writings in Middle English* (and *Supplements*, Yale, 1916 ff.).

Cambridge Bibliography of English Literature (London, 1941) vol. I; *Supplement* (1957).

C. Brown, R. H. Robbins, *The Index of Middle English Verse* (New York, 1943)—see especially pp. 763-4.

C. Brown, *English Lyrics of the XIIIth Century* (Oxford, 1932).

R. H. Robbins, *Secular Lyrics of the XIVth and XVth Centuries* (Oxford, 1952).

There are sections on each of the medieval European vernaculars in *The Year's Work in Modern Language Studies* (since 1931) and the bibliographical section of *PMLA* (international since 1956). The Romance languages are covered more fully by the *Supplementhefte* of the *ZfrP* (Halle, 1878 ff.), and the Germanic by *Germanistik* (Tübingen, 1960 ff.).

CHAPTER 2

'The Background of Ideas': the philosophical texts cited in this chapter have an extensive bibliography (up to 1953) in Étienne Gilson's *History of Christian Philosophy in the Middle Ages* (English ed., London, 1955); the theological texts, similarly, in B. Altaner's *Patrology* (English ed., Freiburg–Edinburgh, 1960), and M. Manitius's *Geschichte der lateinischen Literatur des Mittelalters* (3 vols., München, 1911–31). For a bibliography of the medieval Aristotelian tradition, *Aristoteles Latinus* (Pars Prior, Bruges–Paris, 1957, Pars Posterior, Cantabrigiae, 1955) is indispensable. Among very recent studies in medieval thought, I would mention B. Nardi's *Studi di filosofia medievale* (Roma, 1960), V. Cilento's *Medio evo monastico e scolastico* (Milano–Napoli, 1961), and G. Scholem's contribution to the study of 'Sapiential' language in his *Von der mystischen Gestalt der Gottheit* (Zürich, 1962), pp. 135–92. The *Bulletin de théologie ancienne et médiévale* (Louvain, 1929 ff.) gives an extensive critical bibliography each year.

CHAPTERS 4 AND 5

Medieval Latin love-poetry: a bibliography by manuscripts is given below. There is an excellent general bibliography in F. J. E. Raby's *SLP* (ii. 361–99). Further references to anonymous verse can be found in Walther's *Initia*, to authors, in Raby (loc. cit.) and Manitius (op. cit.). *MGG* contains extensive bibliography on the musical aspects of the Latin lyric, especially in the entries 'Carmina Burana' (II. 853), 'Conductus' (II. 1615), 'Florenz' (IV. 405), 'Ivrea' (VI. 1581), 'Montpellier Handschriften' (IX. 533), 'Notre-Dame Epoche' (IX. 1700), and 'Saint-Martial' (XI. 1262). The bibliographical *Supplementhefte* of the *ZfrP* give the fullest coverage of recent work in medieval Latin (at the time of writing, to 1955), and there is an annual medieval Latin section in *The Year's Work in Modern Language Studies*.

II. ABBREVIATIONS[1]

Abrahams, P. *Les œuvres poétiques de Baudri de Bourgueil* (ed. P. Abrahams, 1926).
AfKdV *Anzeiger für Kunde deutscher Vorzeit.*
AfMW *Archiv für Musikwissenschaft.*

[1] For works of ancient authors, and for the books of the Bible, I use the standard abbreviations of Greek and Latin dictionaries.

814346.2   P

A.G.   *Anthologia Graeca* (ed. H. Beckby, 4 vols., 1957–8).

A.H.   *Analecta Hymnica Medii Aevi* (ed. G. M. Dreves, C. Blume, and H. M. Bannister, 55 vols., 1886–1922).

AHD   *Archives d'histoire doctrinale et littéraire du moyen âge.*

A.L.   *Anthologia Latina* (ed. F. Buecheler and A. Riese, 2nd ed., 2 vols., 1894–7).

ALMA   *Archivum Latinitatis Medii Aevi.*

Annuaire-bull.   *Annuaire-bulletin de la Société de l'histoire de France.*

Archiv   *Archiv der Gesellschaft für ältere deutsche Geschichtskunde.*

Bartsch   *Altfranzösische Romanzen und Pastourellen* (ed. K. Bartsch, 1870).

Baxter–Johnson   *Medieval Latin Word-List* (ed. J. H. Baxter and C. Johnson, 1934).

Brown–Robbins   *The Index of Middle English Verse* (ed. C. Brown and R. H. Robbins, 1943).

BSB   *Sitzungsberichte der Berliner Akademie der Wissenschaften, Philosophisch-historische Klasse.*

CB   *Carmina Burana* (ed. A. Hilka and O. Schumann) I. 1 Die moralisch-satirischen Dichtungen (1930). I. 2 Die Liebeslieder (1941). II. 1 Einleitung; Die moralisch-satirischen Dichtungen (Kommentar) (1930).

CC   *Die Cambridger Lieder / Carmina Cantabrigiensia* (ed. K. Strecker, 1926).

Chailley, J., *École*   *L'école musicale de Saint-Martial de Limoges* (1960).

Chevalier   C. U. J. Chevalier, *Repertorium Hymnologicum* (6 vols., 1892–1920).

CIL   *Corpus Inscriptionum Latinarum* (1863 ff.).

CLP   F. J. E. Raby, *Christian Latin Poetry* (2nd ed., 1953).

CM   *Classica et Mediævalia.*

CN (*Cult. Neo-lat.*)   *Cultura Neolatina.*

Comédie   La '*comédie*' *latine en France au XIIe siècle* (ed. G. Cohen et al., 2 vols., 1931).

Contini   *Poeti del Duecento* (ed. G. Contini, 2 vols., 1960).

Coussemaker, E. de   *Histoire de l'harmonie au moyen âge* (1852).

CQ   *Classical Quarterly.*

Curtius   E. R. Curtius, *European Literature and the Latin Middle Ages* (English ed., 1953).

Denomy, A. J.   *The Heresy of Courtly Love* (1947).

DLD	*Deutsche Liederdichter des 13. Jahrhunderts* (ed. C. von Kraus, 2 vols., 1952–8).
Du Cange	*Glossarium Mediae et Infimae Latinitatis* (9 vols., 1883–7).
EETS	Early English Text Society.
EHR	*English Historical Review.*
Faral, E., *Arts*	*Les arts poétiques du XIIe et du XIIIe siècle* (1924).
Forcellini	Æ. Forcellini, *Lexicon Totius Latinitatis* (ed. F. Corradini, 4 vols., 1864–87; *Onomasticon,* ed. J. Perin, 2 vols., 1913–20).
GA	*Abhandlungen der Göttinger Gesellschaft der Wissenschaften, Phil.-hist. Klasse.*
Gennrich, F.	*Rondeaux, Virelais und Balladen* (2 vols., 1921–7).
GGA	*Göttingische Gelehrte Anzeigen.*
GN	*Nachrichten von der Gesellschaft der Wissenschaften zu Göttingen, Phil.-hist. Klasse.*
Godefroy	F. E. Godefroy, *Dictionnaire de l'ancienne langue française* (10 vols., 1881–1902).
GRM	*Germanisch-romanische Monatsschrift.*
Hagen	*Carmina Medii Aevi maximam partem inedita* (ed. H. Hagen, 1877).
Hauréau, B., *NE*	*Notices et extraits de quelques manuscrits latins de la Bibliothèque Nationale* (6 vols., 1890–3).
Heidelberg SB	*Sitzungsberichte der Heidelberger Akademie der Wissenschaften, Phil.-hist. Klasse.*
Hist. litt. de France	*Histoire littéraire de la France par les religieux bénédictins de la congrégation de Saint-Maur* (1753 ff.).
Hist. Vjs.	*Historische Vierteljahrsschrift.*
Hugh Primas	W. Meyer, 'Die Oxforder Gedichte des Primas', *GN* 1907, pp. 75 ff., 113 ff.
	K. Langosch, *Hymnen und Vagantenlieder* (1954) pp. 148–217.
JTS	*Journal of Theological Studies.*
Lehmann	P. Lehmann, *Pseudo-antike Literatur des Mittelalters* (1927).
Lehmann, *Parodie*	P. Lehmann, *Die Parodie im Mittelalter* (1922).
Levy	E. Levy, *Provenzalisches Supplement-Wörterbuch* (8 vols., 1894–1924).
Lexer	M. Lexer, *Mittelhochdeutsches Handwörterbuch* (3 vols., 1872–8).
Leyser, P.	*Historia Poetarum et Poematum Medii Aevi* (1721).
Liber Floridus	*Liber Floridus, Mittellateinische Studien Paul Lehmann gewidmet* (ed. B. Bischoff and S. Brechter, 1950).

Ludwig, F.   *Repertorium Organorum Recentioris et Motetorum Vetustissimi Stili* (1910).
MÆ   *Medium Ævum.*
Mari, *I trattati*   G. Mari, *I trattati medievali di ritmica latina* (1899).
MARS   *Mediæval and Renaissance Studies.*
Med. Stud.   *Mediæval Studies.*
MF   *Minnesangs Frühling* (ed. C. von Kraus, 1944).
MGG   *Die Musik in Geschichte und Gegenwart* (ed. F. Blume, 1949 ff.).
MGH   *Monumenta Germaniae Historica.*
MIÖG   *Mitteilungen des Instituts für österreichische Geschichtsforschung.*
Mone   *Lateinische Hymnen des Mittelalters* (ed. F. J. Mone, 3 vols., 1853–5).
MSB   *Sitzungsberichte der Bayerischen Akademie der Wissenschaften, Phil.-hist. Klasse.*
NA   *Neues Archiv der Gesellschaft für ältere deutsche Geschichtskunde.*
NE   *Notices et extraits des manuscrits de la Bibliothèque Nationale et autres bibliothèques* (1787 ff.).
Neuphil. Mitt.   *Neuphilologische Mitteilungen.*
Niermeyer   J. F. Niermeyer, *Mediae Latinitatis lexicon minus* (1954 ff.).
NQ   *Notes and Queries.*
d'Olwer, Ll. N.   'L'escola poètica de Ripoll en els segles X–XIII', *Institut d'Estudis Catalans*, vi (1923), 3 ff.
Pauly–Wissowa   *Realenzyklopädie der klassischen Altertumswissenschaft* (ed. A. Pauly and G. Wissowa, 1893 ff.).
PBB   *Beiträge zur Geschichte der deutschen Sprache und Literatur.*
P.G.   *Patrologia Graeca.*
P.L.   *Patrologia Latina.*
PLM   *Poetae Latini Minores* (ed. F. Vollmer and W. Morel, 6 vols., 1910–35).
PMLA   *Publications of the Modern Languages Association of America.*
Poésies   O. Dobiache-Rojdestvensky, *Les poésies des goliards* (1931).
Poetae   *Poetae Latini Aevi Carolini* (MGH, 1881 ff.).
Raynouard   F. J. M. Raynouard, *Lexique Roman* (6 vols., 1836–45).
RB   *Revue Bénédictine.*
Recueil   *Recueil des historiens des gaules et de la France.*
Rev. Fil. Esp.   *Revista de filología española.*
RF   *Romanische Forschungen.*

Riv. Stud. Orient.   *Rivista di studi orientali.*
RMAL   *Revue du moyen âge latin.*
RSPT   *Revue des sciences philosophiques et théologiques.*
Saint-Omer   *Die Lieder Walters von Châtillon in der Handschrift 351 von St. Omer* (ed. K. Strecker, 1925).
SATF   Société des anciens textes français.
SLP   F. J. E. Raby, *Secular Latin Poetry* (2nd ed., 2 vols., 1957).
Spanke, H.,   *Beziehungen zwischen romanischer und mittellateinischer*
  Beziehungen   *Lyrik (GA, 1936).*
—Marcabrustudien   *Untersuchungen über die Ursprünge des romanischen Minnesangs. Zweiter Teil: Marcabrustudien (GA, 1940).*
Strecker 1931   *Studien zur lateinischen Dichtung des Mittelalters. Ehrengabe für Karl Strecker* (ed. W. Stach and H. Walther, 1931).
Streitg[edicht]   H. Walther, *Das Streitgedicht in der lateinischen Literatur des Mittelalters* (1920).
Studi ital.   *Studi italiani di filologia classica.*
Studi med.   *Studi medievali* (N. S.—Nuova serie).
TLL   *Thesaurus Linguae Latinae* (1900 ff.).
Tobler–   *Altfranzösisches Wörterbuch* (ed. A. Tobler and E.
  Lommatzsch   Lommatzsch, 1925 ff.).
Walther   H. Walther, *Initia Carminum ac Versuum Medii Aevi Posterioris Latinorum / Alphabetisches Verzeichnis der Versanfänge mittellateinischer Dichtungen* (1959).
Werner   J. Werner, *Beiträge zur Kunde der lateinischen Literatur des Mittelalters* (2nd ed., 1905).
Wright, T.,   *The Latin Poems commonly attributed to Walter Mapes*
  Mapes   (1841).
Wright, T., SP   *The Anglo-Latin Satirical Poets and Epigrammatists of the Twelfth Century* (ed. T. Wright, 2 vols., 1872).
WSB   *Sitzungsberichte der Akademie der Wissenschaften zu Wien, Phil.-hist. Klasse.*
ZfdA   *Zeitschrift für deutsches Altertum.*
ZfdP   *Zeitschrift für deutsche Philologie.*
ZffSL   *Zeitschrift für französische Sprache und Literatur.*
ZfrP   *Zeitschrift für romanische Philologie.*

III. LATIN MANUSCRIPTS

My aim in the list that follows is to present as complete a conspectus as possible of the medieval Latin poetry concerned with love, and to show at a glance which are the important manuscript collections. Each poem can also be located through the alphabetical index at the end of this volume.

I have tried to include all relevant post-Carolingian poetry which might properly be called 'medieval'. I include manuscripts up to the fifteenth century, but exclude humanist authors. At times, where the love-poetry verges upon the religious, or panegyric, or didactic, or satirical, I have not tried to draw a narrow boundary. I include, for instance, the amatory fabliaux, and verse proverbs and epigrams about love (unless, of course, these are misogynistic).

Each poem is given by its first line under one manuscript, wherever possible under the manuscript containing the earliest complete text. There I also give cross-references to other manuscripts where the poem occurs, or (for widely diffused texts) a brief indication of where further manuscripts are listed or discussed.

I have seen the manuscripts listed under Cambridge, Escorial, Firenze, London, München, Oxford, Paris, Roma, and Saint-Omer, and photographs of pages from many of the others. It seemed worth while, however, to include also the poems I have seen only in a printed text: the risks of sometimes giving manuscript details entirely at second-hand are, I hope, compensated by the gain in comprehensiveness. Thus where the index of Walther's *Initia*, for instance, allows one to find little more than a hundred medieval Latin love-poems, the bibliography that follows charts nearly six hundred.

My indications of date, provenance, and content of manuscripts conform with those in the standard printed catalogue of a library (*v*. P. O. Kristeller, *Latin MS Books before 1600*, revised ed., New York, 1960), unless other sources are given below. I refer as far as possible to the most recent description of a manuscript or edition of a poem (occasionally, for convenience, to a derivative edition). I include older references only where these are of special importance, or have been overlooked in recent scholarship. If no reference to a printed text is given, the poem is, to the best of my knowledge, unpublished. Unless otherwise stated, reference is made to the initial page only of editions or other works cited.

While I have included all relevant material that has been accessible to me, it must be remembered that (as I discussed in *GGA* 1962, 154 ff.) the instruments that would be needed to design a repertorium, complete and accurate in every detail, do not yet exist. The notes that follow are necessarily inadequate, and I should greatly value any additions and corrections.

ADMONT Stiftsbibl. 25, s. XIII. Magnum legendarium Austriacum. Prefaced to the *Vita magistrae monialium Admuntensium*, five lines by an admirer:

> fol. 235ʳ Fulgida vita Dei famulae seu forma trophaei (ed. F. Ohly, *ZfdA* lxxxvii (1956-7), 21)

> MS.: ibid., p. 13; *Analecta Bollandiana*, xvii (1898), 31.

Stiftsbibl. 759, s. XII. Rhetorical treatises and verses (incl. Marbod's *Liber de Gemmis* and the *Disticha Catonis*).

> fols. 189ʳ–199ᵛ *Regulae de Rithmis*, with verse illustrations:
> Advenit aestas, prefulgent rosae
> Adesto, Venus, mater amoris
> Grata Venus iuventuti
> Cetus iuvenum legetur
> Gratus amor puellaris
> (ed. G. Mari, *I trattati*, pp. 29, 30, 33)

AUGSBURG Bischöfl. Ord. 5, s. X. Gregory's *Moralia*, with some interpolated tropes and responses, formerly at St. Magnus in Füssen.

> fol. 1ʳ (s. XII in.—B. Bischoff, private communication) Parce continuis
> (ed. and further references *supra*, p. 341)

AUXERRE 243, written 1358 in Paris at the Collège Saint-Bernard. A collection of Latin verse, incl. *De universitate mundi* and *De planctu Naturae*.

> fol. 17ᵛ Esse quidem dicam rem prosperitatis amorem (also in Paris B.N. lat. 6415, c. 1200, fol. 91ᵛ; ed. A. Vernet, *Mélanges Félix Grat*, ii. 255 ff.)
> fols. 17ᵛ–18ʳ Protrahit in vicium levitas sexum muliebrem (fabliau *De nato Ethiope*, ed. ibid.)
> fol. 18ʳ Ver prope florigerum, flava Licori (also in Bodley Add. A 44; ed. *supra*, p. 374)
> Predantur oculos, captivant animum (ed. *supra*, p. 403)
> Ab ungue primo teneram (also in B.N. lat. 3719; ed. *supra*, p. 378)
> fol. 18ʳ⁻ᵛ Quam velim virginum si detur optio (*v. infra*, B.M. Arundel 384, B.N. lat. 3719; ed. A. Vernet, loc. cit.)
> fol. 18ᵛ Phebeo reditu calescit Aries (ed. ibid.)
> MS.: A. Vernet, loc. cit.

BARCELONA Arxiu de la Corona d'Aragó, Ripoll 74, s. X. Liber glossarum.

> fols. 96ᵛ–101ʳ (s. XII²) Nineteen love-poems (ed. Ll. N. d'Olwer, pp. 41–56, nos. 20–36, 38, 39):
> Aprilis tempore, quo nemus frondibus
> Maio mense dum per pratum
> Sidus clarum
> Sol ramium (corr. radium?) fervens medium dum scandit Olimpi
> Luna velut stellas, sic vincis, amica, puellas
> Dulcis amica mei, valeas per secula multa

Si vera somnia forent, que somnio
Illud si verum fieret, quod somnia monstrant
Conqueror et doleo de te, mea dulcis amica
Grave vulnus amoris
Quot tenet astra polus, aqua pisces, pondera tellus
Si laudare possem florem
Dulcis amica mei, qua non formosior ulla
Noster cetus
Gemma puellarum, valeas, hoc mandat amicus
Felix amor
Redit estas cunctis grata
Heu! dolor inmodicus, mea qui nunc pectora tangit
Quot iuvenes Marti gaudent servire feroci
(Before the last two comes the misogynistic 'Quisquis eris, qui
credideris fidei mulieris', attrib. Marbod in *P.L.* 171. 1684; further
references in Walther 16162.)

MS.: Ll. N. d'Olwer, p. 24. Z. García's description (*WSB* clxix (1913),
39–43) omits the poetry altogether!

BASEL Univ. D. iv. 4, s. XIII–XIV. Chiefly verse miscellany, from the
Dominican house at Basel.

fols. 69ʳ–80ᵛ Sixty-eight medieval poems copied by a clerc in Basel, two-
thirds of them (according to Werner) his own compositions. The
collection includes *CB* 178, 'Dum flosculum tenera' (*v.* Saint-Omer
351), and *Altercatio Ganimedis et Helene* (*v.* Vat. Reg. lat. 344).
fol. 72ʳ Post hiemis rigorem et senium
fol. 73ᵛ Boreali sevicia dulcis concentus avium
Estatis indicium

MS. (and ed. of the unpublished pieces): J. Werner, *GN* 1908, 449 ff.

BEAUVAIS 11, s. XII. Collection of verse by Fulco of Beauvais. Verse-
epistles ed. M. L. Colker, *Traditio*, x (1954), 191 ff. Love-themes occur in
six of the epistles:

fol. 143ᵛ Orpheus in pleno consessu cum Cluvieno (XVI)
fol. 154ʳ In Troiae silva, speciosa quae fuit, Ida (XVII)
fol. 155ʳ Nec vehementer amans nec sis vehementer avarus (XVIII)
fol. 156ᵛ Rixas Lenniacas cur non, sevissime, placas (XIX)
fol. 158ᵛ Tu, qui nec caute nec caste vivere curas (XX)
fols. 159ᵛ–160ʳ Ad morbum medicina fuit cum fratre sorori (XXI)

MS.: M. L. Colker, loc. cit.

BERLIN Hamilton 390—*v*. Toledo, Bibl. del Cabildo s.c.

Lat. fol. 319—*v*. *Lübeck 152.

Lat. fol. 376—*v*. München Clm 14818.

*Lat. qu. 915, s. XII ex. (missing since 1945). Chiefly verse miscellany: incl. Abelard's verses to Astrolabe, *Conflictus ovis et lini*, Thierry of Saint-Trond's *Liber quid suum virtutis*, Vitalis of Blois's *Aulularia* and William of Blois's *Alda* (see below); Bernard of Cluny's *De contemptu mundi;* Serlo of Wilton's 'Dactyle, quid latitas'; 'Quid querar edam' (*v*. München Clm 19488); *A.L.* 635; 'Presbyter Algere' (*v*. Vorau 12).

> fols. 40^{r-v}, 64^{r-v}, 49^r–54^v (originally consecutive) Dum parit Alda perit; Ulfus pro coniuge natam (*Alda*, ed. from six manuscripts, incl. Laurenziana Plut. XXXIII. 31, which is in Boccaccio's hand, *Comédie*, i. 130)

> MS.: E. Muellenbach, *Vitalis Aulularia* (Bonn, 1885), pp. 38–49; K. Holter, *MIÖG* lxiv (1956), 272–6.

Phillipps 1694, s. XII ex. Written at Metz, probably at the monastery of St. Arnulph. Letters of Ivo of Chartres. From p. 133, a poetic miscellany identical with Reims 1275, s. XIII, from fol. 129^r.

> p. 234 (fol. 169^v) Parce, precor, virgo, tociens michi culta videri (ed. W. Wattenbach, *BSB* (1891), 107)

> p. 244 (fol. 173^r) Inclita progenies, patrie flos et specialis (ed. W. Wattenbach, *NA* xvii (1892), 362)

> p. 250 (fol. 175^v) Rarius in terris nihil est quam femina recti (*Sponsus adversus sponsam*, ed. *P.L.* 171. 1453; *Responsio sponse*, ed. *NA* loc. cit.)

> p. 252 (fol. 176^r) Ambrosie flores violeque crocique recentes (*v*. supra, p. 248)

> MS.: W. Wattenbach, *NA* xvii (1892), 351.

Phillipps 1992, s. XII. Formerly at the Collège de Clermont. Augustine *De unico baptismo*; poems of Marbod.

> fol. 81^r Ad sonitum cythare solitus sum me recreare (ed. A. Wilmart, *RB* li (1939), 175 [Wilmart misnumbers this manuscript 1792]; *Liber Floridus*, p. 296)

BERN AA 90. 4, s. XII. A gathering of theological extracts, ending with a verse-greeting (Hagen cxxv) and a love-poem:

> fol. 4^v Carmina missa gravis mihi sunt fomenta caloris (Hagen cxxvi)

211, s. xv. Secular and religious prose and verse miscellany, incl. some French pieces.

For the lines on Abelard and on Héloïse, *v. supra*, pp. 469–71.

568, s. xii ex. Miscellany incl. English historical writings, once owned by Pierre Daniel.

> fols. 15ʳ–17ᵛ Baucis amica sibi, spe lucri sedula nutrix (*Baucis et Traso*, ed. *Comédie*, ii. 70)
>
> fol. 17ᵛ Cuius totus eram, cuius me cura regebat (Hagen cxxiv)
>
> fol. 186ᵛ Occurrunt blando sibi lumina vestra favore (Arnulf of Lisieux, *Ad iuvenem et puellam affectuosius se invicem intuentes*; Hagen cxvi— among a collection of Arnulf's poems, Hagen cx–cxxii, found also in B.N. lat. 16699)

702, s. xii. A collection chiefly of theological and medical writings, once owned by Pierre Daniel.

> fols. 87ʳ–98ʳ Grecorum studia nimiumque diuque secutus (Vitalis of Blois, *Geta*; ed. from seven manuscripts, *Comédie*, i. 34)

710, s. xii–xiii. Anthology of ancient and medieval verse, largely excerpts.

> fol. 96ʳ Virtus in melius vertere queque studet (ed. Werner, p. 196)
>
> MS.: Werner, p. 189.

BRAUNSCHWEIG 103, s. xvi. Sermons and tracts, written in Germany.

> fol. 46ʳ (with music) Amor almus, ardens affectus alacris animi, amenitas appetibilis (ed. *supra*, p. 491)

CAMBRIDGE Caius 418, s. xiii–xiv. Grammatical tracts, problems and verses.

> fol. 94ʳ In vere virencia loca iuvant vere (ed. *supra*, p. 400)
>
> fol. 97ᵛ Mente mea quedam meditor que protinus edam

Corp. 468, ss. xiii, xiv. Miscellaneous verses preceding a Greek–Latin psalter that belonged to Gregory of Huntingdon, Prior of Ramsey (*fl.* 1250).

> fol. xʳ Quot tigridum vil[l]i, quot sunt tellure lapilli (verse-greeting, ed. with many others by H. Walther, *ZfdA* lxv (1928), 273)

Trin. B. 1. 16, ss. xi, xii. Berengaudus super Apocalypsim, Haymo super Cantica (generally attrib. Remigius of Auxerre); preceded by some hymns and fragments.

> fol. 2ʳ (s. xii) [E]pithalamia decantans dulcia (a variation on the Song of Songs, with letter notation over the words; ed. *supra*, p. 515)

Trin. B. 14. 39, *c.* 1300 (K. Sisam, *Fourteenth Century Verse and Prose*, p. 168). English, Latin, and French miscellany, chiefly verse.

fol. 87ᵛ Est amor ut species, timor ut genus, unde timore

Trin. O. 2. 5, s. xɪᴠ. Scientific miscellany.

p. 52 Quid est amor? mentis insania (cf. Oxford, Douce 139, s. xɪɪɪ, fol. 148ʳ)

Nescio quid sit amor: nec amo nec amor nec amavi (for other manuscripts, *v.* Walther 11740, 11741)

Trin. R. 7. 11, s. xɪɪɪ ex. Giraldus Cambrensis, *Symbolum Electorum.*

fol. 40ʳ Mundus ut insignis cunctis ornatibus extat (*Descriptio cuiusdam puelle*)

fol. 40ᵛ Fons erat irriguus cui fecerat arbutus umbram (*De subito amore*)

fol. 41ᵛ Quicquid amor iussit non est contempnere tutum (*Ad quandam puellam litteratam nomen habentem Leticie sed non omen, sub amatoris sui specie*)

All ed. J. S. Brewer, *Giraldi Cambrensis Opera*, i. 349, 352, 356.

Trin. R. 14. 22, ss. xɪɪɪ, xɪᴠ, xᴠ. Rhetorical miscellany.

fols. 91ᵛ–93ᵛ (s. xɪᴠ) Est amor amoris species et causa cruoris (Matthew of Vendôme, 'Pyramus and Thisbe', ed. Lehmann, p. 31)

UL Dd. xi. 78, s. xɪɪɪ. Formerly at St. Albans; much of the manuscript written by Matthew Paris. Collected poems of Henry of Avranches and a few miscellaneous pieces.

fols. 166ᵛ–169ʳ Ut tenebris lux prefertur previsa dierum (debate between *miles* and *clericus*, ed. H. Walther, *Streitgedicht*, p. 248; fragm. also in B.M. Royal 13. A. iv, fol. 24ʳ)

fol. 169ʳ Militat haut aliquis nisi miles; militat autem (ed. ibid. p. 253; also in Wien 1321, s. xɪɪɪ, fol 90ᵛ)

MS.: J. C. Russell and J. P. Heironimus, *The Shorter Latin Poems of Master Henry of Avranches* (1935), p. xiii; R. Vaughan, *Matthew Paris* (1958), p. 260.

UL Ff. i. 17 (1), s. xɪɪɪ (fols. 1–4, 297–300). A songbook, originally complete in itself, probably written in England. Of its thirty-four songs, the majority are religious, three moral–satirical, and four love-songs:

fol. 1ʳ⁻ᵛ Vacillantis trutine (*CB* 108; also in B.M. Arundel 384)

fol. 298ʳ⁻ᵛ Partu prodit arida (ed. O. Schumann, *Studi med.* N. S. xvi (1943–50), 65)

fol. 297ʳ⁻ᵛ Dissoluta glacie (ibid., p. 69)

fol. 300ʳ Olim sudor Herculis (*CB* 63, other references ad loc.)

MS.: O. Schumann, art. cit., p. 48.

UL Gg. iv. 27—*v*. B.M. Harley 3362.

UL Gg. v. 35, s. XI. Large anthology of Christian Latin poetry from the Patristic to the post-Carolingian period, concluded by a (fragmentary) copy of a Rhenish secular and religious songbook. Formerly (s. XII–XVI) at the monastery of St. Augustine in Canterbury, and probably written there.

    fol. 435ᵛ Nam languens (ed. *supra*, p. 275)
    fol. 438ᵛ Iam dulcis amica venito (also in Wien 116 and Paris B.N. lat. 1118)
    Suavissima nunna (ed. *supra*, p. 353)
    fol. 440ᵛ [. . .] Nosti flores carpere (*v. supra*, p. 277)
    fol. 441ʳ Levis exsurgit zephirus
    fol. 441ᵛ O admirabile Veneris idolum (also in Vat. lat. 3227, s. XI ex., fol. 80ᵛ, in a Lombard hand)
    Veni dilectissime, et a et o (*v. supra*, p. 274)

    MS. (and the most reliable ed. of the songs): K. Strecker, *Die Cambridger Lieder*, MGH, Berlin, 1926.

CHANTILLY Musée Condé 1047, s. XV in. A songbook, texts chiefly French, some Latin. Predominantly ballades, with some rondeaux, virelais, and motets. Copied in an Italian hand from a French original written s. XIV ex. 'for the courts of Foix and Aragon' (G. Reaney).

    fols. 69ᵛ–70ʳ Multipliciter amando (Triple)
    Favore habundare (Double)—Motet ed. (with faulty text) U. Günther *Musica Disciplina*, xii (1958), 48

    MS. (and further references): G. Reaney, *Musica Disciplina* viii (1954), 59; (with extracts from texts) L. Delisle, *Chantilly, Le cabinet des livres* (Paris, 1900), ii. 277–303.

DARMSTADT 2780. Completed 1380 'per manus Conrâdi dicti Hânchel' (accepted by Habel; Roth thought 1480). Large verse miscellany, incl. Cato, Avianus, *De contemptu mundi*, *Fagifacetus*, *Physiologus*, *De Troia*, Theodulus, *Vita S. Alexii*.

    fols. 185ʳ–199ᵛ Augurio docti fraudes didici muliebres (Adolphus of Vienna, *Doligamus*; ed. from this and seven fifteenth-century manuscripts by E. Habel, *Studi med.* N. S. xi (1938), 103)

    MS.: F. W. E. Roth, *RF* vi (1891), 29; E. Habel, art. cit.

ERFURT Amplon. fol. 169, s. XIV. Three double leaves, fragments of a collection of motets and notes on musical theory, written in Germany.

fol. ɪɪd [C?]um amoris cella placens dul. . . . [pu–]ella vix decennis
uberum . . . –scere cepere quam . . . .

MS.: J. Handschin, *Acta Musicologica*, vi (1934), 103.

Amplon. oct. 32—*v*. München Clm 4660, *CB* 71.

ESCORIAL O. III. 2—*v*. Vat. Reg. lat. 585.

T. II. 16, s. xv. A small collection of verse, incl. two pseudo-Ovidian
pieces (*De pulice, De lupo*) and Henry of Settimello's *Elegia*.

fols. 68ᵛ–73ʳ [C]antica conponam nunc in me tristia narrans (ed. *supra*,
p. 523)

Z. II. 2—*v*. Clm 4660, *CB* 85, 159.

FIRENZE Bibl. Naz. Landau-Finaly 1416 (1613), *c*. 1265. Italian 'Liber
epistolarum secundum usum curie Romane et aliorum principum' (the
fifteenth-century title), with fables and verses.

fol. 38ᵛ Institor unus erat Pisanus. Nave per altum (amatory fabliau)

MS.: R. Davidsohn, *Quellen u. Forschungen aus ital. Archiven u. Bibl.*
xviii (1926), 373.

Laurenziana Edil. 197, s. xɪɪɪ in. Written in France. Statius' *Thebaid*, fol-
lowed by nine medieval poems fols. 130ʳ–131ᵛ. All except the third (the
planctus of Oedipus) have a love-theme:
Conquerar an sileam? monstrabo crimen amice (possibly by Hildebert;
ed. *A.L.* 794; for other manuscripts *v*. Walther 3173)
In me dei crudeles nimium (ed. M. Delbouille, *Mélanges Paul Thomas*,
Bruges, 1930, pp. 174 ff.)
Diri patris infausta pignora (for manuscripts and eds. *v*. Walther 4511)
O Fortuna quantum est mobilis (ed. M. Delbouille, loc. cit.)
Nescio quid sit amor, noli me sollicitare (ibid.)
Parce continuis (ed. *supra*, p. 341; *v*. also Augsburg Bischöfl. Ord. 5)
Amor habet superos (*CB* 88)
Primo quasdam eligo (ed. *supra*, p. 366)
[D]ant ad veris honorem (ed. *supra*, p. 367)

MS.: W. Meyer, *Studi lett. e ling. dedic. a Pio Rajna* (Milano, 1911), p. 149.

Laurenziana Plut. xxix. 1, s. xɪɪɪ ex. Written in France. A great anthology of
religious and secular, monodic and polyphonic music in the repertoire of
Notre Dame.

fol. 228ʳ⁻ᵛ Flos in monte cernitur
fols. 228ᵛ–229ʳ Veris ad imperia—eya

fol. 352ᵛ Veneris [prosperis] (fragm.—*v*. Oxford Rawl. C 510)
fol. 417ʳ⁻ᵛ Olim sudor Herculis (*CB* 63; other manuscripts ad loc.)
fols. 429ᵛ–430ʳ Vitam duxi iocundam sub amore
fol. 446ᵛ A globo veteri (*CB* 67; also in B.M. Arundel 384)
fol. 469ʳ Iam ver aperit terre gremium
All except the two *CB* ed. *supra*, pp. 390–7.

MS.: L. Delisle, *Annuaire-bull.* 1885, p. 103; F. Ludwig, *Repertorium*, pp. 57–
125; E. Gröninger, *Repertoire-Untersuchungen zum mehrstimmigen
Notre-Dame Conductus* (Regensburg, 1939).

Laurenziana Plut. xxxiii. 31—*v*. Berlin *Lat. qu. 915 and Wien 312.

Riccardiana 688—*v*. Oxford Digby 157.

FRANKFURT Private collection, s.c., s. xiv–xv. An anthology of Latin
and German verse, chiefly amatory and satirical, owned by J. C. von
Fichard, who printed many of the texts in *Frankfurtisches Archiv für die
ältere deutsche Literatur und Geschichte*, iii. Teil, Frankfurt a. M., 1815.
   Deus in adiutorium meum intende
   Amabilis puella
      (two fabliaux in macaronic verse, ed. op. cit., pp. 203, 205.
   The first also in E. Du Méril, *Poésies populaires latines antérieures au
douzième siècle*, 1843, p. 97)

Städt. Bibl. (S. Bartholomaei), 110, s. xiii ex. Ovidian and pseudo-Ovidian
poems.
   p. 26 Nox erat et placido capiebam pectore sompnum (*De sompnio*, ed.
      from this and two fifteenth-century manuscripts by Lehmann, p. 63)
   MS.: Lehmann, loc. cit.

Städt. Bibl. (S. Bartholomaei) 136, s. xv. Glossary, with interpolated verses,
incl. two amatory greetings:
   fol. 393ᵛ Ignis scintillans, terra, lapides, aqua stillans
   fol. 399ᵛ Dulcis amica, vale! carmen dono tibi tale
   MS.: H. Walther, *Hist. Vjs.* xxvi (1931), 295.

GDAŃSK (Danzig) Marienkirche F. 248—*v*. Wolfenbüttel Helmst. 622.

GENT Archive de la Cath. 12, s. xv². Written in Flanders. Ovid's *Fasti*,
with the commentary of Paulus Marsus (1440–84).
   fol. Iʳ⁻ᵛ Constans erat Thetidem parituram natum (ed. *supra*, p. 534)
Univ. 267—*v*. *infra*, p. 597 n. 1.

GLASGOW Hunterian Museum 511, *c.* 1225. *Artes dictandi* and scholastic
verse (French and English authors).

Bibliography
555

fol. 34ʳ Pauca loquar, sed vera loquar, sed fixa loquar; nam (ed. E. Faral, *Studi med.* N. S. ix (1936), 19)

Qui mihi dat quod amat, quod amo sibi velle videtur (ibid., p. 20)

fol. 69ʳ Iupiter Io rapit, Iuno petit infima, virgo

fol. 70ʳ Forma decens Cynarae pariens incendia Myrrhae

fol. 107ʳ Non amor infelix, sed amo; non hamo, sed hamor (ed. ibid., p. 106)

fol. 123ʳ Hic est philosophus Veneris, quem mollis pagina lecti (ibid.)

fol. 136ʳ Consulte teneros non claudit tutor amantes ('Pyramus and Thisbe', ed. E. Faral, *Arts*, p. 330)

fol. 140ʳ Laesi, Phoebe, tuam subit ira cupidinis iram

MS.: E. Faral, art. cit., pp. 18-119.

GÖTTINGEN Lüneb. 2, 1470-1500. Formerly at St. Michael's in Lüneburg. Literary miscellany, incl. ancient, medieval, and humanist verse.

fol. 221ʳ Alias dum synodum clerus celebraret (*De capitulo 15 mulierum; v.* München Clm 14818)

fol. 221ᵛ Pectoribus mores tot sunt, quot in urbe figure (ed. H. Walther, *ZfdA* lxv (1928), 278)

fol. 226ᵛ Si celum pellis, incaustum si mare, stellis (ibid. 287)

HALBERSTADT Domg. 71, s. xv. Verse miscellany, chiefly profane.

fol. 219ᵛ Est tocius mundi gaudium (*v. supra*, p. 297)

MS.: W. Wattenbach, *AfKdV* xxv (1878), 313-20, 345-50.

HOHENFURTH 42—*v.* Oxford Digby 157.

IVREA Cap. 85 fol. Commissioned by Warmund of Ivrea, in the reign of Otto III. *Liber psalmorum*, followed by some hymns.

fols. 21ʳ-23ʳ Cum secus ora vadi placeat mihi ludere Padi (Wido, 'Versus Eporedienses', probably autograph; ed. E. Dümmler, *ZfdA* xiv (1869), 245-53)

MS.: ibid. 259; A. Professione–I. Vignono, *Inventario* (Alba, 1967), p. 34.

Cap. 115, s. xiv. A songbook (64 fols.) compiled in France shortly after 1356. Liturgical tropes, sacred and secular songs, Latin and French. The French are chiefly love-songs; the Latin incl. historical and political pieces, anticlerical satire, didactic songs on the theory of music and of writing.

fol. 8ᵛ Vos qui[d] admiramini (Triple)

fol. 9ʳ Gratissima virg[i]nis species (Double)—Motet, text *supra*, pp. 406 ff.; other manuscripts and references ad loc.

MS.: *MGG*, s.v. *Ivrea* (vi. 1581–4); G. Borghezio, *Archivum Romanicum*, v (1921), 173; A. Professione–I. Vignono, *Inventario*, p. 86.

KØBENHAVN Univ. Fabr. 81 in oct., s. XII. Verse anthology, formerly at the monastery SS. Cosmae et Damiani, Liesborn.

   fol. 93ʳ Virginis insano Iulianus captus amore (ed. P. Lehmann, *Hist. Vjs.* xxx (1935), 54. These ten satirical lines I should attribute possibly to Matthew of Vendôme. A shorter version ed. *A.L.* 912. See also Walther 20470)

   MS.: P. Lehmann, art. cit., p. 20.

KOBLENZ Staatsarchiv ABB VII 1, 124—*v*. Trier 1081.

LAON 465, s. XIV. Collection of *grammatica*, from the Abbey of Cuissy.

   fols. 79ᵛ–80ᵛ *De rhythmico dictamine* contain:
   fol. 80ʳ Cunctis pulcrior puella
      Vilis eram, nunc sum fortis
      (ed. from seven manuscripts by G. Mari, *I trattati*, p. 14, and from a variant text in Paris Arsenal 763, p. 25)

LEIPZIG Univ. 1369—*v*. München Clm 14818.

LENINGRAD O. xiv. 11, s. XV. Miscellany beginning with chiefly satirical verse, written in Bohemia.

   fol. 3ʳ Clerus et presbyteri nuper consedere (*Consultatio sacerdotum de concubinis*; ed. *Poésies*, p. 131; also in München Clm 215, s. XV, fol. 59ʳ; further references in Walther 2929)
   fol. 15ᵛ Salve plus decies quam sunt momenta dierum (verse-greeting; ed. and other manuscripts H. Walther, *ZfdA* lxv (1928), 273)

   MS.: O. Dobiache-Rojdestvensky, *Analecta medii aevi* (Leningrad, 1925), i. 16.

LIÈGE Univ. 77, s. XI ex. Formerly at the Abbey of Saint-Trond (a later part, s. XIII, written at Saint-Trond, contains didactic writings). *Sententiae sapientum*, short scientific pieces, and an autograph of poems by Gautier, sent to Marbod.

   fol. 1ʳ Aeole, rex fortis, ventosae cura cohortis (ed. M. Delbouille, *Moyen Âge*, vi (1951), 222, with variants from three manuscripts. Other manuscripts in Walther 583)
   fol. 72ʳ⁻ᵛ Vernum tempus est amenum (*Laus verni temporis*, Delbouille p. 232)

fol. 72ᵛ Dum transirem Danubium (*Rithmus iocularis*, ibid., p. 235)

fols. 72ᵛ–73ʳ Gaudia nimpharum, violas floresque rosarum (*Puella ad amicum munera promittentem*, ibid., p. 236; also in B.N. lat. 14193; cf. also *Liber Floridus*, p. 290)

MS. (and further references): M. Delbouille, art. cit., p. 215.

LILLE 397, s. XIII ex. Adam de la Bassée, *Ludus super Anticlaudianum*, with corrections by the author. (Ed. P. Bayart, Lille, 1930.)

fol. 31ʳ Amor emptus precio (Bayart, p. 128)

LONDON B.M. Add. 12195, s. XV². Latin and English miscellany, sacred and secular writings, chiefly prose.

fol. 64ᵛ Erat quedam domina (ed. *supra*, p. 419)

B.M. Add. 24199, s. XII. From Bury St. Edmunds. After Prudentius's *Psychomachia* (s. X), a collection of medieval verse (fols. 39–89), especially of Hildebert and Marbod.

fol. 75ᵛ Res mea, dum noctem nondum vocat aurea luna
fol. 80ʳ Cara Matildis, ave! licet haec quae te mihi caram
    Ecce tenes quod amas, tristes depone querelas
fol. 80ᵛ Heu quid peccavi vel quid potui meruisse
    Ergo nec veram nec fictam mitto salutem
fol. 81ʳ Pingitur ales Amor sub causa mobilitatis
    O utinam tactu reddam data basia nutu
    (All ed. A. Boutemy, *Latomus*, ii (1938), 35, 49, 50–52.)

MS.: ibid., p. 30; also *Latomus*, i (1937), 293.

B.M. Arundel 102, ss. XII, XIII, XIV. Commentaries on the Gospels 'olim Carthusiensium prope Moguntiam'.

fol. 1ʳ (s. XIV) Me cogit amore quedam speciosa (ed. *supra*, p. 402)

B.M. Arundel 384, s. XIV². Written in England. Homiletic and ethical writings, ps-Ovid, *De vetula*; after the songs, excerpts of Cicero, an essay on the astrolabe, and an index to Boethius' *Consolatio*.

fols. 232ʳ–237ʳ Twenty-eight songs, ed. W. Meyer, *GA* N. F. xi. 2
    (1908). Seventeen love-songs (probably all composed in the twelfth
    or early thirteenth century), seven sacred songs and four political.
fol. 232ʳ Dionei sideris (ed. Meyer, 1)
    Preclusi viam floris (2)
    Ipsa vivere michi reddidit (3)
fol. 232ᵛ A globo veteri (4; *CB* 67; also in Laurenziana Plut. XXIX. 1)
    Estivali Clarius sublimatus rota (5)
    Brume torpescunt (6)

fol. 233ʳ Plaudit humus Boree (7)
Sevit aure spiritus (8; *CB* 83; also in Vat. Reg. lat. 344)
Dum rutilans Pegasei (9)
fol. 233ᵛ Grates ago Veneri (10; *CB* 72)
In laborem sponte labor (11)
Iam vere fere medio (12; also in Vat. lat. 4389)
fol. 234ʳ O cunctis liberalior (13)
Vacillantis trutine (14; *CB* 108; also in Cambridge Ff. i. 17)
Spoliatum flore pratum (15)
fol. 234ᵛ Partu recenti frondium (16)
fol. 237ʳ Quam velim virginum, si detur opcio (28, 3 sts.; also in B.N. lat.
3719 [fragm.] and Auxerre 243—4 sts., one added, I think spuriously,
between the first and second)

B.M. Cotton Titus D. xxiv—*v. infra*, p. 583.

B.M. Cotton Vitellius A. x, s. xiii ex. Wace's *Roman de Brut*, followed,
after the Latin poem, by historical and legal writings (ss. xiv, xv).

fol. 137ʳ⁻ᵛ Timor (v.l. Rumor) novus Anglie partes pergiravit (*De
convocatione sacerdotum*, ed. T. Wright, *Mapes*, p. 180; further
references and manuscripts in Walther 16929)

MS. (also): *Le Roman de Brut*, ed. I. Arnold (SATF), i. vii.

B.M. Harley 2253, s. xiv in. Miscellany of secular and religious prose and
verse, Latin, French, and English, written in the West Midlands.

fol. 76ʳ Dum ludis floribus velud lacinia (macaronic Latin, French, and
English, ed. G. L. Brook, *The Harley Lyrics*, p. 55)

MS.: G. L. Brook, ibid., p. 1.

B.M. Harley 3362, s. xv in. Verse miscellany (with occasional prose),
written in England.

fol. 10ᵛ Non est verus amor qui vult regnare per horas
fol. 21ᵛ Est 'amo' vox miseri, cui si dederit paragoge (ed. H. Walther,
ZfdA lxxxiv (1952–3), 268–9; also in an earlier manuscript, Berlin
*lat. qu. 915, s. xiii, fol. 94ʳ, missing since 1945)
fols. 90ᵛ–91ʳ A celuy que pluys eyme en mounde (*De amico ad amicam*,
macaronic French, English, and Latin, also in Cambridge UL Gg. iv.
27, s. xv, fol. 10ᵛ—*v*. Brown–Robbins 16)

MS.: H. Walther, art. cit., p. 265.

B.M. Harley 3724, s. xiv in. Written probably in Ireland. Verse and prose
miscellany, incl. Giraldus's *Topographia*, some prayers in English, and the
Epistola Valerii.

fol. 46ʳ Prisciani regula penitus cassatur (*In favorem sacerdotalis coniugii*; ed. *Poésies*, p. 127; fragm. in Oxford Digby 166; further references and manuscripts in Walther 14734)

B.M. Royal 13. A. iv—*v.* Cambridge UL Dd. xi. 78.

Lambeth Palace 118, s. xii. Formerly at Merton Priory. Works of Henry of Huntingdon. In Bk. xi (fols. 188ʳ–191ʳ) are two epigrams:

> Si quis erit quem verus amor per seria ducat (*De vero amore*, *ad lectorem*)
> Qui tenerorum vulnus amorum non reveretur (*De amore*)
> Both ed. T. Wright, *SP* ii. 166, 174

Lambeth Palace 196, *c.* 1150 (W. Meyer). Formerly at Lanthony. Priscian's *Grammatica*.

> fols. Iᵛ–IIʳ Inaspectam nube tectam sero arcton intuens ('Die moderne Leda', ed. W. Meyer, *ZfdA* l (1908), 289)

★LOUVAIN Univ. 139, s. xiii. Formerly at St. Mary of Villers, destroyed in 1914. On the last page was a narrative poem in seventy-three stanzas, about a monk and a nun: 'Erat quidam monachus / corpore non validus / sed grabato deditus . . . .'

> MS.: *Archiv* viii (1843), 482.

★LÜBECK 152, s. xvᴵ. In Lübeck since 1449; missing since 1945. *Epistolarium*, followed by jocular songs and proverbs, Latin, German, and macaronic.

> fol. 80ʳ (among the epistles) Ave, salutaris domina, multum sincerissima
> fol. 242ᵛ Stude, bone clerice, virgines amare
> fol. 243ʳ Institor amabilem obsecravit virginem (ed. W. Wattenbach, *Germania*, xvii (1872), 187–8; also in Berlin lat. fol. 319, s. xv, fol. 210ʳ, inc. 'Rusticius amabilem'—*v. NA* ix (1884), 629)

> MS.: W. Wattenbach, art. cit., p. 181.

MONTPELLIER Bibl. de l'École de Médicine H 196, s. xiii ex. The greatest anthology of thirteenth-century polyphony; both Latin and French texts. Written in the Parisian region, or perhaps at Saint-Germain d'Auxerre.

> fols. 290ᵛ–292ʳ Aucuns vont souvent (Triple)—Amor qui cor vulnerat (Double)
> fols. 378ᵛ–379ʳ Amor potest conqueri (Triple)—Ad amorem sequitur (Double)

> MS. (complete facsimile and transcription): Y. Rokseth, *Polyphonies du XIIIᵉ siècle* (4 vols., Paris 1935–48).

MÜNCHEN Clm 215—*v*. Clm 14818 and Leningrad O. xiv. 11.

Clm 237—*v*. Clm 416.

Clm 416, 'Finitus in Berlin a. 1451'. Secular miscellany, beginning with Andreas Capellanus *De amore* and ending with satirical verse.

> fols. 239ʳ–245ᵛ Ocia si veniunt, iam mens torpescit ab intus ('Pyramus and Thisbe', ed. Lehmann, p. 52; also in Clm 237, s. xv², fols. 121ʳ–128ᵛ)

Clm 641, s. xv. Chiefly secular miscellany, Latin and German.

> fol. 51ʳ Vocativos oculos (*Doctor[is] Noe declina[cio]*, ed. P. Lehmann, *Parodie*, p. 154)

Clm 4350, s. xiv. Secular and religious miscellany, Latin and German, from St. Ulrich, Augsburg.

> fol. 92ᵛ Estas iam redit florida, rosas ferens et lilium (ed. W. Wattenbach, *AfKdV* xxvi (1879), 165)

Clm 4382, s. xiv–xv. Scientific writings, from St. Ulrich, Augsburg. Two illustrations in an *Ars rigmatisandi*:

> fol. 174ʳ⁻ᵛ Iuvencula pulcherrima
> Quadam virgine formosa

Clm 4409, s. xv. Verse anthology from St. Ulrich, Augsburg.

> fols. 167ʳ–174ʳ Moribus et vita quisquis vult esse facetus (*Facetus*, ed. from five manuscripts by A. Morel-Fatio, *Romania*, xv (1886), 224; further manuscripts and references in Walther 11220, 12295, 14438)

Clm 4603, ss. xii, xiii, xiv. Works of Aristotle and Sallust, grammatical and rhetorical commentaries; formerly at Benediktbeuern.

> fol. 135ᵛ (s. xiii) Propter frigus hiemale (ed. *supra*, p. 390)
> fol. 177ᵛ (s. xiv) Sic mea fata canendo solor (*v*. Clm 4660, *CB* 116)
>   Visus et alloquium, contactus et oscula, factum (ed. *CM* xx (1959), 167)

Clm 4660, *c*. 1220–30 (P. D.) [*Carmina Burana*].

> Formerly at Benediktbeuern; written in Bavaria. The largest extant collection of secular Latin lyrics, together with metrical pieces, German stanzas, a Nativity play, and a number of later poetic and dramatic additions.
>
> I give the first lines of the Latin love-poems (ed. O. Schumann, *CB* I. 2, *Die Liebeslieder*; some important corrections by H. Spanke, *Literaturblatt für germ. und rom. Philol.* 1943, 35–46).
>
> Ianus annum circinat (*CB* 56)
> Bruma, veris emula (57)

Iam ver oritur (58)
Ecce, chorus virginum (59)
Captus amore gravi (60)
Cupido mentem gyrat (60a)
Siquem Pieridum ditavit contio (61)
Dum Diane vitrea (62)
Olim sudor Herculis (63; also in Cambridge UL Ff. i. 17, Laurenziana
   Plut. xxix. 1, Bodley Add. A. 44, and Vat. Reg. lat. 344)
Quocumque more motu volvuntur tempora (65)
A globo veteri (67; also in B.M. Arundel 384 and Laurenziana Plut.
   xxix. 1)
Saturni sidus lividum Mercurio micante (68)
Estas in exilium (69)
Estatis florigero tempore (70)
Axe Phebus aureo (71; also in Erfurt Amplon. oct. 32, s. xiii, fol. 89^{r-v})
Grates ago Veneri (72; also in B.M. Arundel 384)
Clauso Cronos et serato (73; also in St. Gallen 383, s. xiii, pp. 158–62,
   and B.N. lat. 1139 [Saint-Martial], fol. 47^v, s. xii ex.)
Letabundus rediit (74)
Omittamus studia (75)
Dum caupona verterem vino debachatus (76)
Si linguis angelicis loquar et humanis (77)
Anni novi rediit novitas (78)
Estivali sub fervore (79)
Estivali gaudio (80)
Solis iubar nituit (81)
Frigus hinc est horridum (82)
Sevit aure spiritus (83; also in B.M. Arundel 384 and Vat. Reg. lat.
   344)
Dum prius inculta (84; also in Vat. Reg. lat. 344)
Veris dulcis in tempore (85, 159; also in Escorial Z. II. 2 [Barcelona],
   s. xiii, fol. 287^r)
Non contrecto (86)
Amor tenet omnia (87)
Amor habet superos (88; also in Laurenziana Edil. 197)
Iove cum Mercurio Geminos tenente (88a; also in B.N. lat. 3719)
Exiit diluculo (90; also in Clm 5539 [Diessen], s. xiv, fol. 35^{r-v})
Anni parte florida, celo puriore (92; *Altercatio Phyllidis et Flore*—also in
   ten other manuscripts)
Hortum habet insula virgo virginalem (93–93a)
Congaudentes ludite (94)
Cur suspectum me tenet domina (95)

Iuvenes amoriferi (96)
O Antioche (97)
Troie post excidium (98)
Superbi Paridis leve iudicium (99)
O decus, o Libye regnum, Carthaginis urbem (100)
Eia dolor (103)
Egre fero, quod egroto (104 I–II)
Dum curata vegetarem (105)
Veneris vincula (106)
Dira vi amoris teror (107)
Vacillantis trutine (108; also in B.M. Arundel 384 and Cambridge UL
    Ff. i. 17)
Multiformi succendente (109)
Quis furor est in amore (110)
O comes amoris, dolor (111; also in the Fragm. Burana)
Dudum voveram (112)
Transit nix et glacies (113)
Tempus accedit floridum (114)
Nobilis, mei miserere, precor (115)
Sic mea fata canendo solor (116; also in B.N. lat. 3719 and Clm 4603
    [Benediktbeuern], s. XIV, fol. 177ᵛ; see also P. Dronke, 'The Text of
    CB 116', *CM* xx (1959), 159)
Lingua mendax et dolosa (117)
Doleo, quod nimium (118)
Dulce solum natalis patrie (119; also in five other manuscripts, incl.
    Stuttgart HB I. 95)
Rumor letalis (120; also in Stuttgart HB I. 95)
Vincit Amor quemque, sed numquam vincitur ipse (120a, one line
    only)
Tange, sodes, citharam manu letiore (121)
Non est crimen amor, quia, si scelus esset amare (121a, two lines; also
    in Oxford Rawl. G 109—*v. supra*, p. 257)
Huc usque, me miseram [Tempus instat floridum] (126)
Cedit, hiems, tua durities (135)
Omnia sol temperat (136)
Ver redit optatum (137)
Veris leta facies (138)
Tempus transit horridum (139)
Terra iam pandit gremium vernali lenitate (140)
Florent omnes arbores (141)
Tempus adest floridum, surgunt namque flores (142)
Ecce gratum (143)

Iam iam virent prata, iam iam virgines (144)
Musa venit carmine (145)
Tellus flore vario vestitur (146)
Si de more (147)
Floret tellus floribus (148)
Floret silva nobilis (149)
Redivivo vernat flore (150)
Virent prata hiemata (151)
Estas non apparuit preteritis temporibus (152)
Tempus transit gelidum (153)
Est Amor alatus puer et levis, est pharetratus (154; also in Clm 17142)
Quam pulchra nitet facie (155)
Salve, ver optatum (156)
Lucis orto sidere (157)
Vere dulci mediante (158)
Veris dulcis in tempore (159; repeats CB 85)
Dum estas inchoatur (160)
Ab estatis foribus (161)
O consocii (162)
Longa spes et dubia (163)
Ob amoris pressuram (164)
Amor telum est insignis Veneris (165)
Iam dudum Amoris militem (166)
Laboris remedium (167 I–II)
Annualis mea (168)
Hebet sydus leti visus (169)
Quelibet succenditur vivens creatura (170)
De pollicito (171)
Lude, ludat, ludite! iocantes nunc audite (172)
Revirescit (173)
Veni, veni, venias (174)
Pre amoris tedio (175)
Stetit puella (177)
Volo virum vivere viriliter (178; also in Basel Univ. D. iv. 4)
Tempus est iocundum, o virgines (179)
O mi dilectissima (180)
Quam Natura ceteris (181)
Sol solo in stellifero (182)
Si puer cum puellula (183)
Virgo quedam nobilis (184)
Ich was ein chint so wolgetan, [virgo dum florebam] (185)
Suscipe, flos, florem, quia flos designat amorem (186)

The love-songs seem to fall into two groups. In the first group (56–121) the compilers of the *CB* drew considerably on an international repertoire (Saint-Martial, Notre Dame, possibly England); in the second (135–86) they collected a local repertoire, usually adding German stanzas. It is noteworthy that (if we exclude a second copy of 85) only two of the Latin pieces in this entire group are found elsewhere: the epigram 154 (in an earlier manuscript from Scheftlarn) and the song 178 (in a later manuscript written at Basel). Between the two groups comes the curious mélange 122–34, which includes songs of Walter of Châtillon and Philip the Chancellor, even lines of Marbod, and only one song (126) that has anything to do with love. One might suppose that the copyists had to return some borrowed non-German manuscript(s) at this stage and wanted to include all they could before returning it, even if it meant disturbing the overall pattern of the love-songs in their own collection. They had already begun to do so a little earlier, to seize the chance of copying such famous pieces as 'Sacerdotes mementote' (91) and 'Pergama flere volo' (101).

MS. (and further references): O. Schumann, *CB* II. 1. 3*–95*. See also P. Dronke, *PBB* lxxxiv (1962), 173.

Clm 5539—*v.* Clm 4660, *CB* 90.

Clm 6432, s. XII. Formerly at Freising. William of Vivaria's verse commentary on the Song of Songs.

> fol. 86^v (s. XIII) Scribere clericulis paro novellis omnibus (ed. P. Lehmann, *Parodistische Texte*, p. 49; see also Clm 18628)

Clm 6911, s. XIII–XIV. Formerly at Fürstenfeld. Grammatical treatises, followed by a small anthology of (chiefly ancient) verse. In John of Garland's *Poetria* (fols. 1^r–22^v):

> Cum citharizat avis silvis dulcedine quavis (ed. G. Mari, *RF* xiii (1902), 894, from this manuscript and Admont 637; with corrs. by E. Faral, *Romania*, xlix (1923), 257—though evidently, as F. writes of 'Bibl. du prince de Monaco 6911' (!), not from manuscript. See also B.N. lat. 11867 for an earlier manuscript of the *Poetria*)

> fol. 102^v Urit in affectu Venus anxia, vexat (v.l. sordet) in actu (text and manuscripts J. Werner, *NA* xxxi (1906), 589)
>
> fol. 128^r In te Natura, que pulchrior omnibus una
> Vite dulcedo, mihi te da, nam tibi me do
> (both ed. *supra*, p. 490)

Clm 8952, s. XV. Commentaries on Vergil and Terence, formerly at St. Augustine's, München.

> fol. 152^v Est Amor hic pictus, cuius pictura figurat (28 lines)

Clm 12725—*v.* Clm 17210.

Clm 14634—*v.* Clm 14818.

Clm 14818, 1457. Formerly at St. Emmeram. Chiefly commentaries on books of the Old Testament, excerpts from Vincent of Beauvais's *Speculum historiale*.

fols. 134ᵛ–136ʳ Alias dum sinodum clerus celebraret (*De capitulo 15 mulierum*; also in Berlin lat. fol. 376, s. xv, fol. 1ᵛ; Clm 215, s. xv, fol. 66ʳ; Clm 14634, s. xv, fol. 3ʳ; Leipzig Univ. 1369, s. xv, fol. 146ᵛ; and Göttingen Lüneb. 2, 1470–1500, fol. 221ʳ; a sequel, probably s. xiii, to 'Clerus et presbyteri nuper consedere'—*v*. P. Lehmann, *Parodie*, pp. 159–65)

fol. 138ʳ Arcubus innumeris mens oppugnatur amantis (4 lines)

Clm 14834, s. xii. Theological and ascetic miscellany, formerly at St. Emmeram.

fol. 26ʳ Iuvenilis lascivia (ed. *supra*, p. 361)
fol. 26ᵛ Virgo Flora (ed. *supra*, p. 362)

Clm 17142, s. xii in. Grammatical and literary miscellany formerly at Scheftlarn, probably written in Regensburg. The eleventh-century love-verses, fifty pieces, are edited in my anthology, *supra*, pp. 422 ff. For first lines see table of Contents, pp. vi–vii.

fol. 107ʳ⁻ᵛ Est Amor alatus puer et levis, est pharetratus (*CB* 154; see also Walther 5818, 12352)

MS.: W. Wattenbach, *MSB* iii (1873), 710–47 (also *Forschungen zur deutschen Geschichte* xiii (1873), 393–7); *supra*, p. 221.

Clm 17210, s. xiii. Grammatical writings and extracts of classical authors, formerly at Scheftlarn.

fol. 40ᵛ Visus et alloquium, tactus, post oscula factum (ed. *supra*, p. 488; also in Clm 12725, s. xv, fol. 16ʳ; further references in Walther 3034, 20651)

Clm 17212, s. xiii. Poetic miscellany from Scheftlarn, incl. verses of Hildebert and Marbod.

fol. 22ᵛ O utinam nobis servetur fedus Amoris
fol. 24ᵛ Horula non hora qua te vidi reputatur
fol. 25ᵛ Cum duo sint quos unus amor conformat in unum
fol. 26ʳ Celitus artifici res elimata paratu
All ed. *supra*, pp. 467 ff.

Clm 17289, s. xiv². A. Rampegolo's 'compendium figurarum moralium', formerly at Scheftlarn.

fol. 144ʳ A. dulcis roris unda (ed. *supra*, p. 410)

Clm 18580, s. xII. Poetic miscellany, formerly at Tegernsee, beginning with poems by Reginald of Canterbury (incl. *De Malcho*).

    fols. 59^r–64^r Non honor acceptus, gradus altus honoris adeptus (*v. supra*, p. 463)

Clm 18628, ss. xI, xIII–xIV. Formerly at Tegernsee. Chiefly poetic miscellany, incl. Sedulius's *Carmen paschale* and Walafrid Strabo's *Visio Wettini*. In the later hand:

    fol. 12^v Fatorum prodigia (ed. *supra*, p. 398)
    fol. 70^r Scribere clericulis (fragm.—*v*. Clm 6432)
    fol. 105^v Rosam et candens lilium (ed. *SLP* ii. 317; fragm. also in Oxford Lyell 50)
    MS.: E. Dümmler, *NA* iv (1879), 278.

Clm 18910, s. xv. Literary and philosophical miscellany, containing anciet t, medieval, and humanist writing, formerly at Tegernsee.

    fol. 59^r Cetera sunt preclusa mihi, tegit omnia vestis
    fols. 106^r–112^r Extracts from the *Facetus* (*v*. Clm 4409, ed. W. Wattenbach as ps-Ovid, *De arte amandi* and *De remediis amoris*, *ZfdA* xxxiv (1890), 277)
    fol. 136^r Sum nuda thalamo nec me formosior ulla est (*Puelle carmina ex Florentia Romam missa*)
    Cetera sunt preclusa mihi . . . . (as on fol. 59^r)
    fol. 201^r *Geta* (*v*. Bern 702)

Clm 19411, *c*. 1160–before 1186. From Tegernsee. *Ludus de Antichristo*; excerpts from Otto of Freising's *Gesta Friderici*; epistles, many to or from Tegernsee, Otto, or Frederick; Albericus *De dictamine*; proverbs and verses.

    fol. 68^v Nobilis, apta, pia, semper letare, Sophia (ed. *supra*, p. 517)
    fols. 69^r–70^r Seven letters (ed. *supra*, pp. 472 ff.)
    S. suo dilecto (*Amico amica*)
    H. quondam carissimo (*Amico amica derelicta*)
    Accipe scriptorum, o fidelis, responsa tuorum
    Affamina salutationis
    C. Cara karissime
    C. super mel et favum dulciori
    G. unice sue rose
        (a few quotations from these letters, with many mistakes, in H. Brinkmann, *Entstehungsgeschichte*, p. 94)
    fol. 70^v Instar solis, ave! totius luminis atque (ed. *supra*, p. 518; fragm. in Zürich C 58/275)
    Ubere multarum, carissima, deliciarum (ed. *supra*, p. 463)

fol. 72ᵛ Iam satis et nimis est quod litera nostra moratur (ed. *supra*, p. 464)

fol. 113ᵛ H. flori florum, redimito stemmate morum ('Dû bist mîn, ich bin dîn', ed. *MF* [1944], p. 318; further references C. von Kraus ad loc., and *Untersuchungen zu MF*, p. 1)

MS.: W. Wattenbach, *NA* xvii (1892), 33; H. Plechl, *Deutsches Archiv für Erforschung des Mittelalters* xviii (1962), 418.

Clm 19486, *c.* 1050. Formerly at Tegernsee, and probably written there. Nineteen double leaves, the (incomplete) autograph of the romance *Ruodlieb* (ed. E. H. Zeydel, Chapel Hill, 1959; K. Langosch, *Waltharius, Ruodlieb, Märchenepen*, 2nd impr. Darmstadt, 1960).

Fragments vi–viii and xvii have fabliau elements; fragments xi, xii, and xiv give a brilliant portrayal of the courtship and marriage of two young lovers. Fragment xi survives only in Sankt Florian Stiftsbibl. 22 (one double leaf).

Clm 19488, s. xii ex. Formerly at Tegernsee. *Medulla Gratiani*, two ethical works attrib. Seneca.

pp. 36–94 Matthew of Vendôme's *Epistolarium* (ed. W. Wattenbach, *MSB* ii (1872), 561). Two love-letters:
Dilectae delegat amans quae Naso Corinnae (ii. 1, ibid. 594)
Dilecto dilecta suo, quodcumque favillam (ii. 2, ibid. 599)
    (ii. 3 and ii. 4 are verse letters to and from a bawd, ibid. 604 ff.)
pp. 95–137 A verse miscellany, including:
pp. 128–30 Profuit ignaris aliquid nescisse: probaris (ed. *supra*, p. 452)
p. 136 Que queror edam: femina quedam me male ledit (ed. W. Wattenbach, *MSB* iii (1873), 707; other manuscripts in Walther 15888)
Sicut cera fluit subito percussa calore (ed. Wattenbach, ibid.; other manuscripts in Walther 18151)

MS.: W. Wattenbach, *MSB* iii (1873), 685.

Clm 24539, s. xv². Chiefly rhetorical miscellany, from Strasbourg.

fol. 69ʳ (among some hymns to the Virgin) Brumalis temeritas (ed. *supra*, p. 420)

NOVARA Bibl. Cap. 64 (cxxxvi), s. xiii ex. 'Grammatica del maestro Syon, vercellese'.

fol. 13ʳ Nimis amor dominatur (ed. G. Mari, *I trattati*, p. 21)

OXFORD Bodley 38, s. xiⁱ. Probably from Fleury (*v. supra*, p. 339); once owned by Pierre Daniel. Late ancient poetry (incl. Maximianus,

Boethius, and Prudentius), a star time-table (*Horologium nocturnum*), some antiphons with music, and three medieval Latin poems.

    fols. 56ᵛ–57ʳ Foebus abierat subtractis cursibus (ed. *supra*, p. 334; fragm. in Vat. lat. 3251)

    MS: (also): R. Poole, *JTS* xvi (1915), 98.

Bodley 315, s. xv in. Formerly at Exeter Cathedral, written in England. Richard Rolle 'super Job', Robert Grosseteste 'de Oculo [morali]', John of Salisbury's *Polycraticus* and *Metalogicon*, some English inscriptions.

    fol. 268ʳ Ite pares pariter, paribus suadete medullis (ed. *supra*, p. 490)

Bodley Add. A 44, s. xiii in. Florilegium (prose and verse) written in England, once owned by Thomas Bekynton.

    fol. 30ʳ⁻ᵛ Anna soror, ut quid mori (ed. A. Wilmart, *MARS* iv (1958), 35; also in Wien 208, s. xv, fol. 113ʳ)

    fol. 45ʳ⁻ᵛ Ridere solitus (moralistic, ed. Wilmart, ibid., p. 37)

    fols. 47ʳ–53ʳ *Miles gloriosus* (*v*. Vat. Reg. lat. 344)

    fol. 70ʳ⁻ᵛ Olim sudor Herculis (*CB* 63; also in Cambridge Ff. i. 17, Laurenziana Plut. xxix. 1, Vat. Reg. lat. 344)

    fol. 70ᵛ Ver prope florigerum, flava Licori (ed. *supra*, p. 374; also in Auxerre 243)

    fol. 71ʳ De terre gremio (from 'Hyemale tempus, vale'—*v*. Zürich C 58/275)

    fol. 71ʳ⁻ᵛ Bruma, grando, glacies (ed. A. Wilmart, art. cit., p. 64)

    fols. 81ʳ–83ᵛ Taurum sol intraverat, et ver, parens florum (*v*. Vat. Reg. lat. 344)

    fols. 83ᵛ–91ᵛ *Geta* (*v*. Bern 702)

    MS.: A. Wilmart, *MARS* i (1941–3), 41.

Bodley Canon. lat. 112, 1325. Copied by Prosdocimo da Cittadella, *custos* of the Duomo at Padova. Bellino Bissolo's *Speculum Vitae* (between 1260 and 1277) and *Liber legum moralium*. The first contains two amatory fabliaux:

    fols. 1ᵛ–3ʳ Femina temporibus nostris fuit una maligno

    fols. 15ᵛ–16ᵛ Magnifice quidam vir quadam dives in urbe (ed. L. Suttina, Strecker 1931, p. 190)

    The *Speculum Vitae* is also in Vat. Ross. 1126 and Perugia 729 (fragm.).

    MS.: R. Weiss, *Archivio storico lombardo*, x (1947), 33.

Digby 53, s. xii ex. Collection of verse and proverbs (esp. Serlo of Wilton), written at Bridlington.

    fol. 11ᵛ Dulce malum Venus est, et opertum melle venenum

    fol. 13ʳ Alteritas sexus quos alterat, unio mentis

fol. 13ᵛ Dulcis amica vale, sine te procul hinc habiturus

fol. 15ᵛ In qua delectant, illam mea lumina spectant
(all ed. *supra*, pp. 510 ff.)

fol. 35ʳ Me dolor infestat foris, intus iugiter omnis (*De Babione*, amatory
fabliau, ed. from five manuscripts by E. Faral, Paris, 1948)

fol. 64ʳ Cuius forma bona Veneri sit femina prona
Cuius amor verus sopor est in pectore serus

fol. 64ᵛ Proxima langori manus est et ocellus amori
Cum procul aspiciunt quod amant, prope gaudia fiunt
(all ed. A. C. Friend, *Med. Stud.* xvi (1954), 179, nos. 41, 43, 44, 47;
other manuscripts given ibid.).

MS.: E. Faral, op. cit., p. xvii; A. C. Friend, art. cit.; P. Meyer, *Archives
des missions*, 2ᵉ série, v (1868), 143.

Digby 157, ss. xii, xiv. *De universitate mundi, Architrenius*, Joseph of Exeter's
De bello Troiano.

fol. 101ʳ (s. xiv) Quidam triplo metro (ed. *A.H.* i. 118, from Hohenfurth 42, s. xv; also in Firenze Riccardiana 688, s. xv, fol. 143ᵛ. A
ribald *meretrix* poem, burlesquing a hymn to the Virgin. Dreves,
A.H., loc. cit., did not see the rhyming principle, and printed the
piece as a—wholly unintelligible—hymn. In this manuscript the nine
stanzas open as follows: Quidam triplo metro / salutando ret..ulit
talia; De imperatrice / facta *meretri*..na deitate; Dum illa chorizat /
fortiter bombici...na tunica; Dum sub umbra quercus / comedit,
tunc ster...nitur floribus; Dum ciphum attingit / quod bibit homo
min...[i]strat aliis; Coma sibi fulva, / magna quoque vul..tus
formositas; Pili quot in mulo, / tot habet in cul.tu monilia; Dum se
lecto ponit / clericus suppo...rtat psalterium; Tunc est sibi cura /
sublevare cru..cis signaculum)

Digby 166, ss. xiii, xiv. Written in England. Mathematical and astronomical
works, followed by a large collection of verse.

fol. 51ʳ (s. xiii) Tria sunt officia quibus laus honoris (ed. K. Strecker,
ZfdP li (1926), 118–19)

fols. 91ʳ–93ᵛ (s. xiv, and in 18 other manuscripts, ss. xiv, xv) Vix
nodosum valeo nodum denodare (here called 'Epilogium fratris
Walteri de Burgo super Alanum in opere suo De planctu nature
contra prelatum sodomitam'; in some other manuscripts attrib. Alanus
himself, perhaps because it was often copied at the end of the *De
planctu* [*v.* R. Bossuat, *Études romanes dédiées à Mario Roques*, Paris,
1946, p. 74 n.]; ed. P. Leyser, *Historia* 1092–5; manuscripts in Walther 20763)

fol. 109ᵛ Fragm. of 'Prisciani regula'—*v.* B.M. Harley 3724.

Douce 137, s. XIII. Legal miscellany, Latin and French, mostly relating to England.

> fol. 111ᵛ En may quant dait e foil et fruit parens Natura parere (macaronic pastourelle, ed. *SLP* ii. 336)

Douce 139, s. XIII. Chiefly English statutes and laws.

> fol. 148ʳ Amor est quedam mentis insania (Latin, French, and English definition of love, ed. C. Brown, *English Lyrics of the XIIIth Century*, p. 14). There is also an English love-song on fol. 5ʳ and a French one on fol. 179ᵛ.

Laud lat. 25, s. XII. Theological writings, chiefly on the Gospels, 'quondam Carthusiensium ord. S. Michaelis prope Moguntiam'.

> fol. 3ʳ Musa iocosa veni, mihi carmina suggere vati (ed. *supra*, p. 450)

Lyell 50, ss. XIIᵎ, XIIIᵎ. Both parts written in Austria or Germany, formerly at Admont. On the last leaf of the second part (fols. 41–63, Honorius's *Elucidarius*), in mirror writing:

> fol. 63ᵛ Te diligo pre ceteris (*v.* München Clm 18628)
> Just below, in another thirteenth-century hand, the words 'Surgite flores'.

> MS.: Typewritten description in the Bodleian Library.

Rawlinson C 510, s. XIII². Written at the Abbey of Bardney. Originally part of a larger volume (with Rawlinson C 504 and D 893), incl. theological writings and the story of Apollonius.

> fols. 1ʳ–20ʳ, 22ʳ–24ʳ, 29ʳ–31ʳ A collection of Notre Dame conductus and motets

> fol. 10ʳ⁻ᵛ Veneris [prosperis] (ed. *supra*, p. 393; fragm. in Laurenziana Plut. XXIX. 1)

> MS. (and further references): R. W. Hunt, *MARS* v (1961), 28.

Rawlinson G 109, *c.* 1200. Probably written in France. Some 200 medieval Latin poems, followed by Ovid's *Rem. Am.* and *Pont.*, and Ranulf de Glanville's *Treatise on the Laws and Customs of England*.

> pp. 3–30 Poems of Hugh Primas (ed. W. Meyer, *GN* 1907, pp. 75 ff.)
> pp. 7–8 Idibus his Mai miser exemplo Menelai (ibid. 127)
> p. 44 Tela, Cupido, tene, quoniam non ille nec illa
> p. 66 Constat et apparet quod amo—nec Amor mihi paret
> p. 67 Cur infirmaris? cur palles? cur maceraris
> (all ed. *supra*, pp. 465 ff.)
> p. 72 Non est crimen amor, quia si scelus esset amare (*CB* 121a)

St. John's 202, s. xɪv. Chiefly theological miscellany, formerly in the monastery of St. Martin at Battle.

  fols. 144ʳ–150ʳ Vir loquitur mulierque simul sic verba serendo (*Altercatio inter virum et mulierem*, analysed by H. Walther, *Streitg.* 137–9, who would date it s. xɪɪ–xɪɪɪ)

PARIS Bibl. Arsenal 763—*v.* Laon 465.

B.N. lat. 1118, 988–96 (Strecker, Spanke, Anglés); Chailley (*École*, p. 92) accepts this only to fol. 101ᵛ, dating the rest s. xɪ, and the gathering containing 'Iam dulcis amica' s. xɪ ex. Troparium and prosarium from Saint-Martial (at least from s. xɪɪ, though not written there acc. Chailley).

  fol. 247ᵛ Iam dulcis amica venito (ed. E. Vuolo, *CN* x (1950), 5; facs. de Coussemaker, *Harmonie*, pl. viii)

  MS. (and further references): J. Chailley, loc. cit.
  See also Cambridge Gg. v. 35 and Wien 116.

B.N. lat. 1139—*v.* München Clm 4660, *CB* 73.

B.N. lat. 3110, s. xɪ ex. Written in France. (s. xɪv, Thomas Aquinas, *De regno.*) Persius' and Juvenal's *Satires*, Priscian's *Institutiones*.

  fols. 59ᵛ–64ʳ Didactic poems, and two invocations to Sapientia:
    Unica regina, specialis Virgo, supina (ed. in part by M.-Th. d'Alverny, *Mélanges Félix Grat,* i. 275)
    Mater materne rationis, adesto superne (ed. *supra,* p. 513)
  MS.: M.-Th. d'Alverny, op. cit. i. 265, 276–8.

B.N. lat. 3718, s. xɪɪɪ. Verse miscellany.

  fols. 28ʳ–48ᵛ Christe, Dei virtus, verbum patris, hostia vera (Karolellus, *Vita Amici et Amelici*)
  fol. 83ʳ Parisius Paridi. Felix tua secula vidi (Serlo of Wilton; also in B.N. lat. 6765 and Vat. Reg. lat. 344; ed. E. Faral, *Romania,* xlvi (1920), 259)
    Voce brevi, sermone levi, tibi paucula nevi
    Fit rea fletque Venus, quod venas Palladi plenus (Serlo; both also in Vat. Reg. lat. 344; ed. Faral, ibid., pp. 260, 265)
  MS.: E. Faral, ibid., p. 231.

B.N. lat. 3719, completed by Bernart Itier, the librarian at Saint-Martial, in 1210; most gatherings in various twelfth-century hands. Songbook, chiefly sequences and conductus.

  fol. 23ʳ (and fols. 37ᵛ–38ᵛ) Ex ungue primo teneram (ed. *supra,* p. 378; also in Auxerre 243)

Quam velim virginum, si detur optio (fragm.; also in B.M. Arundel
384, Auxerre 243)

fol. 23ᵛ Sementivam redivivam (fragm. of 'Hyemale tempus, vale'—
v. Zürich C 58/275)

fol. 28ᵛ Iove cum Mercurio geminos tenente (*CB* 88)

fol. 36ʳ De terre gremio (*v. supra*, 'Sementivam redivivam')

fol. 40ʳ⁻ᵛ Ecce letantur omnia (ed. *supra*, p. 380)

fol. 41ʳ Nisi fallor, nil repertum o (ed. *supra*, p. 382)

fol. 42ʳ De ramis cadunt folia (ed. *supra*, p. 288)

fol. 87ʳ Iocus et letitia (*v. supra*, p. 292)

fols. 87ᵛ, 91ʳ Plures vidi margaritas (ed. *supra*, p. 384)

fol. 88ʳ Sic mea fata canendo solor (*CB* 116)

MS.: H. Spanke, *ZffSL* liv (1931), 308.

B.N. lat. 6415—*v.* Auxerre 243.

B.N. lat. 6560, s. xɪv. Theological works (incl. Honorius, ps-Melitto,
Augustine, Ambrose).

fol. 133ᵛ Quando tellus renovatur (ed. *supra*, p. 520)

B.N. lat. 6765, s. xɪɪ. Written in northern France. After Seneca *De Beneficiis*
(originally separate), a verse miscellany containing poems by Serlo of
Wilton, and concluding with proverbs and epigrams, interspersed with
extracts from *Ysengrimus, Aulularia*, and poems of Claudian. As A. C. Friend
suggests, it may well be a collection of material used by Serlo for his Arts
course. For the fifteen poems ed. above, see my table of Contents p. ix. For
the five proverbs ed. A. C. Friend, see Oxford Digby 53. The remaining
amatory proverbs and epigrams are:

fol. 58ʳ Te sine mendico, sed si te tollis amico

fol. 60ʳ Dum fero langorem fero religionis amorem (ed. *SLP* ii. 114)

fol. 63ʳ Parisius Paridi, felix tua secula vidi (ed. E. Faral from two later
manuscripts—*v.* B.N. lat. 3718)

MS.: B. Hauréau, i. 302; A. C. Friend, *ALMA* 1954, p. 85; J. Öberg,
Serlon de Wilton (1965), p. 16.

B.N. lat. 8121A, s. xɪ². Collection of verse, written in northern France.

fol. 2ʳ Roberto domino, subnixo presulis ostro (Warnerius of Rouen,
satire against Moriuht, containing some amatory adventures; ed.
H. Omont, *Annuaire-bull.* 1894, p. 197)

Followed (fol. 9ʳ) by another poem of Warnerius (Rotberto, doctis
fulgenti semper alumnis), fol. 11ᵛ by the *Querolus*, fol. 28ʳ by a

misogynistic poem on Jezebel (Nomen Abie sonat Ietzabel quia corruit, ah! ah)

fols. 30ʳ–32ᵛ Fama puellaris tauri corrumpitur extis (a mythographic fantasy about Semiramis, wrongly described in the manuscript as 'Liber Secundus' of 'Nomen Abie'. The poems about Jezebel and Semiramis are perhaps also by Warnerius; I am preparing an edition of the second.)

MS.: H. Omont, art. cit., p. 193.

B.N. lat. 11331, s. XII. *Hilarii versus et ludi* (ed. J. J. Champollion-Figeac, Paris 1838—still the best text (corrs. E. Herkenrath, *Strecker* 1931, p. 94); J. B. Fuller, New York, 1930). The following poems show traces of love-language (cf. *supra*, pp. 217 ff.):

Superba, †ne superba nisi solo nomine (eds. no. III)
Omnis expers criminis (IV)
Ave sidus occidentis, sidus lucis unice (V)
Puer pulcher et puer unice (VII)
Ave, puer speciose, qui non queris precium (IX)
Ave, splendor telluris anglice (X)
Puer decens, decor floris (XIII)

MS.: J. B. Fuller, op. cit., pp. 3–6.

B.N. lat. 11412, s. XIII in. Formerly at Saint-Victor. Collection of poems (to fol. 23), followed by philosophical opuscula, verses, fables (in French), and notes.

fols. 14ʳ–17ʳ Taurum sol intraverat, ivi spaciatum (a Summer–Winter debate, central to which is the conflict between two views of love; ed. H. Walther, *Streitg.*, p. 206).

MS.: B. Hauréau, ii. 30–48.

B.N. lat. 11867, s. XIII². Formerly at Saint-Germain-des-Prés, perhaps written there. Selection from Thomas of Capua's formularium; epistles and rhetorical writings (incl. John of Garland's *Poetria*—v. Clm 6911); Petrus Alfonsi's *Disciplina clericalis*; poems of Alexander Neckam. From fol. 98ᵛ till the end of the manuscript (fol. 244), many verses, chiefly secular, incl. some of the most famous satirical *Vagantenlieder*.

fol. 47ʳ Cum citharizat avis silvis dulcedine quavis (v. Clm 6911)
fol. 214ᵛ Et bene sit dedecus et longum decus a[moris] (fragm., Serlo of Wilton)
fol. 216ʳ Langueo—sed pereo (ed. *supra*, p. 486)
fol. 218ʳ Qui michi consuevit vultum pretendere letum

fol. 218ᵛ Arent assiduo tenuata labella labore (fragm. of 'Disce puer tandem'—*v*. Vat. Reg. lat. 585)

Aspectu leni veniens, pectus michi leni
Tu michi leso les vulnus, gemini tibi soles
Que dicis de me? dic si bona, si mala deme (all ed. *supra*, pp. 487 ff.)

MS.: K. Hampe, Heidelberg *SB* 1910, Abh. 8; M. Esposito, *EHR* xxx (1915), 450 (with further references); H. Walther, *MÆ* xxxi (1962), 33.

B.N. lat. 13468, s. XIII. Formerly at Saint-Germain-des-Prés. Theological and moral florilegium, prose and verse, finishing (fol. 129) with a mélange that includes secular proverbial and epigrammatic verses.

fol. 131ʳ Dum fero languorem, fero relligionis amorem (Serlo—*v*. B.N. lat. 6765)

fol. 132ʳ Quot sunt grana salis, quot plumas omnis in alis (verse-greeting; ed. H. Walther, *ZfdA* lxv (1928), 273)

MS.: B. Hauréau, ii. 189–218.

B.N. lat. 14193. Fragments of manuscripts from s. XI to s. XVI, formerly at Saint-Germain-des-Prés. Secular and religious verse and prose, incl. Hildebert, Marbod, Gautier, Peter the Painter, and Matthew of Vendôme.

fol. 1ᵛ Gaudia nympharum violas floresque rosarum (Gautier, *v*. Liège 77)

fol. 8ʳ Cum Linus Pholoen peteret, nec posset habere (? Matthew of Vendôme—*v*. B. Hauréau, ii. 354)

fol. 8ᵛ Eole, rex fortis, ventose cura cohortis (Gautier—*v*. Liège 77)

MS.: B. Hauréau, ii. 349–62.

B.N. lat. 16699, s. XII ex. From Notre-Dame-du-Pré (Amiens). Collection of verse, incl. Sedulius, Arator, Prosper, Arnulf of Lisieux, Serlo of Wilton, Marbod, Peter the Painter; (theological prose fols. 136–72).

fol. 114ᵛ Occurrunt blando sibi lumina vestra favore (Arnulf of Lisieux—*v*. Bern 568)

fol. 173ᵛ Exacta cena, du[c]e luna, nocte serena (Peter the Painter; ed. A. Boutemy, *Latomus*, vii (1948), 53. But the last line reads not 'Anteriore luce facta magistra luce' [!] but 'Anteriore loco facta magistra ioco'.)

MS.: B. Hauréau, v. 202–34; A. Boutemy, loc. cit.

B.N. Nouv. Acq. lat. 153, s. XV². Written in northern France or Flanders. Classical, medieval, and humanist poetry, incl. Vitalis of Blois's *Geta* (*v*. Bern 702), the *Pamphilus* (*v*. Toledo Cabildo s.c.), and 'Vix nodosis (*sic*) valeo' (*v*. Digby 166).

fols. 32^r–37^r Ibam forte via quadam nullo comitante (*De tribus puellis*, ed. *Comédie*, ii. 232)

B.N. Nouv. Acq. lat. 1544, s. xv. Didactic prose, followed (fol. 68) by a verse miscellany, sacred and profane.

   fols. 75^v–80^r *Altercatio Phyllidis et Florae* (*v. CB* 92)
   fols. 91^r–92^v Puer ferens pharetras, iudex iuris scutum (*Causa Acis et Poliphemi pro Galatea habenda*, ed. H. Walther, *Streitg.* 224)
   fols. 92^v–94^r Ave, pater gentium, ave pax et veritas (*Causa viri ementulati et eius uxoris petentis divortium*)
   fol. 108^v Visus et adloquium, contactus, basia, risus (ed. *supra*, p. 488)
   MS.: *NE* xxxii. 1, 253–314 (repr. in B. Hauréau, vi).

PARIS Private collection, s.c., s. xiii in. Poetic miscellany: epigrams, panegyrics, epitaphs, and one love-poem:
   Ve! quid agam? plagam sub mesto pectore gesto
   MS.: A. Vernet, *Bull. Soc. nat. antiq. de France*, 1952–3, p. 52.

PERUGIA 729—*v.* Oxford Bodley Canon lat. 112.

PRAHA Univ. 207 (I. E. 22)—*v.* Wien 5371.

Univ. 1008 (V. H. 31), s. xiv. Philosophical treatises.
   fol. 86^v (with music) Flos florum inter lilia (text in J. Truhlář's Catalogue, ad loc.)

Univ. 2033 (XI. C. 9), s. xv. *Gesta Romanorum; Vision Tnugdals*; Latin and German religious writings, epistles and documents.
   fols. 130^r–131^v Iam entrena plena (ed. *supra*, p. 411; also in *Vipiteno s.c.)

Univ. Germ. 145 (XVI. G. 23), ss. xii–xiv. Medical writings and lapidaries (incl. Marbod).
   fol. 46^v (s. xii–xiii) Quia sub umbraculum (ed. *supra*, p. 364)

QUEDLINBURG Gymnasialbibl. 107, s. xv in. Johannes Noviforensis, *Summa cancellariae Caroli IV.*
   (Flyleaf) Quotquot sunt flores, quot fimbrie sunt et odores (verse-greeting, ed. H. Walther, *ZfdA* lxv (1928), 274)

REIMS 1275, s. xiii ex. Written in France, formerly in Reims Cathedral. Epistles and theological opuscula, and a large anthology of verse.

fols. 67^v–69^v Estatem in Iunio, sicut exstat moris (*Sompnium cuiusdam clerici*, a love-vision of the goddess Philosophia, ed. W. Wattenbach *NA* xviii (1893), 496–504)

fols. 129^r–185^v The collection of verse found in Berlin Phillipps 1694 (q.v.). From fol. 186^r, a second collection not found in the Berlin manuscript.

fol. 190^v Virgo decora, michi cum sis nova causa doloris
Littera vade cito, cito iam quod amamus adito

fol. 191^r Fidus amicus here mandat sine fine valere
Quid queror edam: femina quedam me male ledit (*v.* München Clm 19488)
Sicut cera fluit subito percussa calore (*v.* Clm 19488)
(All ed. from this manuscript by W. Wattenbach, art. cit., pp. 521–3)

MS.: ibid.

ROMA Vat. lat. 1599, s. xv. Ovid (*A.A., Rem. Am., Med. Fac.*), with some ps-Ovidian pieces and the *Facetus*.

fol. II^r O decus, o splendor, vultu generosa benigno (ed. *supra*, p. 484)

Vat. lat. 1602, s. xiv. Ovidian and ps-Ovidian verse.

fol. 48^{r-v} Rebus in humanis non est res altera talis (ed. Lehmann, p. 88; F. W. Lenz, *Rivista di cultura classica e medievale* i (1959), 97)

fols. 48^v–54^r Summi victoris fierem cum victor Amoris (*Ovidius puellarum*, ed. from ten manuscripts and three incunabula, *Comédie*, ii. 141)

MS.: F. W. Lenz, loc. cit.

Vat. lat. 3227—*v.* Cambridge UL Gg. v. 35.

Vat. lat. 3251, s. xii^1. Collection chiefly of Vergil's works with Servius' commentary and other classical and grammatical texts; written in northern Italy, once owned by Filelfo.

fol. 96^r Crus, ocelle (ed. M. Vattasso, *Studi med.* i (1904–5), 122; *SLP* ii. 310, corr. *Das*, ocelle)

fol. 178^v Plangit nonna fletibus (ed. *supra*, p. 357)
Ecce filia[m] regis audierunt (fragm., ed. *supra*, p. 486)
[. . .] equitabat soror effrenis curribus (fragm. of 'Foebus abierat' in Bodley 38, ed. *supra*, p. 335)

MS.: M. Vattasso, art. cit.

Vat. lat. 4389, s. xii. Chiefly moral–philosophical writings.

fols. 173^r–176^v Twelve poems (ed. B. Bischoff, *ZfrP* l (1930), 76)

fol. 176^r Iam vere fere medio (ibid. 94; also in B.M. Arundel 384)

fol. 176^v Invehar in Venerem (ibid. 96)

MS.: B. Bischoff, art. cit.

Vat. Reg. lat. 288—four or five fragments (ss. xII–xIII). One (s. xII ex.) contains Hugh of Rouen's dialogues, Hildebert's *Vita S. Marie Egiptiace*, and Abelard's six *planctus* (of which the best ed. is still W. Meyer's, *Gesammelte Abhandlungen*, i. 340 ff.). In the first, *Planctus Dinae filiae Jacob* (fol. 63ᵛ), Dinah defends her own and Sichem's love; in the last, *Planctus David super Saul et Jonatha* (fol. 64ᵛ), David sings of a love that reaches beyond death. The latter has recently been found with music in a prosarium from Nevers (Paris, private coll., s. xII², fols. 88ᵛ–90ᵛ; *v. Ephemerides Liturgicae* lxxi (1957), 3 ff. and pl. ii).

Vat. Reg. lat. 344, s. xIII in. Alanus's *Anticlaudianus*, and an anthology of medieval Latin poetry, written by two French hands.

 fol. 30ᵛ Te michi meque tibi genus etas et decor equant (*De iuvene et moniali*, ed. W. Wattenbach, *AfKdV* xxv (1878), 319; further references in Walther 19053)

 fols. 31ʳ–32ʳ Taurum sol intraverat, et ver, parens florum (*Altercatio Ganimedis et Helene*, ed. W. Wattenbach, *ZfdA* xviii (1875), 127; manuscripts and further references in Walther 19029)

 fol. 34ʳ⁻ᵛ Primo veris tempore vere renascente ('Jupiter and Danae', ed. ibid. 457–60)

 fols. 34ᵛ–36ᵛ CB 92, 63, 83, 84 (see under München Clm 4660)

 fol. 38ʳ⁻ᵛ Surgens Manerius summo diluculo (ed. *SLP* ii. 310)

 fol. 38ᵛ Nix transit et ymber et frigus horridum (ed. *supra*, p. 364)

 fols. 41ʳ–42ʳ Three poems of Serlo of Wilton ('Parisius Paridi', 'Voce brevi', 'Fit rea fletque Venus')—*v.* B.N. lat. 3718

 fols. 52ᵛ–54ᵛ Vernat eques, vix prima genis lanugo susurrat (*Miles gloriosus*, ed. from this and two other manuscripts, *Comédie*, i. 196)

 fols. 55ʳ–56ᵛ Postquam Pamphileas rumor pervenit ad aures (*Pamphilus, Gliscerium et Birria*, ed. *Comédie*, ii. 93)

Vat. Reg. lat. 479, ss. Ix, x, xI. Eight fragments, chiefly hagiographic.

 fol. 54ʳ (s. Ix) Cara mihi dudum veneranda Polimia virgo

Vat. Reg. lat. 585. A collection of verse (fols. 1ʳ–12ᵛ, s. xII), bound with hagiographic writings of different periods (ss. x–xIII), including several lives of St. Anianus. The poems are identical with those in Escorial O. III. 2, s. xIV, fols. 88ʳ–114ᵛ, which was probably copied from this manuscript or from a common source. Antolín's description of the poetry in the latter manuscript (*Catálogo*, iii, 226–7) contains several omissions. After Proba's *cento* comes a group of eighteen (not fifteen) poems, seven of which have love-themes:

 fol. 4ᵛ (98ʳ⁻ᵛ) Ira quidem prodest, quia corda reformat amantum (ed. *supra*, p. 448)

(99ʳ) Iam michi signa patent affectus interioris
fol. 5ʳ⁻ᵛ (100ᵛ⁻101ʳ) Nisum querebam, Nisos mihi mittis, amice
fol. 5ᵛ (101ʳ) Disce puer tandem quid amor, quid forma valeret (*v.* also
    B.N. lat. 11867)
    Ecce redit species et amoris grata voluptas (ed. *supra*, p. 449)
    (101ᵛ⁻102ʳ) Expectata diu puero responsa daturus
fols. 5ᵛ⁻6ʳ (102ʳ⁻ᵛ) Non placet hic adamans quem das adamanteus ipse
The eighteen poems appear to be by one author, who has affinities with
    the so-called 'school of Angers'. There follow (fols. 7ʳ⁻12ᵛ; 103ʳ⁻114ᵛ)
    Hildebert's prose and verse *De querimonia et conflictu carnis et animae,*
    his poem *Cur deus homo,* and Simon Chèvre d'Or's *De Troia.*

MS.: B. Montfaucon, *Bibliotheca Bibliothecarum,* i. 45 (1315).

Vat. Reg. lat. 598. Gatherings, often fragmentary, of the most diverse
periods (ss. x–xv) and subject-matter, which await detailed investigation.
(Some brief indications in B. Montfaucon, *Bibl. Bibl.* i. 45 [1382]). One
fragment (fols. 61ʳ⁻62ᵛ, s. x–xi) contains

fol. 61ʳ Gratior [. . .]
    Duccemus letum lucis honore diem (eight distichs in praise of
    love, the first line fragmentary)
    O cordi nostro dulcissime semper amice (verse-epistle on friendship)
The manuscript concludes with astronomical writings and excerpts in a
    northern French hand, s. xi–xii in., including Hermannus Contractus,
    De utilitatibus astrolabii and *De mensura astrolabii.* (On this section, *v.*
    J. Millás Vallicrosa, *Assaig d'història de les idees físiques i matemàtiques a
    la Catalunya medieval* [Barcelona, 1931], chs. vi and vii, *passim.*)

Vat. Reg. lat. 1351, s. xii¹. The poetry of Baudri of Bourgueil.

fols. 12ᵛ⁻17ᵛ Quae vestrum nomen latum vulgavit in orbem
fols. 17ᵛ⁻24ʳ Fama tuum nomen nostram celebravit in aurem
    (*Paris Helenae; Helena Paridi;* ed. Lehmann, pp. 65 ff., Abrahams
    pp. 29 ff.)
The second verse-epistle to Constance (fols. 140ʳ⁻143ʳ, Abrahams,
    p. 337), and Constance's reply (fols. 143ʳ⁻146ʳ, Abrahams, p. 344),
    also bear traces of love-language.

MS.: Abrahams, pp. xiii–xx.

Vat. Reg. lat. 1357, s. xii. Formerly at Fleury. The poems of Rodulfus
Tortarius (ed. M. B. Ogle and D. M. Schullian, Roma, 1933). Rodulfus's
second verse epistle (fols. 106ʳ⁻111ʳ) 'Pro meritis, Bernarde, tuis tibi verba

salutis' (p. 256) tells the romance of Amis and Amiles; his sixth (fols. 121^r–124^v) 'Sincope, formosae custodia provida Florae' (p. 289) also has a love-theme.

MS.: ed. cit., p. xxxii.

Vat. Ross. 1126—*v*. Oxford Bodley Canon lat. 112.

SAINT-OMER 351, s. XIII^1. Thirty-three songs by Walter of Châtillon.

    fol. 17^v Declinante frigore (ed. K. Strecker, *Saint-Omer*, 17)
        Importuna Veneri (18)
    fol. 18^r Inperio eya (19)
        Verna redit temperies (20)
        Autumnali frigore (21)
        Dum queritur michi remedium (22)
    fol. 18^v Dum flosculum tenera (23; also in Basel D. iv. 4)
        Vetus error abiit (24)
        Dulcis aure temperies (25)
    fol. 19^r Anno revirente (26; song for the Feast of Fools?)
    fol. 19^v Ver prodiens in virore (28)
    fol. 20^r Redit estas preoptata (31)
        Sole regente lora (32)

    MS. (and further references): Strecker, *Saint-Omer*, p. viii.

SANKT FLORIAN Stiftsbibl. XI. 58. Theological writings, incl. four by Boethius.

    fol. 83^v (s. XI, P. D.) Cantant omnes volucres (ed. *supra*, p. 352)

Stiftsbibl. 22—*v*. München Clm 19486.

SANKT GALLEN 383—*v*. München Clm 4660, *CB* 73.

STUTTGART HB I. 95, s. XIII. Songbook, chiefly religious, written in Germany, though containing some Notre Dame music. According to Dreves and Hilka–Schumann (*CB* I. 1, 1930, p. x), the manuscript is from Weingarten, but Spanke (1931) disputes a precise location.

    fols. 20^r–21^r O quam formosa (ed. *supra*, p. 387)
    fol. 73^r Cogito plus solito (ed. *SLP* ii. 320)
    fol. 73^{r-v} Vale tellus, valete socii (fragm. of *CB* 119)
    fols. 77^v–78^r Rumor letalis (*CB* 120)

    MS. (and further references): H. Spanke, *ZfdA* lxviii (**1931**), 79.

TOLEDO Bibl. del Cabildo; .c., s. XIII. Probably written in Italy. Ovid, *Pont.* and *Rem. Am.; Disticha Catonis; Dogma moral. phil.*

fols. 63ʳ–73ʳ Vulneror et clausum porto sub pectore telum (*Pamphilus*; ed. from this manuscript by A. Bonilla y San Martín, *Una comedia latina del siglo XII*, Madrid, 1917. This manuscript, which apart from Berlin Hamilton 390, fols. 114ʳ–156ʳ, seems to be the only complete thirteenth-century text of the *Pamphilus*, has been ignored by other editors and by Walther. The Berlin text, incl. the Venetian transl., ed. A. Tobler, *Archivio glottologico italiano*, x (1886–9), 177). Other manuscripts (and further references): *Comédie*, ii. 169 ff., Walther 20868 (also Walther's Ergänzungen 20868).

TŘEBOŇ (Wittingau) Archiv A. 4, s. xv. Formerly at Praha (Collegio regis Wenceslai). Miscellany, chiefly verse, Latin and Czech. Classical excerpts, proverbs, secular and religious verse, medical treatises.

fol. 408ᵛ Filia, si vox tua (satire on a *romance*, ed. J. Feifalik, *WSB* xxxvi (1861), 169–70)

MS. (also): J. Feifalik, *WSB* xxxix (1862), 630.

Archiv A. 7, s. xv (Coll. reg. Wenceslai). Latin and Czech prose and verse. Historical, religious, alchemical writings; satires.

fol. 157ʳ Fuit una domina (ed. J. Feifalik, *WSB* xxxvi (1861), 166)
fol. 164ʳ⁻ᵛ De iuvene et moniali (*v.* Vat. Reg. lat. 344)

MS. (also): J. Feifalik, *WSB* xxxix (1862), 628.

TRIER (S. Matthiae Trevir.) 1081, ss. xi–xiii. Cicero *De Senectute*, *Ad Herennium*, extracts of Gregory, Augustine and others. pp. 1–6 (second pagination, s. xii) *Idibus Aprilis habitum est concilium hoc in monte Romarici*:

Veris in temporibus sub Aprilis idibus
(also in Koblenz Staatsarchiv ABB VII. 1, 124: a Bullarium from Römersdorf, s. xiii–xiv; ed. from both manuscripts by W. Meyer, *GN* 1914, pp. 1–19).

MSS.: W. Meyer, ibid.

★VIPITENO (Sterzing), s.c., 4°, s. xiv ex. German and Latin miscellany, chiefly verse; some songs with music. Lost since 1945.

fols. 35ᵛ–36ʳ Iam entrena plena (ed. *supra*, p. 411, from Praha Univ. 2033)
MS.: I. Zingerle, *WSB* liv (1866), 293; H. Rietsch, *Die deutsche Liedweise* (1904), pp. 215–46 (melody of *Iam entrena*, p. 224).

VORAU 12, s. xii ex. Legends of saints, followed by a group of secular poems.

fol. 140ᵛ Prespiter Algere, tibi consilium dare vellem (ed. W. Wattenbach, *NA* ii (1877), 398; also in Berlin *lat. qu. 915)

MS.: W. Wattenbach, *Archiv*, x (1851), 627.

WEIMAR Staatsbibl. Qu. 39, s. xᴵ (B. Bischoff, in *MGH Poetae*, v. 2, 553). Formerly at Sts. Peter and Paul, Erfurt. Theological miscellany, incl. works of Hrabanus Maurus, Augustine, Jerome, and Chrysostom.

fol. 126ʳ (preceding Jerome's *De lapsu virginum*) Deus amet puellam (ed. B. Bischoff, loc. cit.)

MS.: B. Wirtgen, *Die Handschriften des Klosters St. Peter und Paul zu Erfurt* (Diss., Berlin, 1936), p. 116.

WIEN CV 116, s. x. Formerly at Salzburg. Alcuin, Cicero, and Marius Victorinus on rhetoric.

fol. 157ᵛ Iam dulcis amica venito (ed. E. Vuolo, *CN* x (1950), 5; facs. E. de Coussemaker, *Harmonie*, pl. ix; see also B.N. lat. 1118 and Cambridge UL Gg. v. 35)

CV 208—*v.* Oxford Bodley Add. A 44.

CV 303, s. xiv. Chiefly secular verse anthology, incl. *Pamphilus, Facetus, Ovidius puellarum, Geta, Miles gloriosus, Alda,* and (only here and in Wien 312)

fols. 155ʳ–158ʳ Hamus amoris edax et rete capacius orbe (Matthew of Vendôme, *Milo,* ed. from both manuscripts, *Comédie,* i. 168)

CV 312, s. xiv. Formerly at Salzburg. Anthology of ancient and medieval poetry, almost wholly secular, incl. *Miles gloriosus, Milo, Alda,* and (only here and in Boccaccio's anthology, Laurenziana Plut. xxxiii. 31).

fols. 31ᵛ–40ᵛ Postquam prima equitis ludentis tempora risit (*Lydia,* ed. from both manuscripts, *Comédie,* i. 226)

CV 1321—*v.* Cambridge UL Dd. xi. 78.

CV 1565, s. xiii in. St. Bruno's commentary on the Pentateuch, followed by religious verse.

fol. Iʳ Usus vite veteris (ed. *supra,* p. 369)

CV 2521, s. xii. Miscellany of ancient and medieval verse.

fol. 138ʳ Lilia ceu flores, sic vincis, amica, sorores (*v. supra,* p. 489)

CV 5371, s. xv. From Bohemia. Medical writings.

fols. 185ʳ–234ʳ *Summa recreatorum,* also in Praha Univ. 207, 1412, fol. 51ᵛ

fol. 216ʳ Iam vernalis amenitas (ed. *supra,* p. 416)

fol. 216^{r-v} Auxilia mundo prebens apparuit (spring-song)

MS.: A. Hilka, *Strecker* 1931, p. 97.

WOLFENBÜTTEL Helmst. 622, s. xv. Secular prose and verse.

fols. 146^r–156^v Grecia (here *Precia*) summorum fecunda parens studiorum (*Filo*, ed. A. Hilka, *Mitteil. d. Schles. Ges. f. Volkskunde*, xix (1917), 58–69; in *ZfdA* lix (1922), 334, Edward Schröder dates the poem 1150–1250, and Hilka gives the variants from Gdańsk, Mar. F 248, s. xv, fols. 14^r–16^r)

fols. 168^r–175^r Carmina fingo, licet iam nullus carmina curet (Theodoricus, 'Pyramus and Thisbe', ed. from six fifteenth-century manuscripts by Lehmann, p. 36)

fols. 175^r–180^v Querat nemo decus in quo vult pingere cecus (anon. 'Pyramus and Thisbe', ed. from four fifteenth-century manuscripts, ibid., p. 46)

ZÜRICH C 58/275, s. XII. Probably written at Schaffhausen. Chiefly theological and verse miscellany, also a German *Arzneibuch* and German glosses. The love-poems are all ed. by J. Werner, *Beiträge* (1905).

fol. 5^r Omine felici te Musa salutat amici (Werner 48)
Dulcis amica mea, speciosior es Galatea (49)

fol. 5^v The epitaphs for Abelard and Héloïse (*v. supra*, p. 470)

fol. 6^r Instar solis ave! tocius luminis atque (*v. supra*, p. 519)
[   ] Utque patet, levis est aut tua nulla fides (fragm., 66)

fol. 11^v Omnia vilescunt, artusque dolore liquescunt (116)

fol. 12^r Conpar nulla tibi me teste valet reperiri (117)
Avertat penas deus et tibi donet amenas (118)
Si cuiquam capto vel tetro carcere clauso (119)

fol. 12^v Omnia postpono, te pectore diligo toto (120)

fol. 16^v Hyemale tempus, vale (149; fragms. in B.N. lat. 3719 and Oxford Bodley Add. A 44; *v.* also Walther 4167, 17480; *MARS* iv (1958), 62)

fol. 41^r Mens mea tristatur, virtus mea debilitatur (Marbod, *Dissuasio intempestivi amoris sub assumta parabola*; 201, also *Liber Floridus*, p. 288)

fol. 158^r Unus ero tecum, si nos fedus liget equum (373)

MS.: full references in the Catalogue (Zürich, 1951), p. 33.

C 62/282 Two twelfth-century manuscripts (Statius' *Thebaid* and grammatica) bound with a tenth-century one.

fol. 202^r (s. XII) Quibus placet fabula iocunda vel seria (fragm. on the love of *miles* and *clericus*, ed. W. Meyer, *GN* 1914, p. 1)

★

The following poems with amatory themes by Marbod of Rennes and by Saxo Grammaticus have not survived in manuscripts, but occur first in the *editiones principes* (Marbod, Redonis, 1524; Saxo, Parisiis, 1514).

Marbod (*v. supra*, pp. 213 ff.)

Lingua nequit fari, mens nulla valet meditari (*Ad amicam repatriare parantem*, ed. W. Bulst, *Liber Floridus*, p. 289)

A te missa michi gaudens, carissima, legi (*Rescriptum ad amicam*, ibid., p. 290)

Hec est votorum, carissima, summa meorum (*Rescriptum rescripto eiusdem*, ibid., p. 291)

Sum felix tandem, quia nunc scio quid tibi mandem (*Ad puellam adamatam rescriptum*, ibid., p. 292)

Si tam iusta foret de te michi causa querendi (*Ad puellam iniuste accusantem*, ibid., p. 292)

Ploro, cum ploras, labor est michi, quando laboras (*Ad eandem resipiscentem*, ibid., p. 293)

Fraude puellarum perit omnis amator earum (*Ad amicam zelantem*, ibid., p. 293)

Ei michi si tantum gemitus imitaris amantum (*Ad amicam gementem*, ibid., p. 294)

Saxo (*v. supra*, pp. 243 ff.)

Quid tibi vaga fluit (*Gesta Danorum* I. viii. 2, ed. J. Olrik–H. Ræder, p. 21)
Num meis mavis monitis adesse (VII. iv. 5, p. 188)
Si captum genitor tuus
Me crede tecum, care, velle commori (VII. vii. 9–10, p. 195)
Ocius, o iuvenes, correptus in aera tollar (VII. vii. 16, p. 198)
Patris sceptra relinquens
Fragili moderamine rerum (VII. ix. 18–19, p. 205)

ADDENDA

[LONDON] B.M. Cotton Titus D. xxiv, *c.* 1200. Compiled at the Cistercian abbey of Rufford. Chiefly moral and religious poetry, epitaphs, and occasional verse; poems by Marbod, Hildebert, Laurence of Durham; extracts from Henry of Huntingdon's *Historia Anglorum*.

fol. 29ᵛ Stephane, Guido tuus te corde salutat et ore (epanaleptic distichs, using language of love) fol. 31ʳ Anglia tota gemit cum sit tristis mea Phillis (ed. J. H. Mozley, *MÆ* xi (1942), 22)

MS.: J. H. Mozley, ibid. 1–45.

[CAMBRIDGE] Trin. O.2.45, *c.* 1250. From Cerne Abbey. Miscellany (fragm.): scientific writings, tables, calendar, religious and satirical verse and prose (incl. French), proverbs and epigrams. For love-verses, *v. supra*, p. 489.

[MÜNCHEN] Univ. 4° 810, s. xv². Treatises on rhetoric, spelling, and 'de naturis rerum'; alphabets, proverbs, epistolaria. Owned by a doctor in München, Sigmund Gotzkircher († 1474/5).

fol. 203ʳ Femineum plene si vis formare decorem (ed. H. Walther, *ZfdA* xcv (1966) 240)

fols. 204ᵛ–205ʳ Nobilis pre ceteris (ibid. 237)

MS.: H. Walther, ibid. 237–42; P. Lehmann, *Festschrift für Georg Leidinger* (1930), pp. 160–4.

INDEX

I. GENERAL

This index includes brief glosses of certain technical terms used in the book. Others, which are not glossed here, are explained at their first occurrence in the discussion.

II. MEDIEVAL LATIN LOVE-POETRY

The entries here are not in every case complete first lines, which are given in the Bibliography (pp. 546–83).

594

Index

---

[1] Stanzaic love-letter in Gent Univ. 267, s. XIII ex., fol. 16ᵛ, ed. D. Schaller, *Latomus* xxiii (1964), 483–90, when this book was in proof. Manuscript: further references ibid.

III. MOTIFS AND IMAGES

This index relates to all the poetry discussed or edited in the book. It is necessarily selective, and designed chiefly to give quick access to a range of material that may be illuminating for comparative studies.

PRINTED IN GREAT BRITAIN
AT THE UNIVERSITY PRESS, OXFORD
BY VIVIAN RIDLER
PRINTER TO THE UNIVERSITY